THE SECOND ECONOMY IN MARXIST STATES

Also by Maria Łoś

ASPIRATIONS AND MILIEU
ATTITUDES OF POLISH SOCIETY TOWARDS MORALITY AND LAW
(*co-author with A. Podgórecki, J. Kurczewski and J. Kwaśniewski*)
MULTI-DIMENSIONAL SOCIOLOGY (*co-author with A. Podgórecki*)
WELFARE AND JUSTICE
*COMMUNIST IDEOLOGY, LAW AND CRIME:
A Comparative View of the USSR and Poland

Also published by Macmillan

The Second Economy in Marxist States

Edited by

Maria Łoś

Professor at the Department of Criminology
University of Ottawa
Canada

MACMILLAN

First published 1990

Published by
THE MACMILLAN PRESS LTD
Houndmills, Basingstoke, Hampshire RG21 2XS
and London
Companies and representatives
throughout the world

Printed in Hong Kong

British Library Cataloguing in Publication Data
Łoś, Maria, *1943–*
The Second economy in Marxist states.
1. Socialist countries. Private enterprise
I. Title
338.6'09
ISBN 0–333–43758–6

This publication was prepared in part under a grant from the Kennan
Institute for Advanced Russian Studies of the Woodrow Wilson
International Center for Scholars, Washington, DC. The statements
and views expressed herein are those of the contributors and are not
necessarily those of the Wilson Center.

Dedicated to the memory
of Adam Łoś (1905–62)

Contents

List of Tables   ix
Acknowledgements   x
Notes on the Contributors   xii

1 Introduction
   Maria Łoś   1

2 The Second Economy in the Soviet Union
   Louise I. Shelley   11

3 The Dynamics of the Second Economy in Poland
   Maria Łoś   27

4 The Second Economy in Hungary
   Istvan Kemeny   50

5 The Second Economy in Romania
   Horst Brezinski and Paul Petersen   69

6 Unofficial Economic Activities in Yugoslavia
   Ivo Bićanić   85

7 The Cuban Second Economy in Perspective
   Raymond J. Michalowski and Marjorie S. Zatz   101

8 The Second Economy in Nicaragua is the Second Front:
   Washington's Efforts to Destabilise any Succeeding
   American Revolution
   W. Gordon West   122

9 The Second Economy in Socialist China
   Xin Ren   141

10 The Second Economy in Angola: *Esquema* and
   Candonga
   Daniel dos Santos   157

11 The Second Economy in Tanzania: its Emergence and
   Strategies of Control
   Andrew S. Z. Kiondo   175

Contents

12 Dynamic Relationships of the First and Second
    Economies in Old and New Marxist States
    Maria Łoś   193

Index   231

List of Tables

5.1 The share of private livestock, private meat production
    and other agricultural products (1970–85)   72

6.1 Negative features of the immediate working
    environment as perceived by the adult population   92

6.2 Citizens of Yugoslavia found guilty of criminal offences
    against the economy (1976–86)   96

8.1 Police-recorded criminal occurrences   126

9.1 The result of 'New Democratic Reform'   143

9.2 Mobility of labour in economic structure (1949–57)   144

Acknowledgements

I acknowledge with thanks a research grant from the Solicitor General of Canada which enabled me to secure the help of a research assistant, Wanda Jamieson, who helped with the data collection, co-ordination and editing of this book. I appreciate very much her contribution to this project.

The work on the final theoretical synthesis of the material, as well as the time-consuming tasks of editing individual chapters and preparing the final version of the book, were made easier by a research grant from the Wilson International Center for Scholars/ Kennan Institute for Advanced Russian Studies in Washington, DC. While at the Kennan Institute, Daniel Williams helped, in a most conscientious way, with many aspects of my research. I also wish to thank the staff at the Kennan Institute, and especially its Secretary, Peter Reddaway, who showed unqualified faith in the feasibility of a ten-country comparative project spanning five continents and very diverse levels of development. I appreciate his support.

The unique intellectual atmosphere at the Wilson Center made thinking easier and writing less arduous. Among many Center fellows and scholars, Abdullahi An-Na'im, Anders Åslund, René Fox, Anthony French, Philip Pomper and Khosrow Shakeri influenced my research the most, as much through intellectual discussion and stimulation as through their warm friendship and exceptional human qualities.

The authors of the individual national studies made this book possible. They showed great patience in the face of my requests for revisions and clarifications. I could not have wished for better collaborators on this project. I would like to stress, however, that I am solely responsible for the final interpretation and synthesis of the material they provided.

I would also like to thank my colleagues, chairperson Ross Hastings and secretaries in the Department of Criminology, University of Ottawa, who always encourage me in my research endeavours.

I am very appreciative of the efforts of Chi Hoang, who typed the endless pages of this book with both expertise and a smile. Louise Clément also assisted in typing and correcting the manuscript. I am grateful to Springer Verlag Publishers Inc. of New York for permission to reproduce in the present book a table (9.1) from *Economic Development and Social Change in the People's Republic of China* by Willy Kraus (1982); to *Social Justice* for permission to use material from Vilma Nuñez's 'Justice as the Control of Crime', *Social Justice*, no. 23; and to *Capítulo Criminológico*, no. 14, 1986, pp. 187–200, for permission to use material in the chapter by W. Gordon West. Finally, I wish to thank Mr T. M. Farmiloe, my publisher, for his interest in my work, and Mr Keith Povey and Mrs Barbara Docherty for their skilful copy-editing of the typescript.

MARIA ŁOŚ

Notes on the Contributors

Ivo Bićanić, born in Zagreb, Yugoslavia, completed a B.Phil. in Economics at Oxford University and later received a doctorate from the University of Zagreb, where he has been teaching since 1977. He has published articles on topics such as theory, economic history and the Yugoslav economy. His main research interest is the study of income inequality with special reference to Yugoslavia.

Horst Brezinski is Assistant Professor at the University of Paderborn, Department of Economics. His main research interests are in comparative economic systems and international economic relations.

Daniel dos Santos, Assistant Professor at the Department of Criminology, University of Ottawa, knows Angola, the subject of his chapter, from academic research and from first-hand experience. He has studied in Lisbon (economics), Geneva, and Montreal (sociology). His current main research interest is in the area of Law, Justice and Development in Angola. He has published, among other articles, 'Cabinda: the Politics of Oil in Angola's Enclave' in Robin Cohen (ed.), *African Islands and Enclaves* (Beverly Hills: Sage, 1983); 'L'Etat périphérique', *Critiques Socialistes*, 3 (Autumn 1987); 'The Political Struggle and the Construction of the Angolan Social Formation', in *Studies in Political Economy* (forthcoming).

Istvan Kemeny is a Fellow of the Ecole des Hautes Etudes en Sciences Sociales in Paris. He has published widely on contemporary Hungarian social and economic issues, including the second economy.

Andrew S. Z. Kiondo is a Lecturer in Political Science with the Department of Political Science at the University of Dar es Salaam. Currently, he is a PhD candidate with the Department of Political Science at the University of Toronto, where he is working on a thesis titled 'The Politics of Economic Liberalization in Africa: A Case Study of Tanzania's Policy Changes, 1977–1987'. His recent works include, 'The Emergence of Parallel Economies in Sub-Saharan

Africa: A Comparative Study of Zaire, Uganda and Tanzania' (mimeo, University of Toronto, 1985).

Maria Łoś is Professor in the Department of Criminology, University of Ottawa, and Adjunct Professor at the Institute of Soviet and East European Studies, Carleton University. She has taught and conducted research at the Universities of Sheffield and Warsaw (from where she obtained her MA and PhD) and at the Polish Academy of Science. She is the author of *Communist Ideology, Law and Crime, Welfare and Justice, Multi-Dimensional Sociology* (with A. Podgórecki; also published in Portuguese), *Aspirations and Milieu*, and *Attitudes of Polish Society towards Morality and Law* (with A. Podgórecki, J. Kurczewski and J. Kwaśniewski) and numerous articles in several languages.

Raymond J. Michalowski is Professor of Sociology at the University of North Carolina at Charlotte. He is the author of *Order, Law, and Crime* as well as an eclectic collage of articles about topics ranging from vehicular homicide to corporate crimes by transnationals. He is currently studying the practical applications of socialist legality in Cuba.

Paul Petersen is an engineer and freelance writer based in Hamburg, West Germany.

Xin Ren received her BA in philosophy and sociology from the People's University of China and Nankai University, China, and her MA in Criminology from the University of Ottawa, Canada. Formerly a research associate at the Institute of Sociology, Chinese Academy of Social Sciences, she is currently a doctoral candidate at the Criminal Law and Criminology Center, University of Pennsylvania at Philadelphia. Her research interests include the state and crime, juvenile delinquency, corrections and comparative criminology.

Louise I. Shelley is a Professor in the Department of Justice, Law and Society and the School of International Service at the American University (Washington, DC). She is the author of *Crime and Modernization* and *Lawyers in Soviet Work Life* as well as numerous articles. She has received Fulbright, Guggenheim, IREX and Kennan Institute fellowships.

W. Gordon West, Associate Professor at Ontario Institute for Studies in Education, and Centre of Criminology, University of Toronto, has published on the topics of serious theft, schooling and juvenile delinquency, youth culture, juvenile courts and diversion. He has done on-site research in Nicaragua five times and spent his sabbatical there in 1985 as a researcher at La Corte Suprema. He serves as a member of the Nicaraguan team of the Comparative Social Control project of the Grupo Critica de Criminologia. He is presently jointly editing (with CIDE/PIIE) a collection on *Education and Work: North and South*, Santiago: PIIE/CIDE and Toronto: OISE), and drafting a monograph on *Just Revolution: Popular Insurrection, Sandinista Justice, and Imperial State Terror in Nicaragua*.

Marjorie S. Zatz is an Associate Professor in the School of Justice Studies, Arizona State University, Tempe, Arizona, USA. She received her PhD in Sociology with a minor in Latin American Studies in 1982 from Indiana University. Most of her research has focused on the situation of Latinos in the USA, and particularly on racial–ethnic discrimination in court processing and sanctioning. She is currently completing a monograph on the intersection of class, ethnicity, and the emergence of recent immigration legislation in the US, and is beginning to work on a study of the emergence of socialist legality in Cuba and Nicaragua.

1 Introduction

Maria Łoś

INITIAL CLARIFICATIONS

This book is conceived as a broad comparative study of ten countries whose political structure and dominant ideology justify the application of the 'Marxist State' label. However, while these countries are ruled by parties strongly influenced by Marxist ideology and vision, their acceptance of and adherence to the Soviet model of communism varies considerably as do their links to the Soviet Union. The levels of centralisation and nationalisation of their economies are also highly varied; nonetheless, the latter can be identified as important ideological ingredients in the party philosophy and policies within each country.

The reason for choosing nations with diverse historical traditions is simple enough: it is the only way to test the limits and pertinence of the generalisations regarding the official and unofficial economic relationships which have been hitherto derived mainly from research on the Soviet Union, Hungary, and some other East European countries. Due to a limited cross-national research effort, it has been methodologically impossible to arrive at definitive conclusions as to the role and importance of such diverse factors as the Marxist ideology, its specific embodiment in the Soviet model, the series of poor harvests, or the czarist heritage of corruption. The inclusion of a larger number of countries, particularly non-European ones whose emancipatory and revolutionary movements have had distinct roots and outcomes, is highly instructive. The national case studies comprising this volume focus on the second economies of the Soviet Union, Poland, Hungary, Romania, Yugoslavia, Cuba, Nicaragua, China, Angola and Tanzania. They account for cultural specificity, the impact of the colonial past, and underdevelopment and dependency, which many of these societies have experienced.

Based on the typology of comparative research proposed by Kohn (1987) the approach in this research may be described as both an investigation of certain institutions in their specific context in different countries and as a consideration of these countries as units of

1

analysis, whereby they are classified along several dimensions to test certain hypothesised relationships. It is not, however, a rigorous and definitive research, but rather a first attempt to assess the viability of such an approach in this particular area, to stimulate a broader theoretical orientation in the field where such an orientation is conspicuously missing, to propose hypotheses for future research endeavours and, finally, to face a challenge which is admittedly formidable.

THE ADOPTED DEFINITION OF THE SECOND ECONOMY

Definitions of the second economy have focused on legal criteria ('illegal economy'; see Shelley, 1983); moral criteria (illegal and 'contrary to accepted economic morality'; see Wiles, 1987); institutional criteria (income-producing transactions not included in official records and statistics; see Feige, 1987); quantitative criteria (all those economic activities which can be somehow measured and counted but have not been yet accounted for); or ideological criteria – the latter option, having been chosen as the most suitable for the purposes of this research, is elaborated below. The legal definition has been rejected as too narrow, the moral definition as too relative, the institutional definition as too bureaucratically oriented, and the quantitative definition as based either on a mistaken vision of reality which assumes that what cannot be counted does not exist, or the misinformed view of research which assumes that what cannot be counted should not be studied.

According to the adopted definition, the second economy includes all areas of economic activity which are officially viewed as being inconsistent with the ideologically sanctioned dominant mode of economic organisation. In addition to the illegal and semi-legal economic activities, the second economy also includes those types of activity that are formally legal but ideologically suspicious and therefore officially discriminated against and assigned a clearly inferior status.

This definition does not include the informal economy connected with routine tasks of maintaining a household and a family (cooking, cleaning, nursing, minor repairs), although these activities, performed mainly by women, constitute an enormous unpaid contribution to the economy. While these activities are not normally directly controlled by communist states, they cannot be perceived as incompatible with the dominant ideology, as the pure Marxist ideals of commune feeding and child rearing have either been abandoned by those countries which – like the USSR – were initially inclined to implement them, or have not been incorporated at all into the official doctrine.

The present project is predominantly qualitative in nature because of the sheer impossibility of obtaining hard data whose quality would be compatible across differing nations. The use of existing scattered studies in this area is not viable for the purposes of quantification because of the great variety in adopted definitions of the second economy and wide ranges of various quoted estimates. The absence in some studies of clear definitions and reliance on dubious sources of information justify doubts as to the reliability of the input data.

By the same token, any attempts at cross-systemic comparisons, even purely qualitative and theoretical, have to be treated with caution as they entail comparing phenomena whose structural location and social meanings are bound to be fundamentally different. Indeed, the definition of the second economy chosen for the present, intra-systemic research makes it even more difficult to speak of comparability of second economies across ideological borders. Furthermore, it is a definition which may be more easily applied in communist countries where paramountcy of the official ideology is emphasised, and the economy is directly and explicitly administered by ideological and political decisions. On the other hand, in Western capitalist countries periods of ideological clarification and their direct translation into economic policies are rather exceptional (for example, the United Kingdom and the United States in the 1980s). However, despite, these obvious difficulties, some very general inter-systemic comparisons will be undertaken in the final pages of this book as a tentative bridge between the hitherto unconnected attempts at analysing second economies generated under different conditions.

While the use of the adopted definition may present special difficulty in cross-systemic comparisons, it is also anything but easy in an intra-systemic project. It must be expected that Marxist-inspired ruling élites vary greatly in their ideological interpretations in both cross-national and cross-temporary fashion. Furthermore, their official ideologies or doctrines usually differ from the operative ones (Moore, 1950; see also Zaslavsky, 1982). Although the official 'superideology' may remain quite stable over time, the operative ideology may shift, a hidden agenda may be incorporated, strategical

manoeuvres justified and instrumental declarations may be made for
international purposes or as a tool in an internal power struggle. In
the present project, attempts have therefore to be made to assess
short-term shifts and long-term trends within the dominant ideology.
Moreover, the co-existence of different economic formations within
individual countries is bound to create complex ideological pressures
which may shape and modify the official ideology. These considerations are very important in a research which undertakes to compare
countries with such different histories of Marxist rule as, for example,
the 70-year-old Soviet Union and the new-fledged revolutionary
Nicaragua.

Nonetheless, despite the complex problems of its application, the
ideology-based definition of 'second economy' seems to be particularly appropriate for countries where the ruling party's ideology determines policies of discrimination against unorthodox or ideologically
alien economic activities. It is important to note that, unlike Western
countries, the acknowledged rule in many communist societies is not
that what is not forbidden is permitted, but that what is not explicitly
recommended is forbidden (see, for example, Vasilyev, 1987: 17).
And even what is ostensibly permitted may be delegitimised by
numerous administrative regulations, *ad hoc* decrees and party
resolutions.

Finally, it is worth making a conceptual distinction between
dispersed second economy activities and the actual second economy,
which implies the existence of a well-developed network of second
economy practices, both statistically and functionally important
enough to be perceived as an economic system in itself, albeit
intertwined with the first economy.

PROJECT FORMAT

Several authors have agreed to write concise research reports on the
second economy and its control in the selected countries. A fair
measure of co-ordination and comparability was achieved by a set of
initial guidelines and instructions, as well as numerous exchanges
through correspondence and personal meetings. These national
reports, five of which were presented and discussed during a session
of the Annual Conference of the American Society of Criminology in
November 1987 in Montreal, constitute the primary basis for the final
comparative essay which closes this volume (Chapter 12). They are,

however, supplemented liberally by information and data from other sources and publications.

In addition to the working definition of 'second economy', each author received the following information and general guidelines, based to a great extent on earlier inquiries into the second economy of Soviet bloc countries (see especially Łoś, 1987). The limitations of the stock of knowledge from which this project had been conceived were clearly acknowledged and communicated to its participants.

The Authors' Guidelines

Existing studies of the Soviet Union and Eastern Europe suggest that the 'real life' economies inspired by the Marxist model tend to provoke a parallel growth of a 'second economy' that openly defies Marxist ideology. The official economy becomes, thus, threatened from within and from without. It is threatened from within, because a centrally planned economy lacks self-regulating mechanisms, and therefore tends to become rigid and divorced from the social reality. It is also threatened from without as the vigorous and flexible development of the parallel 'second economy' inevitably undermines the credibility of the official economy.

The waves of criminalisation of unorthodox economic activities seem to be the favoured response by the Soviet style party-states faced with the problem of the 'second economy'. On the other hand, however, they tend to depend ever more on this economy's productive, redistributive and socio–psychological functions.

Yet, in the absence of comparative studies which would include those non-European societies whose economies have been guided by Marxist ideas, any theoretical generalisations concerning these processes must be treated as tentative. The proposed book, which would bring together, compare, and analyse the USSR, East-European and non-European Marxist states should help explain the nature of the impact of the society's politico–economic organisation on the relationships between the official and unofficial economic sectors and methods of their control.

For the purpose of this study, a distinction will be made between the 'first' (official, dominant, ideologically promoted) and the 'second' (secondary, contrary to the dominant ideology) economies. Four types of second economy activities will be analysed: (i) the legal second economy inside the first economy (for example, legal semi-

private contracts, enterprises and subsidiary shops within the state-
owned firms); (ii) the illegal second economy inside the first economy
(for example, illegal private production within state enterprises); (iii)
the legal second economy parallel to the first economy (for example,
licensed private economy, 'barter' economy) and (iv) the illegal
second economy parallel to the first economy (for example, unlicensed private production and distribution, black markets, contraband). The meaning and application of these categories in the context
of different societies will depend on the specific economic model
adopted, and its officially articulated interpretation. Of special
importance will be the extent of the ideological and actual emphasis
on the state ownership of the means of production and the centralised
state control over the market.

Given the known inefficiency of the centralised model of the state
economy, it is expected that in all countries studied the ruling élites
(parties) have been moved to accept extensive areas of the second
economy as vital to securing a minimum level of consumer needs
satisfaction. The specific choice of favoured types of the second
economy would depend on the unique configuration of historical,
economic and political factors in each case. Since the question of the
private ownership of the means of production is, in the Soviet-
controlled countries, particularly sensitive it is presumed that they
would tend to favour the development of some forms of legal private
activities within the framework of the first economy over a legitimate
parallel private economy that would openly recognise such an
ownership. In the area of the illegal second economy activities, it may
be expected that the parallel rather than internal private initiatives
would be treated with more tolerance, the latter being of a largely
parasitic nature, while the former are economically vital and lend
themselves to private exploitation by the members of the élite.

*To the extent the studied countries have adopted the model of the
centralised planned economy* the following predictions may be formulated:

1. Contrary to its underlying assumptions, the centralised economy
    offers almost unlimited illegal opportunities for making private
    profits. They result from:

    –   mechanical allotments of materials, machines, time, and person-
        nel according to the abstract plan (leaving room for corruption
        and private initiative in manipulating the quantities of the

planned supplies and using surplus resources for unofficial production);
- limited incentives to increase productivity within the first economy;
- stress on the quantitative goals of the Central Plan, whereby quality is of secondary importance (an easy opportunity to profit illegally by sacrificing quality for quantity);
- omnipresent waste which contributes to the perception of the low value of state property; and
- widespread shortages (the possibility of charging inflated prices and fees for goods and services which the state cannot supply adequately).

2. Though the second economy is perceived as indispensable, the central authorities employ a number of strategies to render it politically relatively harmless and ideologically acceptable. They include:

- legalisation of registered small-scale private business portrayed as an economically insignificant craft sector;
- authorisation of certain forms of informal arrangements and contracts with the state economy employees;
- overregulation and overtaxation of registered private enterprises to make them vulnerable to prosecution and to check their expansion;
- criminalisation of unplanned or unregistered economic activities which allows the authorities to keep the size of the underground economy under some control; and periodical scapegoating campaigns portraying black-marketeers as evil people who pray on innocent people by selling state products for black-market prices, thereby deregulating and destabilising the otherwise healthy economy.

Finally, it is presumed that the second economy, like the first, is stratified and produces both its own financial élite – which tends actually to overlap with the official élite – and its own underclass. At the very top there are, first of all, those high officials who, due to their positions as the top party functionaries, ministers in important branches of the economy, chief representatives of law enforcement, executives in major industrial organisations, and so forth, often treat the state economy as their private fiefdom. The official economy

treated as a private economy becomes a second economy insofar as it
serves individual needs of the members of the party élite and not the
interests of the ruling party as a whole. The élite enjoys all the rights
of private ownership without having the obligations and responsibilities which normally come with it.

At the top of this stratified world of the second economy are also
exceptionally successful private businessmen and black-marketeers
who are actually able to reinvest their capital in various profitable
ventures and have close enough ties to the influential members of the
élite to operate in relative safety. They may also have important
international connections. Although they lack the actual political
power and are at the mercy of the official power élite, they have the
financial means to protect their interests.

In the middle, there are numerous registered private entrepreneurs
and craftsmen, successful private physicians and artists, full-time
hard-currency dealers and black-market operators, as well as organis-
ers of large-scale illegal production and trade within the state
economy. Moreover, this category includes middle-level functionaries who, through their local mutual favour networks, use state
resources for their private purposes.

Below the middle level of this stratified second economy, but still
better off than the average wage earner, are those state employees
who land important private contracts with their employers; who
derive untaxed income from moonlighting; who speculate in scarce
goods on a limited or irregular basis; and who, being employed in
retail trade, warehouses, and transport, routinely take bribes from
their clients in addition to their regular wages.

At the very bottom of the second economy stratification are those
who have actually dropped out of the official economy, or have never
been integrated into it. Their involvement in the second economy
constitutes a desperate attempt at survival. Their profits are meagre,
and the rate of police harassment and prosecution high. They
produce and sell moonshine and speculate in agricultural products,
foodstuffs, and cheap consumer goods.

In addition to the money-based second economy, there occurs the
involvement of almost the entire population in an informal exchange
economy. Intimate networks of relatives and friends make opportunities available to individuals for needs satisfaction. Not unlike the top
officials, but on a much more humane basis, ordinary people try to
secure access to various goods and services through those whom they
know and with whom they may exchange favours. For their survival,

ordinary members of these societies have to rely on informal exchange economy networks. While their etiquette and secondary characteristics will differ from country to country, as well as in urban and rural areas, these networks inevitably involve goods snatched from workplaces; private services rendered during work hours; private utilisation of state machines, tools, or transport; procuring goods from 'under-the-counter'; contraband and illegal trafficking. Thus, in addition to the 'objective' stratification which indicates economic differentiation among entrepreneurs and other players in the money-based secondary markets, there exists also an intricate web of subtle stratification within informal, exchange-economy networks and circles. The status within the latter depends to some extent on personal characteristics and the dedication to one's circle. But most important of all is the ability to intercept desired state goods, commodities and services, and channel them into the network.

In sum, the second economy is believed to contribute to the continuation of the dominant economic relationships while at the same time eroding the ability of the bureaucratic party-state effectively to control and manage the society. If this contradiction characterises the essence of the second economy's role within the societies studied, it may also explain the ambivalent nature of the policies adopted by the authorities.

While the above ideas and hypotheses are derived mainly from my inquiries into the Soviet Union and East European countries, it is especially instructive to test them within societies whose histories and routes towards the Marxist party rule have been radically different. The cultural and religious specificity, the impact of the colonial past, and the various forms of exploitation, dependency and conflict ravaging these societies create a complex reality which must be analysed to assess the economic implications of the adoption of the Marxist ideology in diverse social contexts.

Each chapter should contain:

– A brief historical overview of the developments in the area of the 'second economy' and the methods of its control since the introduction, revolutionary or otherwise, of a Marxist-inspired political order in the given country. (Including references to the pre-Marxist period in order to illuminate such issues as change and continuity, possible impact of national cultural and political traditions, level and character of economic development, colonial heritage, etc.)

- A theoretical analysis of the relationships between the Marxist-inspired political change and various forms of 'second economy' in the given country. (Including references to the official economy and a discussion of the relationships between the two.)
- A theoretical analysis of the style of control of the 'second economy' and hypothetical explanations of shifts in methods of control at different stages or periods in the development of the given society. (Including attempts at control through moral incentives and peer pressure, economic sanctions, penal measures, etc.)
- Conclusions: proposed generalisations about the processes in question and their historical, political and economic meaning. Possible implications for the Marxist theory.

REFERENCES

Feige, E., 'The Anatomy of the Underground Economy', in S. Alessandrini and B. Dallago (eds), *The Unofficial Economy* (Aldershot: Gower, 1987) pp. 83–106.

Kohn, M. L., 'Cross-National Research as an Analytic Strategy', *American Sociological Review*, 52 (6) (1987) pp. 713–31.

Łoś, M., 'The Double Economic Structure of Communist Societies', *Contemporary Crises*, XI (1987) pp. 25–58.

Moore, B. Jr, *Soviet Politics – The Dilemma of Power* (Cambridge, Mass.: Harvard University Press, 1950).

Shelley, L. I., 'Law and the Soviet Second Economy', *Research in Law, Deviance and Social Control*, 5 (1983) pp. 3–24.

Vasilyev, A., 'Ways of Restructuring the Legal System: The Law is an Instrument of Renewal', *Pravda*, 3 May 1987, excerpted in *The Current Digest of the Soviet Press*, XXXIX (18) p. 17.

Wiles, P., 'The Second Economy, Its Definitional Problems', in S. Alessandrini and B. Dallago (eds), *The Unofficial Economy* (Aldershot: Gower, 1987) pp. 21–33.

Zaslavsky, V., *The Neo-Stalinist State: Class, Ethnicity, and Consensus in Soviet Society* (Armonk, N.Y.: M. E. Sharpe, 1982).

2   The Second Economy in the Soviet Union

Louise I. Shelley

INTRODUCTION

The Soviet economy is a model for many nations that have followed the socialist form of economic development. Many of these states adopted a centrally-controlled and state dominated economy. An examination of their economies reveals that many socialist nations have followed the same pattern as the USSR. A centralised planning process, a system of fixed wages, established price controls, and extensive regulations govern the official economy. But alongside the official economy, a large unofficial economy, popularly called the second economy,[1] has arisen, adding much flexibility to the economic system.

The extensive second economy is a major force outside the officially regulated economy. But the flexibility it provides the Soviet system has come at great costs. Widespread corruption of the governing *apparat*, particularly in Asian[2] but as well in Slavic republics (Simis, 1982) has alarmed the present day leadership. Furthermore, the pervasive second economy has had significant demographic effects. Beneficiaries of the second economy, in particular rural residents of Central Asia (Lubin, 1984), rarely move to urban areas with strong industrial economies where less potential of unofficial earnings exists. Consequently, the second economy is a deterrent to a distribution of manpower beneficial to the official state-regulated economy.

Mikhail Gorbachev, in an effort to reduce corruption and regulate some of this unofficial sector, had enacted legislation on private labour initiative ('V Politbiuro . . .', 1986). This much heralded legislation does not usher in a new NEP (New Economic Policy) (a period in the 1920s when large-scale private enterprises and businesses existed and a legitimate wealthy business class emerged in the USSR), but attempts to serve the neglected consumer sector by authorising certain private economic activities.

DEFINING AND DESCRIBING THE SECOND ECONOMY

This study adheres to the definition of the second economy presented in the Introduction of this book (Łoś). It divides the analysis of the second economy into its legal and illegal components. It does not include stealing from the state which is an ordinary criminal offence, or 'eyewash' (*ochkovtiratel'stvo*) which is a crime against the central planner (Pomorski, 1978).

The Legal Second Economy

The legal second economy encompasses a broad range of activities and it is often difficult to draw the line between legal and illegal private activity.[3] The most important activity of participants in the parallel economy is the sale of agricultural products raised on private plots by state and collective farm workers. The private cultivation by individual farmers contributes significantly to the national economy; products raised on these plots contribute one-fourth the output of total Soviet agriculture (Grossman, 1977: 26). Agricultural workers are permitted to sell their products in collective farm markets where they set their own prices, and recently have been able to sell from trucks in urban neighbourhoods. As fruits, vegetables and meat are in perennial short supply in the Soviet Union, farmers often profit substantially, but their efforts sometimes place them in legal jeopardy (Kairzhanov, 1963; 'Private Sector . . .', 1985). In some cases, needed fertilisers and food for livestock may be acquired only illegally (Osipenko, 1985). Middlemen may be illegally retained by farmers to market goods in distant communities (Brovkin and Gorbuntsov, 1986: 9, 13).

Other Soviet citizens participate legally in private exchange. Individuals rent *dachas* (vacation cottages) that they own to their fellow citizens. Furthermore, individuals may hire other citizens to work for them as domestic employees (Lane, 1985: 5), although this involves a rather small category of Soviet citizens.

The new legislation on individual labour activity enacted in November 1986 and in force since 1 May 1987 increased the areas of permissible second economy activity. It permits 'cottage industry and handicrafts and consumer services as well as other types of activity based exclusively on the personal labour of citizens and of members of their families'. The new law authorises individuals to produce clothing and footwear, furniture, carpets, pottery as well as a wide range of other consumer products. It will now be possible to legally hire someone for tutoring,[4] house and garage repair and construction, clothing, furniture, and carpet repair. Private photographers, hairdressers, and secretarial services are now authorised, as well as private transport services along with private care for the elderly and the disabled ('V Politbiuro . . .', 1986: 3). This significantly expands the areas of permissible activity.

The legislation provides for careful control over taxation and licensing fees. As the services of those in the private sector are at a premium, this new legislation may lead to a group of financially successful medical personnel, skilled craftspeople and production personnel whose incomes far exceed those in the official economy. As supplies are limited in the official economy, it is likely that many participants in the private labour initiative will illegally obtain materials needed to produce clothing, repair cars and run cafés. But these groups will then become vulnerable to prosecution, as the state seeks to maintain close control over the 'legitimised' second economy.

Yet such predictions remain speculation. Although Soviet authorities have reported the opening of private restaurants in Moscow, a dating service in the Baltics and on-call private repair services for the home and automobiles, initial numbers of participants are not great. In Kiev, by 1 May 1987, 4000 individuals had registered as private servicemen and craftsmen and in such smaller cities as Tallinn, Vilnius, Kishinev and Alma-Ata over 1000 registrants in each were recorded ('Zakon vstupaet v silu', 1987: 11).

In Moscow, independent entrepreneurs now sell individually manufactured clothing, art work and crafts. Unlicensed yet undeterred by the *militsiia*, these individuals indicate that the society is changing faster than the laws authorising the second economy. Gorbachev's legitimation of a wide variety of second economy activities indicates that he seeks to remedy existing problems without a dramatic restructuring of the economic apparatus. The legislation recognises that the second economy is indispensable to the Soviet state, but renders it relatively harmless and ideologically acceptable by legitimising the production and provision of some of its most needed goods and services.

The legislation does not provide for a dramatic reshuffling of the means of production, control over which remains firmly in the hands of governmental authorities. Instead, the legislation seeks to satisfy a minimum of consumer needs by adding increased flexibility to the service and consumer sector while retaining control over the licensing, marketing and income of those involved.

This law only legitimises the activities of those who choose to register with the authorities. It does not provide the incentives for many individuals to forego their illegal economic activity. It is therefore unlikely that many of the 17 to 20 million people, reported by *Izvestiia* as working privately in the service sector annually (Taubman, 1986: A9), will be affected by the new law. Large numbers of moonlighters will probably continue to operate outside the official economy.

This law may bring into the open certain previously underground activity but it will not lead to the control, or eradication, of the pervasive illegal second economy.

The Illegal Second Economy

The illegal second economy is much larger and more complex than the legal second economy. The forms that it takes are 'limited [only] by human ingenuity' (Grossman, 1977: 29). The second economy has expanded in the last three decades because legal restrictions have been reduced while the increasingly affluent Soviet citizen can not fulfil his desires by officially available goods (Shelley, 1984: 98; Perevoznik, 1980: 21–9).

The centralised planned economy that stymies private initiative, the endless regulations, as well as poor quality production, ensure that consumer goods are in chronic short supply. Much needed flexibility is absent as 'the macroeconomic decisions, especially the plan, cannot be criticised or adapted to the changing needs of society; their premises are secret, their directives legally binding' (Łoś, 1980: 121). Management problems compound those inherent in the planning process (Bauman, 1986: 22–3). Individuals capable of managing and innovating in the workplace find their talents unappreciated in the official economy as most managers, until recently, have been rewarded more for their party reliability than for their skills in running a complex economy.

The discussion of the illegal second economy will be divided, as in the Introduction to this volume (Łoś), into two parts: the illegal second economy inside the first economy and the illegal second economy parallel to the first economy. The illegal second economy inside the first economy encompasses both individual activity as well as the collective activities of large numbers of individuals engaged in production.

Internal Illegal Economy

Soviet research indicates a very high degree of embezzlement within the consumer economy, particularly in trade organisations and the food industry (Utkin, 1980). For example, restaurant employees sell choice items out the back door rather than to the customers, causing the constant reply of Soviet waiters '*netu*' (not available) to the queries of customers. Pharmacists set aside needed antibiotics for friends and customers who are willing to pay a premium. The same goes for the sales personnel of any desired commodity such as theatre tickets, clothes and shoes (see, for example, Katsenelinboigen, 1977: 75–9). Profits from items withheld from sale are often divided with managers, and bribes are paid to law enforcement personnel to protect them from arrest and prosecution (Simis, 1977–78: 41). Individuals not only withhold goods from sale but purchase them and resell them at a profit, making themselves liable for prosecution both for misuse of their positions as well as the crime of speculation.

The reasons given for the proliferation of theft with the purpose of resale are not only the absence and poor distribution of goods, but also the monopoly over the distribution process and the close links between the criminals and the items they seek to steal (Utkin, 1980). Although serious problems exist at the distribution stage, objects often do not reach the stores as there is massive theft of goods from the railways (Tenson, 1980) and other means of transport.

The problem is particularly pronounced in the agricultural sector. Soviet radio, for instance, reported that in one Ukrainian region, a commercial dispatcher with four accomplices diverted 23 metric tons of flour and groats intended for sale in the shops. Furthermore, the same broadcast asserted that the practice of falsifying agricultural inventories in stores in order to embezzle livestock feed is very widespread (Osipenko, 1985). A major Soviet newspaper reported that in the Central Asian Republic of Kazakhstan, over half of farm machines delivered from the factory arrive in an unusable state, having lost numerous parts en route.

Although much attention is paid by Soviet authorities to the criminality of store and trade personnel, individuals higher up in the chain of command also benefit from their ability to allocate and influence the distribution of consumer goods. Such positions are so desirable that some individuals pay large sums to procure them (for details, see Simis, 1977–8: 42). The notary who certifies the sale of private homes and *dachas* is often 'rewarded' for completing the appropriate paperwork. Employees of organisations allocating cars and housing often take bribes to move individuals up the waiting list or even provide them with these desired items years ahead of schedule. In Georgia, a former *ispolkom* (local unit of government) chairman was sentenced to death for collecting 88 000 rubles in bribes for facilitating the illegal exchange and acquisition of apartments (Fuller, 1980).

Corruption is also widespread in education. Although only some heads of educational institutions have been thrown out for accepting bribes to admit students, the practice seems to be widespread (Simis, 1977–8: 42). One of the most notable cases of this was the recent dismissal of the law faculty dean at Moscow State University. Entrance to law school had become very desirable because of the potential for obtaining large illegal incomes among members of the criminal justice apparatus (Zemtsov, 1985: 11; Simis, 1982: 96–125). The extent of this corruption is evidenced by the Azerbaidzhan Party Secretary Aliev's closure of that republic's law school to the offspring of all justice personnel (Grigo, 1981: R17).

The *shabashniki* or wildcatters are individuals who earn money by working illegally or semi-legally within the official economy. Unlike the employees of the consumer sector whose positions enable them to obtain small or large illegal payments, it is the physical labour of *shabashniki* which gives them their income. The tangible benefits the *shabashniki* provide the official economy often make Soviet officials look the other way, but the popular resentment of their large incomes, as well as the state's ideological commitment to the centralised allocation of labour resources, often causes them to run foul of the law.

Shabashniki are usually men 25 to 40 years of age who work in the construction trades or as agricultural workers on state and collective farms (Murphy, 1985: 48). Other times they are college-aged students who earn extra money during their summer vacations. As manpower is in constant short supply in the agricultural sector brigades, *shabashniki* hire themselves out to farms ('Private Sector . . .', 1985; Murphy, 1985: 50–1). *Shabashniki* account for half the construction workers in some regions of the USSR (Murphy, 1985: 51–2).

Although the *shabashniki* perform services that are useful for the official economy, they are frequently fined by the police for violating passport laws and are even sometimes prosecuted for 'private entrep-reneurial activity' (Article 153 of the Russian Socialist Federal Soviet Republic Criminal Code) or for bribery (Simis, 1982: 259).

Another form of illegal labour activity is the addition by managers of so-called 'dead souls' (or 'ghost' workers) to the payroll. Workers take a second job but appear only at their places of primary employment. They are paid wages as if they appear at the job and they are forced to share these illegal wages with those who hire them. Prosecutions for such activities are not unknown and the penalties meted out to the masterminds of such schemes are often substantial (Turovsky, 1981: 161–3).

In the industrial sector a wide range of illegal activity exists within the official economy. These illegal activities occur, as two Polish social scientists explain, because 'managers find the social goals underlying the plans and orders of the Central Planners obscure or impossible to interpret. As a result, these goals cannot serve as the basis of the managers' activity' (Kurczewski and Frieske, 1977: 493). As one western commentator has added, 'the highly centralised character of management over all types of organisation nourishes a pervasive tendency to indulge in false reporting about organisations' performance' (Lampert, 1984: 367). Compounding these difficulties are the problems of delivery, inadequate supplies and labour shortages that frustrate their efforts to meet production norms.

Perhaps the most flagrant example of illegal activity within the official economy is the existence of underground factories that operate 'behind the protective facade of a state owned factory or collective farm' (Grossman, 1977: 31). Raw materials may be diverted from the official state enterprise to an underground factory that produces a consumer item in short supply. A complex cover operation has to be developed to mask the work that the employees are to be doing in the official factory and significant pay-offs have to be made to inspectors and ministerial employees that supervise the government operation. Despite the great potential risks for the managers of these 'factories', such ventures sometimes flourish for years until they are uncovered and their leaders prosecuted.

Parallel Illegal Economy

The previous discussion has focused on the many forms of second economy activity that occur within the official economy. But many forms of such activity exist parallel to the first economy. These consist of unlicensed private production and sales, black markets as well as contraband.

As in the capitalist economies of the West, the so-called victimless crimes lead to illegal markets. Alcohol production is tightly controlled by the state but many individuals turn to illegal markets to satisfy their demands. The Soviet proclivity for alcohol makes *samogon* or home brew the largest field of private production and sale; while there is a smaller degree of production in urban areas, many rural inhabitants manufacture alcohol and sell it to supplement their incomes. The illegal production of wine, beer and other forms of alcohol is on a massive scale. It has been estimated that the value of illegal annual alcohol production is between one and two billion rubles (Treml, 1986). Although Soviet authorities since the onset of the anti-alcohol campaign in May 1985 have made an initial effort to suppress private alcohol production by destroying vineyards on private plots and distilling equipment, *samogon* production has continued on a massive scale, primarily because the law enforcement campaign lost its impetus, home brewers have become more skillful in evading detection and the demand has increased due to the limited availability of vodka in state stores ('Stop the Home Brewer', 1987: 20).

Although drug addiction is much less of a problem than alcoholism, since the early 1970s there has been a growing use of illicit drugs and an illegal traffic in opium derivates to meet this demand ('Growing Concern . . .', 1986; Gabiani, 1987: 9–10; Sergeev, 1987: 12). This problem has been exacerbated since the Soviet war in Afghanistan. Illegal drug cultivation occurs primarily in Central Asia and Azerbaidzhan (Katsenelinboigen, 1977: 85) and drugs are then transported throughout the country by complex networks. Soviet authorities have combatted *samogon* production for decades, but their inexperience in combatting illicit drug activity renders them relatively ineffective ('*Growing Concern* . . .', 1986: 2–3).

In addition, prostitution is now an administrative though not a criminal offence (Mysyakov and Yakubovich, 1986: 21–2). As in other areas of illicit activity, participation is stratified, ranging from part-time prostitutes to full-time 'street walkers' and to those who cater to foreigners and serve the Soviet élite (Kislinskaya, 1987: 1–4).

Illegal or black markets have arisen in a diverse range of items. Some of these markets, run by speculators, deal in consumer items that are in continuous short supply – a consequence of the problems inherent in a centrally planned economy. Other black markets deal with goods that are unavailable through official sources due to official state controls over the press and the means of mass communications, such as forbidden books (Bush, 1986), records and videos. Still other markets have arisen in such items as gold and precious jewels, commodities that Soviet citizens are not permitted privately to buy and sell.

The largest black market is that of ordinary consumer goods, since it addresses the needs of most Soviet citizens. In certain situations, these markets exist out in the open with only occasional interference by Soviet law enforcement officials. In other cases, the trade occurs in semi-public places like public bathrooms. In the case of gold and precious jewels, the trade is often highly clandestine and occurs only with the involvement of highly placed officials who are bribed generously to look the other way (Simis, 1982: 56–9).

The existence of the illegal second economy at the workplace and outside of it has led to widespread corruption. Corruption, defined according to the Soviet criminal code as abuse of authority (RSFSR Criminal Code, Article 170), or bribery (RSFSR Criminal Code, Articles 173–174) (Kvitsinia, 1980) is pervasive at all levels of the Soviet system. Most, but not all, individuals manage to participate in the illegal parallel markets without negative consequences. As the following section indicates, Soviet citizens are prosecuted for their participation in the second economy particularly during periods of political transition.

Law Enforcement and the Second Economy

'"Economic crimes" represent one of the central themes of Soviet criminal legislation, law enforcement and criminal law theory' (Pomorski, 1978: 293). Recurrent campaigns against illegal economic activity, especially since Brezhnev's death,[5] underline the importance which control over the economy has to the Soviet leadership. 'Yet the Soviet form of political management itself helps to create an environment in which illegal practices flourish' (Lampert, 1984: 367). The Soviet leadership is, therefore, torn between cracking down on participants in the second economy and allowing the system the flexibility it needs to survive.

Prosecutions of participants in the second economy comprise a significant part of all criminal prosecutions. National Soviet crime statistics reveal that in the 1960s 9 per cent of total convictions were of individuals accused of economic and official crimes (Ostroumov, 1970: 298). In Georgia (a republic known for disproportionate participation in illegal activity), in the late 1970s, over 15 per cent of all convictions were for economic crimes and another 7 per cent were for official crimes (Gabiani and Gachechiladze, 1982: 86–108).

The sentences imposed for participation in the shadow economy can range from fines, correctional labour, and minor terms of incarceration to the death penalty for large scale embezzlement of state property. Almost a third of all death sentences, a figure estimated at several hundred a year, are meted out to those involved in large scale corruption or illegal business activity (Kline, 1987).[6] The type of sanction involved depends on the relationship of the offence to the official economy. As one Western analyst suggests, second economy activities which do not benefit the official economy encounter little toleration, whereas second economy activities that support the official economy are often tolerated. Furthermore, milder criminal sanctions seem to be applied when there are moderate financial gains, high status offenders, or the offence has been perpetrated in the Caucasus (Feldbrugge, 1984: 542).

Party members who participate in the second economy and misuse their positions may be disciplined through the party instead of the courts. As party members must first be expelled from the party before they stand trial, party leaders are hesitant to lose skilful managers even if they have been involved in illegal activity. Consequently, 90 per cent of managers accused of economic offences in the early 1970s received party sanctions rather than criminal sentences (Korobeinikov, 1973: 72). The total number of criminal prosecutions and individuals sanctioned by the party for illegal economic activity, while representing a large number of cases annually, is still a small number relative to the total number of Soviet citizens participating in the second economy (Pomorski and Ginsburgs, 1980).

With so many Soviet citizens eligible for prosecution, the question remains who is singled out to receive penalties. The reasons for prosecution are both economic and political. Many prosecutions for economic crimes occur in waves as campaigns are launched against these offences. As Łoś contends, it is the five year economic planning cycle that influences prosecutions. Procurators in the first three years of a plan are encouraged to prosecute a diverse range of offences. In the fourth year of a plan, as pressures on managers to reach their quotas increase, prosecution of economic crimes like theft and embezzlement which threaten production are targeted. In the fifth and final year of the plan, prosecutions are heightened for report padding and falsification of records, as managers attempt to fulfill their plans (Łoś, 1983: 52–3).

Those who have been singled out for prosecution are often multiple offenders (Kvitsinia, 1980: 126–7) whose blatant conduct makes them particularly vulnerable. But they may also be individuals who, having served their political utility, are conveniently removed by means of corruption charges (Shelley, 1987). Furthermore, prosecutions are often 'aimed at mobilising official agencies and public opinion in support of general goals fixed by the party and central planning agencies' (Łoś, 1983: 52).

A complex system exists to ensure that both managers and workers abide by the law. Elaborate systems of controls exist within organisations as well as at the ministerial level (Lampert, 1984: 372–5). Furthermore, the OBKhSS (the Department for the Struggle Against the Theft of Socialist Property) under the Ministry of Internal Affairs has a system of informants in organisations and enterprises to detect bribery, embezzlement and other forms of economic misconduct. The ordinary police (the *militsiia*) as well as the KGB (in cases of large scale illegal economic activity) share responsibility with the OBKhSS. The procuracy is the organisation with general oversight authority (Berenzon and Iastrebov, 1974: 37–8) as well as the concrete obligation to prosecute cases of illegal economic activity.

Yet the success of the campaigns against economic crime is not determined solely by the effectiveness of these organisations, as a 'tension between law and illegality' (Lampert, 1984: 384) exists. Members of the law enforcement system can be influenced by financial payments as well as by the exercise of party and personal connections. The individual's success in forestalling prosecution is determined by the extent of his connections and his financial resources.

CONCLUSION

The socialisation of the means of agricultural and industrial production as well as the system of centralised planning and control have led to government domination over the official Soviet economy. Yet an extensive second economy existing both within and outside the official Soviet economy has developed during the past seventy years. This growth of the second economy is a consequence of the inefficien-

cy of the planned economy, as well as the inability of the official
economy to meet the needs of many of its citizens.

Contrary to expectations that a centrally planned economy would
effectively hinder private initiative and illegal activity, many conditions have facilitated the emergence of illegal activity. Salaried
workers see limited financial advantage in hard work or longevity of
service, and limited incentives exist for managers to increase production. Consequently, all levels of Soviet personnel have looked for
additional compensation outside of the planned economy. Managers
sometimes shortchange their enterprises but they are able to meet
their production plans by manufacturing substandard goods. The
omnipresent waste that is inherent in the poorly co-ordinated and
centrally planned system has led workers to undervalue state property. Consequently, many Soviet citizens see embezzlement of socialist
property as being inherently different from theft of private property.
Finally, the widespread shortages of items needed for production and
to satisfy consumer demands lead to illicit markets within and outside
the official economy.

The second economy provides the flexibility that the Soviet system
needs to survive. Although the authorities realise its utility, they seek
to control the unofficial economy by means of the law enforcement
apparatus when they believe that illegal economic activity is stifling
the effectiveness of the official economy, or becoming so pervasive as
to undermine support for the existing political system. Periodic
campaigns are launched against various participants in the second
economy (black-marketeers, speculators, *samogon* producers) in an
effort to limit their activity and to establish for the general population
the parameters of permissible activity.

Gorbachev has recently taken a bold step in legitimising parts of
the second economy. The recent adoption of the legislation on
private labour initiative legalises certain small scale private business
and permits informal arrangements between individuals and Soviet
enterprises. But this newly enacted legislation legitimises only a small
share of the illegal activity that presently exists. Nonetheless the
recognition that certain activity outside the official economy is
permissible does much to diffuse the perceived threat of the unofficial
economy. Furthermore, this legislation was an important preliminary
step before the adoption of Gorbachev's dramatic economic initiative
at the June 1987 Central Committee meeting which changed the
system of fixed pricing and total dependence on centralised planning
(Lee, 1987: A25, A31).

The emergence of the large Soviet second economy has led to a stratified system with its own élite. Contrary to expectations, the social structure of the second economy is not entirely distinct from that of the state run economy, because there is much overlap between the official and unofficial élite. At the top of the unofficial economy are the large-scale underground businessmen who organise sizable operations to produce or distribute goods. Although many of these individuals do not hold significant positions in the official economy, their survival depends on their ties to members of the official élite. Consequently, a significant proportion of the ill-gotten gains of the leaders of the unofficial economy are transferred to members of the party élite.

Below this level are the large numbers of small-scale private businessmen, moonlighting professionals and full-time black-marketeers. Many of these individuals survive as a result of their influence with mid-level government functionaries and their pay-offs to law enforcement personnel. Although many of the businessmen and professionals are now able to do legitimately what was previously outside the law, it can be presumed that many individuals will continue to operate in these areas without registering with the authorities.

At the bottom of the second economy are those numerous citizens who supplement their meagre incomes through some form of illegal or semi-legal activity. This includes small-scale producers of moonshine, petty thieves in factories as well as shop personnel who set aside merchandise for favoured customers. Individuals who try to fend off prosecution through bribes frequently become the victims of various law enforcement campaigns directed against participants in the second economy.

The diverse levels of the second economy enjoy a complex relationship with the official political and economic élite. The web of associations between the official and the unofficial economy, as well as the state-directed economy's need for the second economy ensures its perpetuation even in the face of numerous party orchestrated campaigns. The ambivalent relationship of the state and the party leadership towards the Soviet unofficial economy reveals the difficulty of securing and maintaining effective centralised control over all forms of economic activity.

24 *The Soviet Union*

NOTES

1. For a discussion of the origin of the term second economy, see Grossman, 1977: 25 and Holzman, 1981: 111–14. For an extensive bibliography on the subject see Grossman, 1985.
2. The accumulation of capital, the strong family networks (Mars and Altman, 1983; Amir, 1985), and the potential for prosecution contribute to what many consider the endemic corruption in the Asian republics.
3. This difficulty exists because 'the former often serves as a front for the latter and both support one another' (Grossman, 1977: 25).
4. Instruction and tutoring can be provided only in subjects that are already approved as part of Soviet curricula. For example, private religious or Hebrew instruction would remain illegal as these are not authorised subjects.
5. The most important of these is the recent campaign against unearned income (Kurkov, 1987; Shokhin, 1986: 4–5), which took effect in July 1986.
6. See, for example, the recent executions for bribery (Ovechkina, 1987: R11).

REFERENCES

Amir, M., 'Georgian Jews from the USSR: Problems of Criminality and Adaptation to Israeli Society', *Crossroad* (14) (1985) pp. 57–77.
Bauman, Z., *Hidden Economy – East and West* (Washington, D.C.: National Council for Soviet and Eastern European Research, 1986).
Berenzon, A. D. and V. B. Iastrebov, *Bor'ba s khishcheniami na predpriiatiakh* (Moscow: Iuridicheskaia Literatura, 1974).
Brovkin, V. and D. Gorbuntsov, 'Is the Cucumber Guilty', *Current Digest of the Soviet Press*, XXXVIII (28) (1986) pp. 9, 13.
Bush, K., *Books on the Soviet Second Economy* (Washington, D.C.: National Council for Soviet and East European Research, 1986).
Feldbrugge, F. J. M., 'Government and Shadow Economy in the Soviet Union', *Soviet Studies*, XXXVI (4) (1984) pp. 528–43.
Fuller, E., 'Georgian Official Sentenced to Death for Bribery', *Radio Liberty Research* (290/80) (1980).
Gabiani, A. A., '"White Death" in the Mirror of Sociology', *Current Digest of the Soviet Press*, XXXIX (8) (1987) pp. 9–10.
Gabiani, A. A. and R. G. Gachechiladze, *Nekotorye voprosy geografii prestupnosti* (Tblisi: Izd. Tbilisskogo universiteta, 1982).
Grigo, A., 'Let Justice Prevail', *FBIS Daily Reports* (2 December 1981) pp. R15–24.
Grossman, G., 'The "Second Economy" of the USSR', *Problems of Communism*, 26 (5) (1977) pp. 25–40.
Grossman, G., *The Second Economy in the USSR and Eastern Europe: A*

Bibliography (Paper 1, Berkeley–Duke Occasional Papers on the Second Economy in the USSR, 1985).

'Growing Concern over the Drug Scene', *Current Digest of the Soviet Press*, XXXVIII (34) (1986) pp. 1–3.

Holzman, F., 'The Second Economy in CMEA: A Terminological Note', *ACES Bulletin*, XXIII (1) (1981) pp. 111–14.

Kairzhanov, E. I., 'Nekotorye voprosy bor'by s prestupnonebrezhnym ispolzovaniem i khraneniem sel'skokhozaiistvennoi tekhniki', *Voprosy ugolovnogo prava i protsessa* (Alma-Ata) (7) (1963) pp. 80–95.

Katsenelinboigen, A., 'Coloured Markets in the Soviet Union', *Soviet Studies*, XXIX (1) (1977) pp. 62–85.

Kislinskaya, L., '"Easy Virtue" on the Scales of Justice', *Current Digest of the Soviet Press*, XXXIX (11) (1987) pp. 1–4.

Kline, G., *Capital Punishment for Crimes against Property in the USSR* (Washington, D.C.: Kennan Institute Occasional Paper, 1987).

Korobeinikov, B. V., 'Bor'ba s prestupnymi narusheniiami gosudarstvennoi distipliny v narodnom khozaistve (Otvetststvennost' i preduprezhdenie)', *Sovetskoe Gosudarstvo i Pravo* (10) (1973) pp. 72–4.

Kurczewski, J. and K. Frieske, 'Some Problems in the Legal Regulation of the Activities of Economic Institutions', *Law and Society*, XI (1977) pp. 489–505.

Kurkov, A., 'The Citizen, Society and the Law', *JPRS* (4 February 1987) pp. 100–4.

Kvitsinia, A. K., *Vziatochnichestvo i bor'ba s nim* (Sukhumi: Alashara, 1980).

Lampert, N., 'Law and Order in the USSR: The Case of Economic and Official Crime', *Soviet Studies*, XXXVI (3) (1984) pp. 366–85.

Lane, D., *Soviet Economy and Society* (New York: New York University Press, 1985).

Lee, G., 'Party Girds Gorbachev for Reform Fight', *Washington Post* (28 June 1987) pp. A25, A31).

Łoś, M., 'Crime and Economy in the Communist Countries', in P. Wickman and T. Dailey (eds), *White Collar and Economic Crime* (Lexington, Mass.: Lexington Books, 1982) pp. 121–37.

Łoś, M., 'Economic Crimes in Communist Countries', in I. L. Barak-Glantz and E. H. Johnson (eds), *Comparative Criminology* (Beverly Hills: Sage, 1983) pp. 39–57.

Lubin, N., *Labor and Nationality in Soviet Central Asia* (Princeton, N.J.: Princeton University Press, 1984).

Mars, G. and Y. Altman, 'The Cultural Bases of Soviet Georgia's Second Economy', *Soviet Studies*, 35 (4) (1983) pp. 46–60.

Murphy, P., 'Soviet Shabashniki: Material Incentives at Work', *Problems of Communism*, XXXIV (6) (1985) pp. 48–57.

Mysyakov, D. and P. Yakubovich, 'Subject for Reflection: "Lady" with a Tip', *Current Digest of the Soviet Press*, XXXVIII (41) (1986) pp. 21–2.

Osipenko, P. G., 'USSR Procurator Discusses Grain Embezzlement', *JPRS USSR National Affairs* (20 May 1985) pp. R17–18.

Ostroumov, S. S., *Sovetskaia Sudebnaia Statistika* (Moscow: Iuridicheskaia Literatura, 1970).

Ovechkina, O., 'From the Courtroom: To Be Shot for Bribes', *FBIS Daily Reports* (9 February 1987) pp. R11–12.
Perevoznik, P. F., *Otvetstvennost' za melkie khishcheniia* (Moscow: Znanie, 1980).
Pomorski, S., 'Crimes against the Central Planner: "Ochkovtiratel'stvo"', in D. Barry, G. Ginsburgs and P. Maggs (eds), *Soviet Law after Stalin*, Part II (Leyden: A. W. Sijthoff, 1978) pp. 291–317.
Pomorski, S. and G. Ginsburgs, *Enforcement of Law and the Second Economy* (Washington, D.C.: Kennan Institute Occasional Paper, 1980).
'"Private Sector" Thrives in Soviet Countryside', *Current Digest of the Soviet Press*, XXXVII (24) (1985) pp. 1–3.
Sergeev, I., 'Kto daet im narkotik', *Literaturnaia Gazeta* (14 January 1987) p. 12.
Shelley, L., *Lawyers in Soviet Work Life* (New Brunswick, N.J.: Rutgers University Press, 1984).
Shelley, L., 'The Political Function of Soviet Courts: A Model for One Party States?', *Review of Socialist Law*, 13 (3) (1987) pp. 241–62.
Shokhin, A., 'Economics and Morality: Where Unearned Income Comes From', *Current Digest of the Soviet Press*, XXXVIII (16) (1986) pp. 4–5.
Simis, K., 'The Machinery of Corruption', *Survey*, XXIII (4) (1977–78) pp. 35–55.
Simis, K., *USSR: The Corrupt Society* (New York: Simon & Schuster, 1982).
'Stop the Home Brewer', *Current Digest of the Soviet Press*, XXXIX (10) (1987) pp. 20–1.
Taubman, P., 'Soviet Law Widens Private Business', *New York Times* (20 November 1986) p. A9.
Tenson, A., 'Piracy on the Soviet Railroads', *Radio Liberty Research*, (276/80) (1980).
Treml, V., *Alcohol in the Soviet Underground Economy* (Washington, D.C.: National Council for Soviet and Eastern European Research, 1986).
Turovsky, F., 'Society without a Present', in L. Shapiro and J. Godson (eds), *The Soviet Worker*, (New York: St Martin's Press, 1981) pp. 156–93.
Utkin, M. S., 'Kriminalisticheskaia kharakteristika khishchenii', in L. A. Iantsen (ed.), *Aktual'nye problemy kriminalizatsii i dekriminalizatsii obshchestvenno opasnykh deianii* (Omsk: Omskaia vysshaia shkola militsii, 1980) pp. 129–37.
'V Politbiuro TsK KPSS', *Pravda* (21 November 1986) pp. 1, 3.
'Zakon vstupaet v silu', *Literaturnaia Gazeta* (29 April 1987) p. 11.
Zemstov, I., *The Private Life of the Soviet Elite* (New York: Crane Russak, 1985).

3 The Dynamics of the Second Economy in Poland[1]

Maria Łoś

THE FIRST (STATE) ECONOMY

In the period immediately following the Second World War and the imposition of the Soviet-backed communist government in Poland, only large and medium-scale plants were taken over by the new state (on 3 January 1946), while retail trade, services, crafts, and small-scale industrial industrial firms remained in private hands (Zieliński, 1974; Åslund, 1984: 429). But the years 1947–8 witnessed an ideological battle over trade between the Communists and more moderate Socialists in which the latter were defeated (Kaliński, 1970). By the end of the 1940s all industries were effectively nationalised and private trade and craftsmanship liquidated. This was achieved by 'a combination of ruthless, inconsistent laws, withdrawal of licences, prohibitive taxation, unprofitably low fixed prices, lawless persecution, etc.', all of which was officially labelled as a 'sharp class struggle' (Åslund, 1984: 429, 430; also Åslund, 1985a: 25–33; Kaliński, 1970).

Poland's rapid expansion of industry, which took place in 1950–5, copied faithfully the Soviet model of industrialisation, whereby industries producing means of production were given absolute priority and the whole organisation of production was subordinated to military goals. Those branches of the economy which had been particularly successful before the war, such as light industry, crafts and agriculture, were completely neglected (*Raport. . . .* , 1986: 53).

The military reorientation of the Polish economy was initiated in 1948 with Stalin's momentous decision ordering Poland rapidly to build a large military–industrial complex. It was 'organized over a three-year period by simply taking over a large portion of existing and much needed civilian factories' (Chęciński, 1983: 32). Moreover, 'totally new and very large factories were built and equipped with a

27

growing flow of Soviet machines useful only for producing military goods' (Chęciński, 1983: 35). By 1953, employment in military-related industry constituted 8 to 10 per cent of total industrial employment (Chęciński, 1983: 35).

Reforms of the official economy undertaken in Poland following the so-called 'Stalinist' period have been both numerous and remarkably unsuccessful. Perhaps the most weighty changes took place in the second part of the 1950s, the years of political liberalisation and economic decentralisation. Yet, preceded by the liquidation of the workers' councils in 1958–9, even these reforms were restricted in the 1960s, the period of gradual political and, above all, economic de-liberalisation. The late 1960s brought intensified anti-reformist feelings among a significant part of the political apparatus who were apprehensive of any prospects of weakening the full and direct party control of the economy (see Zieliński, 1974: 71–2). As Zieliński concluded, based on the period 1956–70, Polish reforms of that period were rather spurious, as they tended to focus on limiting the central command aspect while simultaneously extending the parametric state management. The latter is characterised by the manipulation of wages, prices, taxes, and interest rates to achieve centrally fixed economic objectives, as opposed to the traditional reliance on the direct administrative management based on the legally binding directives of a detailed Central Plan (Zieliński, 1974: 45, 66).

In the 1970s, Poland experienced a second wave of industrialisation based on foreign credits, which aimed at the selective modernisation of its industrial base. Once again, however, the focus of new investment was almost exclusively on heavy industry. The technology of the rapidly developing electronic industry was never applied in the consumer goods area, nor was it used to streamline the existing, highly wasteful technologies in heavy industry (*Raport. . . .* , 1986: 62). Furthermore, compared to other Eastern European countries, Poland was burdened with a disproportionate share of the cost of the Warsaw Pact's arms policy. During the years 1969–79, 'Poland had a negative arms trade balance totalling nearly US$ 400 million', and it was thus forced to 'finance its net arms imports with a large portion of its earnings from non-military exports' (Chęciński, 1983: 39).

The 1970s was a decade that inevitably brought a possibility of a greater integration of the Polish economy with Western markets, yet those prospects were nullified by the general failure of adopted policies, the misapplication of foreign credits, and unrestrained corruption. Thus, as a result of both the dissipation of Western loans and the imposition of the martial law in 1981, Soviet control of the Polish economy has once again been firmly reinstated. Indeed, a momentous economic agreement was signed by the two states on 7 October 1985, which included provisions for Soviet use of Polish industrial capacity (Kusin, 1986: 49). Thus has begun a new stage of a rapidly increasing Soviet presence within the state economy of Poland, including mergers of Soviet and Polish firms whereby the latter are required to adjust their production to the Soviet economic plan (see, for example, 'Ekonomiczeskaja Gazieta', 1987: 6). Clearly, in addition to the continuous subordination of the whole Polish heavy industry to the Soviet military programmes, the post-Solidarity period has witnessed an intensified effort to make the whole Polish economy inseparable from the Soviet one.

Following the suppression of the Solidarity Union's economic proposals in the 1980s, yet another attempt at reforming the ailing economy was announced. Despite a relatively open discussion of the merits of a market-based economy, the reforms of the 1980s have focused once again on 'decentralising' the nationalised economy – a futile undertaking when the dogma of the monopolistic state management remains intact.

THE PARALLEL URBAN LEGAL ECONOMY

The rather barren economic reforms implemented after the Stalinist period have been accompanied by certain changes in the generally restrictive policies towards private entrepreneurship (see Åslund, 1985a: 19–117 for an excellent discussion of the private economy in post-war Poland). The 1970s brought some changes – albeit inconsistent and erratic – in the status of small-scale industrial and handicraft enterprises which had been revived in post-Stalinist years. These changes signalled the green light for their final lawful inclusion into the private sector. The sorry state of the nationalised economy and the society's mistrust towards the loudly publicised economic reforms have led in the 1980s to further reluctant concessions to the 'private economic initiative' (*prywatna inicjatywa*). The 1981 resolution (No. 112) of the Council of Ministers proclaimed the equal treatment of handicrafts and other branches of the small-scale economy, both private and 'socialised' (Åslund, 1985b: 23), which had been demanded by the Solidarity Union. This signalled a certain ideological climate rather than a real attempt legally to equalise private and public sectors.

While in the late 1970s individual leaseholding within the state economy (involving boutiques, restaurants, and so forth) was the most dynamic of all types of entrepreneurship, in the early 1980s, small-scale private ownership seemed to be preferred, and favoured treatment was offered to the so-called 'Polonian' enterprises. The latter, small-scale manufacturing firms wholly owned by foreigners or Poles residing abroad, had been allowed by the legislation of 1976, but were more actively encouraged only at the beginning of the 1980s (Åslund, 1985a: 115–16). In only two years from 1982 to 1984 the number of Polonian firms jumped from 250 to 500 – employing 25 000 persons – in swift reaction to the new favourable terms governing their operation. Predictably, however, their high productivity and the high wages they offered soon provoked new restrictions and negative publicity in the media (see Åslund, 1984: 429, 1985b: 29; Łoś, 1987: 36; Rymwid, 1985: 13; Zarzecki, 1983: 6). Even despite the policy of active harassment, including raised taxes and restricted possibilities of transferring export revenues abroad, this type of ownership proved to be quite resilient, and in 1987 there were already 670 foreign firms employing approximately 62 000 people ('Perspektywy . . .', 1987: 2). Poland has not been able, however, to attract serious foreign investors, with a proven business record, who understandably prefer more stable and predictable environments.

The changes that took place in the 1980s also include a revision of the restrictions which forbade private producers to sell their produce to state companies. This has extended the scope of their production, but has simultaneously increased their integration and inter-dependency with the official economy. Despite the considerable expansion of the industry-oriented production and services, the main lines of private trade and services remain targeted at individual clients including retail outlets in vegetables, fruit, clothes, and crafts, as well as catering, tailoring, carpentry, home construction and repairs, travel and taxi services. New electronic services, related to the boom in the private importation and construction of computers, video equipment, etc. have also been noticeably active in recent years.

The bureaucracies authorised to issue licences for individual entrepreneurs are exceedingly slow and formalistic, demand numerous diplomas and qualifications certificates, and are known to extort bribes (Warzocha, 1988: 4). Nevertheless, according to the official

data, the number of registered, non-socialised (private) economic
units more than doubled in the early 1980s: from 357 142 in 1987 to
897 175 in 1984, while the number of their employees climbed from
654 075 to 897 175 respectively (995 600 in 1986). In 1984, the crafts
sector employed 74 per cent of all private employees; transport of
people and goods, 12 per cent; retail trade and catering, 8 per cent,
and foreign firms employed roughly 5 per cent ('Perspektywy . . .',
1987: 2; *Rocznik* . . . , 1985: 390–1; *Mały Rocznik*, 1987: 47).

For their part, the authorities are involved in a constant effort to
make the private sector compatible with the centrally planned
economy, through strictly limiting supplies of materials, restricting
employment quotas, imposing price controls, and implementing
restrictive taxation policies. Faced with the rigidly alloted quotas of
supplies – which make profitable operation of these businesses all but
impossible through legitimate channels – entrepreneurs have no
choice but to pay black-market prices or to bribe employees of the
state supply agencies in order to secure the additional materials
essential to their production. They also frequently employ more
people than permitted, in order to carry out their illegally expanded
production. In addition, they sell at least part of their output for
inflated black-market prices to make up for their covert costs, like
bribes and black-market purchases. The policy of state imposed
prices paralyses the operation of market mechanisms, subordinates
the private sector firmly to the central command system and necessitates massive and obtrusive state control operations.

Moreover, Poland's unrealistic and ever-changing tax policy seems
to be based on an assumption that private entrepreneurs will always
cheat the authorities, and will be able to find illegal ways of making
their business operations worthwhile. For example, the tax policy
recognises only in a minimal degree the costs of initial investments,
the risks and fluctuating profits inherent in a market economy and the
need to pay higher wages to the employees who relinquish certain
perks and benefits related to state employment to work in the
private sector. This discourages private investment in more technologically sophisticated production and any reinvestment of profits.
Moreover, the highly progressive taxation provokes dishonesty as
'every illegal concealment of a fraction of total revenues gives
disproportionally large reductions in taxes' (Kowalczyk, 1985: 5; this
and all subsequent quotations from Polish sources have been translated by this author). Constant changes in the tax policy, which lead
to an extreme sense of insecurity among entrepreneurs, reveal the

fundamental ideological and political problems that the private sector poses to the communist authorities. The policy oscillates between incompatible goals of enhancing production on the one hand, and punishing entrepreneurs for their unorthodox success on the other. They are also convenient scapegoats blamed for causing labour shortages, inflation, excessive economic inequality, and a revival of the bourgeois mentality.

The vulnerable political situation of the private sector creates an opportunity for corruption and embezzlement whereby all those involved in supplying, taxing and controlling of private businesses expect additional payments or favours. Even according to the official sources, bribery has been increasing faster than any other crime, with the exception only of economic mismanagement, which shows similar increases (see the report of the Prosecutor General for 1986, 'Posiedzenie Rady . . .', 1987: 2). As the president of the National Crafts Council remarked in a 1984 interview published in the official weekly *Polityka*: 'if almost every purchase requires greasing someone's palm, how can we talk about absolute honesty? Corruption does not plague just the private sector' (Modzelewski, 1984: 4). Another interviewee, the president of the Association of Private Trade and Services (Warsaw Branch) maintains that public opinion is completely misinformed about the problems facing the private sector, and that the media conduct a never-ending smear campaign against private entrepreneurs, refusing to acknowledge their vulnerability. According to her, 'if craftsmen often refuse to give an invoice, it is because they have to cover the "extra" cost of conducting their economic activity under abnormal circumstances, when virtually nothing can be purchased in a straight way' (Nowakowska, 1984: 4).

Despite the prevalent reliance on bribery, also in dealing with the law enforcers, the offending businesses are not always able to avert punishment. For example, a Polish daily reported in 1987 that in merely three months, 2149 controls and fiscal investigations of both registered and unregistered private businesses were completed leading to 1484 charges, out of which, however, only 686 were against registered firms; the remaining charges were being levelled against the operators within the hidden/illegal economy ('Wysokie grzywny . . .', 1987: 6). While the law enforcement is selective, the risk of detection is generally high due to widespread illegalities, and the potential punishment is likely to include incarceration. The risk of criminal sanctions notwithstanding, however, the class of entrepreneurs has grown in the 1980s and its social composition has changed dramatically, attracting increasing numbers of college graduates disillusioned with the limited official opportunities open to them. The earlier social indignation and stigma attached to private money-making ventures seem to have faded and instead private businessmen have become 'objects of envy and adoration' (Rykowski and Władyka, 1988: 5; see also ZG PTS, 1987: 52). On the other hand, the pauperised intelligentsia appears to be losing its traditional status of prestige and moral influence.

The programme of economic reforms of the mid-1980s emphasised the importance of the state and co-operative small businesses in order not to lose ground completely to the rapidly growing private initiative in manufacturing. Yet, according to the state Commission on the Economic Reform, 'after a brief period of activisation, the socialised small producers show again in recent years a tendency to stagnate', and despite the introduction of new policies and legislations, 'the practice presents a totally different picture than the official declarations' ('Biurokracja . . .', 1987: 1). Services – which employ only 5–7 per cent of the total labour force – constitute another chronically troubled and underdeveloped sector of the state economy that seems unable to compete with private entrepreneurship. The official party–governmental commission concluded in 1987 that the existing socialised service sector was unable to fulfil its function, and it recommended '[revising] the existing legal regulations on speculation in order to ensure that entrepreneurship which could stimulate the development of services would not be portrayed as speculation and would be instead supported in all possible ways' ('Stanowisko . . .', 1987: 6). It stated further that the prevalent practices of 'protecting the state interests, sheltering them from possible competition [would] have to be eliminated' (p. 6). An editorial in the main Warsaw daily makes clear, however, that any support for free competition between these two sectors should be qualified. Commenting on a proposal for joint ventures involving both private and state businesses, it argues that: 'the possibility of the utilisation of the private sector to revive the economy does not constitute a threat to the socialist system. For it is possible to set a limit beyond which a private company would be automatically converted into a mixed state-private share-holding firm' ('Orientacja . . .', 1987: 2).

The non-agricultural private sphere is thus not seen as an economic sector in its own right, but as a desperately needed stimulator of the small-scale state economy. Consequently, its own economic success – just as its success in fulfilling its officially defined mission – is expected to contribute to its demise. The private sector appears to be caught between the temptations of expansion and profit-making and the ever-present threat of outliving its direct usefulness to the first economy.

THE PARALLEL RURAL LEGAL SECOND ECONOMY

Private farms account for almost three quarters of the cultivated land in Poland (*Rocznik* . . . , 1985: 277). Yet, as indicated in the 1985 report prepared by a group of independent experts in Poland, private agriculture has been systematically subjected to both economic and political exploitation. The first consists in extracting all the economic surplus in order to finance heavy industry and subsidise inefficient collectivised farming. The political exploitation, on the other hand, is based on the official view that private agriculture constitutes the most backward sector of the economy and, therefore, does not deserve full political recognition (*Raport*. . . , 1986: 72). Polish peasants have for decades been treated as ideologically retarded, second-rate citizens and deliberately kept in a state of extreme insecurity. They have been subjected to various forms of direct economic and political oppression – ranging from violent attempts at collectivisation in the early 1950s to compulsory deliveries of their output in the 1950s and 1960s, to the imposition of detailed plans of production for each individual farm in the 1970s.

Following the total resistance to the early efforts at compulsory collectivisation in 1948-56, whereby only 23 per cent of the cultivated land had been successfully collectivised, the ruling party had to assume more subtle forms of pressure. While the policy of coercion was officially called off in 1957, the heavily subsidised 'socialised' agricultural sector has continued to be given political and economic priority. The administrative controls over the private sector, relaxed only temporarily in the late 1950s, grew rapidly in the following decade. A new policy introduced by Edward Gierek, who took over the party leadership in 1970 did, however, offer some degree of deregulation and other favourable changes in the treatment of farmers. They were given permission to acquire lands from the state land fund; compulsory deliveries were abolished, and prices paid to farmers were raised. As a result, agricultural production grew in 1970–3 by approximately 6 per cent per year (Gałęski, 1986: 91). However, in 1973 this policy was reversed. It started with the creation of the co-operative agricultural circles, 'which controlled the farmers' access to machinery and other resources. In 1974, local chairmen were authorized to make decisions on the production profile of individual farms' (Gałęski, 1986: 92). Moreover, the state retained the monopoly over trade in grain and meat, two crucial agricultural products.

The preferential treatment given to the 'socialised' sector, and especially co-operatives, is well illustrated by the fact that in 1974 the value of investments per hectare exceeded 12 000 *zlotych* in co-operatives, 7000 in state farms and amounted to a mere 1900 in the private sector. Three years later, in 1977, the value of investment in the latter remained the same while it more than doubled for co-operatives (Fallenbuchl, 1980: 35). Income *per capita* in farmers' families fell drastically and the share of private land fell to the all-time low of about 69 per cent of the cultivated land. The economic results of this policy were disastrous. In the words of a renowned Canadian specialist on the Polish economy, 'if someone decided to destroy agricultural production in Poland, he could not choose a more effective policy to achieve it' (Fallenbuchl, 1980: 35).

In 1981, the Rural Solidarity Union demanded equality of farmers and industrial workers, full independence for individual farmers, as well as equal treatment of private and public agricultural sectors. Eventually, fearful of the newly developing solidarity between peasants and workers, the authorities granted certain privileges to the former, while scolding and disciplining the latter. The deepening economic crisis of the 1980s brought a renewed interest in revitalisation of agriculture as the last resort for saving the sinking economy. To remove – if only symbolically – the ever-present threat of collectivisation, a constitutional amendment was passed on July 1983 which stated that the family farm was to be recognised as a permanent feature of the socialist system. Moreover, it was made easier for peasants to purchase the necessary machinery and equipment as well as to buy land from heirless elderly farmers. Yet, private agriculture has remained highly regulated by the two state monopolies: 'the monopoly over the supply of means of production, machines, chemicals and construction materials, as well as the purchasing monopoly over the agricultural product' (*Polska 1985*, 1985: 3).

The neglect by industry of the needs of the rural economy is well expressed in the fact that only about 5 per cent of Poland's industrial production was used in the mid-1980s for the purpose of aiding agriculture (*Polska 1985*, 1985: 35). Moreover, private farmers have also been discriminated against in the availability of credits. In 1985 total credits allotted to 'socialised' farms were only 15 per cent lower than those received by private farms. Yet the former cultivated only 4451 thousand hectares, while the latter 14 425 thousand hectares. On the other hand, the private producers' contribution to the GNP is almost seven times greater than that of state farms (Spaliński, 1987: 3). Even official supporters have to admit that state-owned agriculture brings losses and represents an economic burden to the country (for example, in 1983–4 the value of output per hectare was 14 600 *zlotych*, while subsidies amounted to 18 300 *zlotych* per hectare; Kierul, 1985: 5).

Thus, based on an analysis of the preambles to relevant statutes, the author of an article in a Polish weekly concludes: 'The state "*protects*" and guarantees the legal status of individual farms. It gives "*support and assistance*" to agricultural cooperatives. And it "*develops and fortifies*" state farms' (Spaliński, 1987: 3; emphasis added).

THE ILLEGAL PARALLEL SECOND ECONOMY

The illegal economy flourished during the Stalinist period, when Polish society was subjected to the rigid but arbitrary police state with its proliferation of inconsistent regulations and *ad hoc* legislations, concentration on heavy industry, and flagrant disregard for the needs of the population (see Åslund, 1985a: 52–3). Many of the illegal entrepreneurs legalised their businesses following the liberalisation of 1956. This relaxation of policies towards private crafts was short-lived, however, and subsequent restrictions pushed many entrepreneurs back into the black market and increased the need for bribery and the activities of illegal middlemen.

The policies of the Gierek era stimulated the underground economy even further due to the 'propaganda of success' and notorious market imbalances which jointly contributed to a sharp increase in the material aspirations of the population. The corrupt élite did not seem too concerned with curbing lower level corruption and illegality as long as they themselves could profit from the second economy while maintaining their overall control over the society (Łoś, 1984). The deep economic crisis of the 1980s has brought a further expansion of the parallel illegal second economy which has assumed many functions of the virtually paralysed first economy. This process has been described as a self-defence reaction to the sharp deterioration of the population's living standard (Bednarski, 1987: 231).

Compared to legal private entrepreneurship, which is circums-cribed by the restrictive policies and in which profits are curtailed by the prevailing regulations and taxation, illegal production and trade offer more freedom and flexibility. In their most inconspicuous and usually safest form they involve individuals who render unregistered, but desperately needed services to their acquaintances and recom-mended clients. They usually hold jobs in the state economy and more often than not utilise materials, tools or time stolen from the work place. At the other end of the spectrum, large-scale parallel illegal production and services tend to use fronts provided by registered private businesses. This, of course, necessitates bribing numerous controllers and tax inspectors.

Besides the widespread production and services, another common form of the illegal parallel economy is the unlawful distribution (and redistribution) of goods. Private middlemen and speculators play an important role in an elaborate world of illegal and semi-legal traffic of foodstuffs, vodka, consumer goods, building materials, and other scarce commodities. They, in effect, introduce to the communist economy the capitalist market laws of supply and demand (see Łoś, 1987: 39; MK, 1985: 8; 'Nielegalny . . .', 1984: 6; Podemski, 1985: 4; Popkiewicz, 1984: 1, 4). Nowhere is it more evident than in the black market in foreign currency. Since the Polish *zloty* has a limited value and its purchasing power has been additionally undermined by the unprecedented rates of inflation in the 1980s, the shift towards the use of dollars as a real currency has become quite noticeable. In 1986 individual dollar accounts – which hold only a small part of the privately owned 'hard' currency – totalled $2 billion (Bugaj, 1987: 3), much of it sent by relatives living abroad or earned (often illegally) by Poles visiting foreign countries. With the increased need of the state for Western currency, more and more products can be obtained only (or mainly) for dollars, either in official 'hard-currency stores' or on the black market, which to some extent appears to be also controlled and exploited by the state (see, for example, Steven, 1982: 47–67). This situation effectively channels individual energies into efforts to obtain dollars. The 'black' value of the dollar is usually approximate-ly five times that of the official one.

The 'struggle' against speculation is among the most persistent preoccupations of the Polish authorities. The mass media tend to devote much attention to the dangerousness and moral repulsiveness of illegal markets, but they usually focus on small-scale vendors and speculators who deal with items stolen from the workplace, buy up goods in state stores in order to resell them for higher prices, or illegally sell agricultural products from their farms (see, for example, 'Amatorzy . . .', 1984: 8, 1987: 2; 'Kary . . .', 1985: 8; 'Kontrola . . .', 1981: 3; 'Kronika . . .', 1985: 4; 'Spekulacja . . .', 1984: 6; 1985: 8). Yet, in addition to this widespread small-scale speculation, highly organised and often 'well-connected' criminal rings exist which intercept large quantities of newly manufactured goods before they reach state stores. They normally act in collusion with the managers of state enterprises, who even go so far as to adjust their production to the needs and preferences of the speculators ('Narada . . .', 1984: 2; 'Nowe . . .', 1982: 2; 'Siedemdziesiąt cztery-osobowa . . .', 1984: 6; 'Spekulacja . . .', 1984: 6). Often, for instance, goods are received at the factory gates and sold on the black market while the stores for which they are intended are offered cash equivalents calculated according to the official prices and augmented by bribes. It seems that in the context of the chronic market imbalance, producers are able to terrorise the state trade to the point where the stores are forced to accept with gratitude substandard or dated articles while large quantities of state-produced goods are diverted from the state market altogether (Łoś, 1987: 40).

Legal tools of controlling speculation are constantly revised and sharpened although, in the end, even the Commission on the Struggle Against Speculation had to admit that 'the best strategy would be to increase production' ('Posiedzenie . . .', 1985: 2). A very stringent Law on Combatting Speculation was passed in 1984. It resulted in a relentless law-enforcement activity. While in 1983 speculation charges had been levelled against 14 723 persons, in 1984 the number rose to 20 829 (*Rocznik . . .* , 1985: 505) and the majority of sentences typically involved both the deprivation of freedom and fines ('Surowsze . . .', 1984: 8). By comparison, the number of speculation charges in 1980 had been 5229. Taken together, however, the charges for crimes against state property and state economy constituted in 1980 30 per cent of the total number of charges for all crimes, while in 1984 their share was 26 (*Rocznik . . .* , 1985: 505).

'Speculation' is defined in the Introduction to the bill of 1984 as 'a transaction which involves purchase-sale of goods, securities, money or even real estate, by unauthorised persons with the purpose of reselling them with a profit. It thus introduces into the circulation of goods, a redundant, intermediary link' (Janiszewska-Talago, 1984: 4–5). Yet, this 'redundant' link, which brings profits to the involved individuals (from state employees to full time black-marketeers) would not be there if it did not meet some unsatisfied economic needs. Inequitable distribution of goods and their insufficient supply, as well as the waste of goods within the state economy seem to both trigger speculation and justify it in the eyes of the population.

Indeed, the extent of waste and faulty output is quite staggering. According to the official data, the State Trade Inspection found in 1980 that 37.2 per cent of bread and pastries, 40 per cent of processed foods, 60.5 per cent of soft drinks, 29.9 per cent of canned fruit and vegetables, 35 per cent of washing powder, 51 per cent of paints, and 75 per cent of woollen fabrics were substandard. 'Retail trade outlets were reluctant to protest in the fear of not receiving anything at all from producers next time round' (W.O., 1987: 2). Likewise, those state plants which receive faulty parts and other supplies from their co-operators 'do not have any choice – they can either complain and halt production or accept what is sent' (Kastory, 1987b: 3). In 1985, 42 per cent of the industrial output was judged substandard, in 1986, 51 per cent. According to the information submitted to the Polish Diet, losses caused by faulty production in that year reached 25–40 per cent of the GNP (Kastory, 1987b: 3).

In a monopolised market where chronic shortages exclude any effective consumer control over quality, multiplying the formal controls of the production standards and distribution is a spurious exercise (Zieliński, 1974: 101). Yet the Polish Politburo commenting in June 1987 on the notorious quality problems, demanded further reinforcement of control mechanisms as the only viable remedy ('Obradowało . . .', 1987: 6).

Not surprisingly, faced with such a dissipation of their labour and the lack of meaningful reforms, state employees do not identify with their workplace, and look for economic opportunities outside the official system. When conscientious and diligent work within the 'first' economy is an object of ridicule or disdain and legal economic regulations appear to be void of any moral authority, the black economy may present a welcome forum for economic activities and exchanges free of the pressure of the centralised bureaucracy.

THE LEGAL SECOND ECONOMY ACTIVITIES WITHIN THE FIRST ECONOMY

Given the ideologically controversial nature of the private ownership of the means of production, certain forms of private initiative within the state economy have been called upon to counteract the success of the parallel economic system. For example, in 1983 Poland legalised the practice of subcontracting teams (or 'autonomous groups') whereby employees of state enterprises may be offered negotiated quasi-private contracts to fulfil some short-term or continuous projects within their plants, but outside their normal working hours (Baczyński, 1984; 'Nowa filozofia . . .', 1987: 1; Dunin-Wąsowicz, 1987: 3). With the chronic labour force shortages, general apathy, and the outflow of the best workers to the private sector, subcontracting creates for the employee an additional source of revenue and allows the introduction of a direct material interest in the production outcomes. Compared, however, to Hungary, where quasi-private contracting of employees is widespread, Polish state companies have been so far rather reluctant to implement it.

Another much discussed novelty which still awaits appropriate legislation are the so-called innovative firms charged with developing and implementing new technological solutions. They would receive preferential tax treatment and offer good financial prospects for particularly creative individuals. It is clear that this proposal has been prompted by the competition from private employers: 'It is necessary to change the present situation whereby one has to become a private vegetable grower or work in a "Polonian" firm to achieve substantial material rewards', argues the author of an article in a major Polish daily (Chadzyński, 1987: 3; see also Kastory, 1987a: 3).

Yet another proposal has been given certain publicity, namely the anti-monopoly bill which is expected to be passed in 1988 ('Bliżej . . .', 1987: 1–2). It redefines the state monopoly over the economy in such a way as to create an appearance of free competition among state producers – a clear ideological concession for a state based on the principle of a centrally planned economy.

The reform package proposed in 1987 also contained a proposal for share-holding corporations, whose shares would be available both to companies and private individuals. It would allow for a mixed, state–private ownership and a greater reliance on market mechanisms ('Orientacja . . .', 1987: 2; 'Konferencja . . .', 1987a: 6, 1987b: 6). A different bill, which was actually passed in the Diet in 1987, authorises joint capital ventures open to foreign investors as long as Poland controls at least 51 per cent of shares ('Odważny..., 1986: 11).

In sum, certain ideological concessions are being made – or at least contemplated – to revive the 'first' economy, to attract capital and manpower, and to counter the threat of competition from the separate private sector.

THE ILLEGAL SECOND ECONOMY WITHIN THE FIRST ECONOMY

The new rhetoric of the official economic reform of the mid-1980s has stressed the need for the recognition of market forces and the release of individual initiative and energy. It is well exemplified by the following comment made by a professor of economics in the leading official daily: 'Since we have now certainty that neither slogans nor commands will solve the fundamental problems of our economy, we have to bank on the economic [i.e., market] mechanism' (Orfin, 1987: 3). This new approach has resulted above all in a series of price increases in order to establish 'realistic price levels', which would suppress demand for goods in short supply. Thus, instead of increases in the supply of goods, the recommended remedy would attempt to stop people from actively looking for many scarce items which they would no longer be able to afford. Since private entrepreneurs (both legal and illegal) and speculators adjust their prices accordingly, the only source of cheaper goods is within the state economy, and the only way of obtaining them is through workplace theft. Goods stolen from the state economy has become a rapidly growing factor in the family economy. Moreover, familial and friendship ties with individuals whose work involves producing, guarding or handling goods in short supply are perceived as vital preconditions of survival.

Simple theft of state property, however, is not the only method of private exploitation within the state economy. Lack of incentives, waste and mismanagement practically invite efforts to introduce illegal incentives in order to achieve additional output, destined for private appropriation. The quality of goods is often sacrificed for the quantity of goods produced. Furthermore, with a surplus of state supplies, or additional private purchases, unplanned goods can be processed on the state enterprise's equipment, simultaneously with the official production. In each case, the surplus product is sold on

the black market or through the services of bribed employees of the
state agencies, with the profits being pocketed by private entrepreneurs. On the other hand, non-production is often represented as
production in order to obtain special financial bonuses connected
with the fulfilment or overfulfilment of the plan.

In the state-run services, second economy activities provide a
sizable extra income to numerous individuals. By rendering poor-
quality services, turning down clients, or placing them on lengthy
waiting lists, the employees of state agencies encourage private
arrangements whereby services are delivered more efficiently for an
extra fee. In catering services, part of the food alloted for consumption is often sold directly on the black market, while the quality and
weight of the served meals are substantially lowered. In the majority
of cases, illegal economic activities within the first economy involve
some form of appropriation of state property and bribery. (For
discussion and examples of this type of second economy see: 'Afera
. . .', 1984; 'Amatorzy . . .', 1984; Bleja, 1984; 'Inspektorzy . . .',
1984; Łoś, 1980, 1982, 1987; Majchrzak, 1965; Markiewicz, 1984,
1985; Pawłowski, 1981; Zagrodzka, 1981).

It is worthwhile to note that in most cases these illegal operations
could not have been carried out without support from the influential
party and economic administration officials. As indicated by a Polish
criminologist,

> [m]any of the organized crime groups are not located outside the
> economic upper world . . . but are situated within the structure of
> the public enterprises in which they play double-sided roles, both
> legal and illegal. In fact, key members of criminal groups often
> inhabit high-ranking positions in governmental agencies (Marek,
> 1986: 164; see also Łoś, 1984 and 1988: 147–204).

In retail trade, the shortages of goods engender corruption which is
taken for granted by both clients and authorities. One day in June
1985, police inspectors ordered the closing down of 80 per cent of all
furniture stores in Warsaw due to the disclosure of massive illegalities, whereby 60 per cent of furniture was allegedly sold 'through the
back door'. This did not seem to surprise anyone. The pressing
unsatisfied demand for furniture and long waiting lists of eager
customers encouraged the staff to dictate their own prices and sale
conditions. The press reacted with a blasé, *déjà vu* attitude. 'Do you
know a store which carries attractive goods where the personnel do
not take bribes?' asked one reporter in a popular weekly, and he

quoted a furniture sales clerk's remark: 'One cannot live on wages alone. When they fix our income they already assume that everybody will earn something extra on the side' (Markiewicz, 1985: 11).

The malaise of the official economy has several aspects. In addition to other well-known problems of the centrally-planned, state-monopolised economy, the cheapness of labour in the situation of state-fixed wages appears to constitute a serious barrier to economic growth and innovation. Wages do not fulfill their nominal objective when employees have to seek other sources of income to meet their most vital needs. The cost of labour does not exceed 15 per cent of the value of production. It is cheaper to expand employment than invest in new machines or equipment. Additional manpower compensates for the irregularities in the supply of materials, disorganisation of the productive processes and outdated machinery. Sheer human effort is expected to make up for the deficiencies of the whole economic organisation, and technological modernisation becomes automatically too costly an option when increased numbers of workers can perform the task at a lesser cost and a lesser risk (*Polska 1985*, 1985: 22; 'Co się komu . . .', 1987: 2). Accordingly, Skalski argues that 'low wages . . . are more a cause of the inefficiency of the economy than its consequence' (1986: 7).

Yet, the recent expansion of the legal non-agricultural private economy, where 10 per cent of the total non-agricultural workforce is employed, has caused an unprecedented exodus from the state economy of the most energetic individuals, contributing further to the hostility of the official economic managers towards this sector. Unable to match the wages and efficient organisation of most private businesses, state managers have no choice but to tolerate illegal enterprise, perks and corruption within their economic realm.

THE PAST AND PRESENT SECOND ECONOMIES

The second economy which has developed in Poland in recent decades cannot be perceived as a continuation of any pre-war illegal economic traditions which might have emerged as a reaction to the landlordship system in agriculture and the marginalisation of the urban poor in the early phases of the capitalist industrialisation. On the other hand, the years of German occupation (1939–45) were undoubtedly conducive to the development of an all-pervading system of an unofficial economy antagonistic to the Nazi-imposed economic order and legitimated by the society. The accumulated experience of those years might have contributed to the ease with which Poles set up their second economy under the subsequent communist rule, but its importance should not be overestimated.

Under the German occupation, the economy was organised to assist the occupants in the war effort. Food was rationed, work assignments were strictly enforced and closely supervised, compulsory foodstuff deliveries from the countryside were in the large part shipped off to the Reich. The death penalty was introduced for those who tried to sabotage these arrangements (Gross, 1979: 107). The draconian penalties notwithstanding, 'more than 80 per cent of the [deprived] population's needs [were] provided [for] by the black market, [and] the extralegal economy grew to unheard-of dimensions ... All legitimate businesses had to deal on the black market and maintained two bookkeeping systems' (Gross, 1979: 109). Corruption was rampant and not only morally absolved by the oppressed Poles, but also tolerated by Germans in spite of 'frequent police raids against the black market and vicious propaganda campaigns against "speculators" and "profiteers" ' (Gross, 1979: 157). Jan T. Gross, who conducted an extensive historical study of German-occupied Poland, argues that only a ruling group which actually tries to establish its legitimacy may be damaged by corruption in the state bureaucracy.

> But, if the ruling élite is not really concerned with establishing its legitimacy, as in the case of the German occupation of Poland, corruption may very well serve its purposes by moderating the effects of some of the irrationality of the state's policies, and it may provide a certain minimal degree of coalescence and interaction in the system (Gross, 1979: 158).

While the nature and extent of corruption and unofficial economy in the period of occupation bear many similarities to those found in contemporary Poland, this reality cannot be fairly explained by the historically learned habits of Polish people. Certain commonalities in both structural situations should not pass unnoticed. The present, Soviet-backed communist rule has not been chosen by the Polish population and is still perceived as a result of the Red Army's seizure of the Polish territory at the end of the war. The methods of the imposition of the strictly controlled economic order during the Stalinist years were not unlike those used by the Nazi authorities, inasmuch as they included the central economic administration, compulsory work assignments, stringent criminal penalties for absenteeism, forced deliveries of agricultural products, anti-speculation campaigns and – significantly – the death penalty for economic infractions. Most of these forms of economic control have been preserved in the post-Stalinist era, albeit in a somewhat restrained version.

It should not come as a surprise that an imposed, restrictive economy – backed by a political order which has not gained the support of the society – creates a need for an alternative sphere of economic exchanges outside the state bureaucracy. This is especially likely when the official economy does not seem to benefit the population and is not geared to its needs. Yet this counter-economy does share certain features and problems with the official economy. Undeniably, it operates in the economic environment created and structured by the first economy. It constitutes a response to the latter and not a freely chosen economic option. Also, just as the first economy, it depends on the ideological climate and political decisions made by the ruling party. As a result, both the first and second economies are marked by a myopic, short-term orientation which precludes real economic advancement. The first economy continues to be centrally planned, which in effect 'reduces time horizon of the enterprise to one year and causes indifference towards long term profits, as they would be appropriated by the state by the way of increased production quotas' (Zieliński, 1974: 90). As well, this situation discourages innovation and technological progress as such developments cannot be planned in advance. They also involve risk and, consequently, a threat of penalties against the managers involved. Corruption and party privileges are thus the surest way for these managers to attain the level of wealth and consumption they feel they are entitled to as compensation for their thankless tasks within the unprofitable state economy. The second economy, on the other hand, is oriented towards quick profits and conspicuous consumption because the changing ideological moods, official policies and legal regulations provide an unsuitable environment for long-term commitments and reinvestment of profits.

In sum, given the overall constraints, neither sector appears to be particularly economically effective, and each introduces its own mode of inequality, contributing to and perpetuating a double structure of economic oppression of the deprived society. The second economy is legitimised both by the economic necessity and by its opposition to the dictates of the state economy in a manner which bears some functional similarity to the processes of moral justification of the underground economy under the German occupation. One of the major functions of the second economy seems to lay in securing a minimum level of needs satisfaction of the population. Its special political significance is based on the fact that the second economy – including non-monetary informal barter exchanges – constitutes a large terrain of non-state activities which, combined with the thriving second culture, introduce a measure of plurality into the party-state monolith.

NOTE

1. In this chapter, special attention is paid to the legal, parallel second economy as I offered a comprehensive analysis of the illegal second economy, corruption and economic crimes in several earlier publications (Łoś, 1980; 1982; 1983; 1984; 1987; 1988).

REFERENCES

Abbreviations:

ZW – Życie Warszawy, a leading Polish daily, Warsaw.
Pol. – Polityka, a leading Polish weekly, Warsaw.
TP – Tygodnik Powszechny, a leading Polish Catholic weekly, Cracow.
'Afera mięsna w Białymstoku' (Meat Gang in Bialystok), *ZW* (12 October 1984) p. 4.
'Amatorzy spekulacji nie rezygnują' (Speculators do not give up), *ZW* (16 February 1987) p. 2.
'Amatorzy szybkiego bogacenia się' (Those Who Like to Get Rich Fast), *ZW* (13 November 1984) p. 8.
Åslund, A., 'The Functioning of Private Enterprise in Poland', *Soviet Studies*, XXXVI (1984) pp. 427–44.
Åslund, A., *Private Enterprise in Eastern Europe* (London: Macmillan, 1985a).
Åslund, A., 'Yellow Light for Private Enterprise in Poland?', *Osteuropa-Wirtschaft*, XXX (1) (1985b) pp. 21–9.
Baczyński, J., 'Policzyć sztuki, godziny i do kasy' (Count Items, Hours, and Get Paid), *Pol.* (8 December 1984) p. 19.
Bednarski, M., 'Gospodarka "drugiego obiegu" a kryzys lat osiemdziesiątych' (The Second Economy and the 1970s crisis), in M. Marody and A. Sułek (eds), *Rzeczywistość Polska* (Warsaw: University of Warsaw, 1987).
'Biurokracja hamuje drobną wytwórczość' (Bureaucracy Hinders Small-Scale Production), *ZW* (5 May 1987) p. 1.

Bleja, A., 'Działkowanie' (Sharing), *Pol.* (8 December 1984) p. 6.

'Bliżej antymonopolowej ustawy' (Closer to an Anty-Monopoly Bill), *ZW* (15 January 1987) p. 1.

Bugaj, R., 'Z perspektywy roku 1986' (Looking Back at Year 1986), *TP* (10 May 1987) p. 3.

Chadzyński, H., 'Jak zarobić na technice' (How to Make Money on Technology), *ZW* (14 January 1987) p. 3.

Chęciński, M., 'Poland's Military Burden', *Problems of Communism*, XXXII (3) (1983) pp. 31–44.

'Co sie komu opłaca' (What Works for Whom), *ZW* (20 May 1987) p. 2.

Dunin-Wąsowicz, M. 'Ostrożnie i nie za wszelką cenę' (Cautiously and Not at Any Price', *ZW* (20 May 1987) p. 6.

'Ekonomiczeskaja Gazieta', *ZW* (4 May 1987) p. 3.

Fallenbuchl, Z. M., *Polityka Gospodarcza PRL* (Polish Economic Policy) (London: Odnowa, 1980).

Gałęski, B., '40 lat polityki rolnej PRL' (40 Years of the Polish Agricultural Policy), in I. Lasota (ed.), *40 Lat Władzy Komunistycznej w Polsce* (London: Polonia, 1986) pp. 79–97.

Gross, J. T., *Polish Society under German Occupation* (Princeton, N.J.: Princeton University Press, 1979).

'Inspektorzy kontroluja ceny' (Inspectors Control Prices), *ZW* (19 December 1984) p. 6.

Janiszewska-Talago, E., *Ustawa o Zwalczaniu Spekulacji* (The Law on Struggle against Speculation) (Warsaw: Wydawnictwo Prawnicze, 1984).

Kaliński, J., *Bitwa o Handel 1947–48* (The Battle over Commerce) (Warsaw: KiW, 1970).

'Kary dla spekulantów' (Penalties for speculators), *ZW* (24 April 1985) p. 8.

Kastory, B., 'Jednostki innowacyjne' (Innovation Units), *ZW* (16 February 1987a) p. 3.

Kastory, B., 'Wyrastanie z bylejakości' (To Outgrow Shody Production), *ZW* (6 March 1987b) p. 3.

Kierul, Z., 'Wyniki i uniki' (Results and Avoidance Strategies), *Pol.* (14 December 1985) p. 5.

'Konferencja prasowa rzecznika rządu' (Press Conference of the Governmental Spokesman), *ZW* (1 April 1987a) pp. 1, 6.

'Konferencja prasowa rzecznika rządu', *ZW* (15 April 1987b) pp. 1, 6.

'Kontrola rynku' (Market Control), *ZW* (12 August 1981) p. 3.

Kowalczyk, H., 'Rzemieślnik o podatkach' (An Artisan on Taxes), *Pol.* (23 February 1985) p. 5.

'Kronika sądowa. Wyroki w aferach spekulacyjnych' (The Court Diary. Sentences for Gangs of Speculators), *ZW* (7 January 1985) p. 4.

Kusin, V. V., 'Gorbachëv and Eastern Europe', *Problems of Communism*, XXXV (1) (1986) pp. 39–53.

Łoś, M., 'Economic Crimes from a Comparative Perspective', in G. R. Newman (ed.), *Crime and Deviance* (Beverly Hills: Sage, 1980) pp. 251–93.

Łoś, M., 'Crime and Economy in the Communist Countries', in P. Wickman and T. Dailey (eds), *White Collar and Economic Crime* (Lexington, Mass.: Lexington Books, 1982) pp. 121–37.

Łoś, M., 'Economic Crimes in Communist Countries', in I. L. Barak-Glantz and E. H. Johnson (eds), *Comparative Criminology* (Beverly Hills: Sage, 1983) pp. 39–57.

Łoś, M., 'Corruption in a Communist Country', *International Annals of Criminology*, XXII (1–2) (1984) pp. 194–206.

Łoś, M., 'The Double Economic Structure of Communist Societies', *Contemporary Crises* 11 (1987) pp. 25–58.

Łoś, M., *Communist Ideology, Law and Crime* (London: Macmillan; New York: St Martin's Press, 1988).

Majchrzak, I., *Pracownicze Przestępstwo i Jego Sprawca* (White Collar Crime and its Perpetrator) (Warsaw: KiW, 1965).

Mały Rocznik (Small Yearbook) (Warsaw: GUS, 1987).

Marek, A. E., 'Organized Crime in Poland', in R. J. Kelly (ed.), *Organized Crime* (Totowa: Rowman & Littlefield, 1986) pp. 159–71.

Markiewicz, W., 'Poemat pedagogiczny' (Pedagogical Poem), *Pol.* (8 December 1984) p. 6.

Markiewicz, W., 'Sklep nieczynny z powodu aresztowania personelu' (Store Closed due to Arrests of Staff), *Pol.* (29 June 1985) p. 11.

MK, 'Spekulant' (A Speculator), *TP* (21 July 1985) p. 8.

Modzelewski, K., 'Jak być uczciwym w sektorze prywatnym' (How To Be Honest in the Private Sector), *Pol.* (2 June 1984) p. 4.

'Narada w Warszawie' (A Meeting in Warsaw), *ZW* (27 January 1984) p. 2.

'Nielegalny handel maszynami rolniczymi' (Illegal Trade in Agricultural Machinery), *ZW* (14 December 1984) p. 6.

'Nowa filozofia pracy' (New Work Philosophy), *ZW* (14–15 March 1987) pp. 1, 2.

Nowakowska, I., 'Jak być uczciwym w sektorze prywatnym' (How To Be Honest in the Private Sector), *Pol.* (2 June 1984) p. 4.

'Nowe oblicze spekulacji' (New Face of Speculation), *Trybuna Ludu* (3 November 1982) p. 2.

'Obradowało Biuro Polityczne KC PZPR' (The Politburo Held A Meeting), *ZW* (11 June 1987) p. 6.

'Odważny projekt ustawy' (A Bold Bill), *Ład* (23 February) (Warsaw, 1986) p. 11.

Orfin, W., 'Co zamiast rynku' (What Instead of Market), *ZW* (23 April 1987) p. 3.

'Orientacja rynkowa' (Market Orientation), *ZW* (8 May 1987) p. 2.

Pawłowski, W., 'Bez upojenia' (Without Euphoria), *Pol.* (21 March 1981) p. 7.

'Perspektywy rozwoju drobnej wytwórczości' (Prospects of Small-Scale Production), *ZW* (15 July 1987) p. 2.

Podemski, St., 'Niech lecą wióry' (Let the Shavings Fly), *Pol.* (4 May 1985), p. 4.

Polska 1985 (Poland 1985) (Paris: Biblioteka Libertas, 1985).

Popkiewicz, J., 'Nierównowaga i spekulacja' (Imbalance and Speculation), *Pol.* (26 May 1984) pp. 1, 4.

'Posiedzenie Centralnej Komisji do Walki ze Spekulacją' (A Meeting of the Central Commission for the Struggle against Speculation), *ZW* (15 March 1985) p. 2.

'Posiedzenie Rady Państwa' (A Meeting of the State Council), *ZW* (27 March 1987) pp. 1, 2.

Raport. Polska 5 Lat po Sierpniu (Report. Poland 5 Years after August (London: Aneks, 1986).

Rocznik Statystyczny (Statistical Yearbook) (Warsaw: GUS, 1985).

Rykowski, Z. and Władyka, W., 'Biedni i bogaci' (The Rich and the Poor), *Pol.* (2 January 1988) pp. 1, 5.

Rymwid, J., 'Nie chcę być właścicielem' (I Don't Want to Be an Owner), *Pol.* (23 November 1985) p. 13.

'Siedemdziesiąt cztero-osobowa grupa przestępcza spekulowała w Legnicy' (A Criminal Gang of 75 Members Have Speculated in Legnica), *ZW* (10 January 1984) p. 6.

Skalski, E., 'Praca, płaca' (Work, Wage), *TP* (15 June 1986) pp. 5, 7.

Spaliński, L., 'Równość czyli jedno rolnictwo' (Equality: One Agriculture), *TP* (3 May 1987) p. 3.

'Spekulacja i marnotrawstwo mięsa' (Speculation and Wastage of Meat), *ZW* (28 September 1984) p. 6.

'Spekulacja w minionym roku' (Speculation during the Past Year), *ZW* (4 January 1985) p. 8.

'Stanowisko komisji partyjno-rządowej' (A Declaration of the Party-Government Commission), *ZW* (1 July 1987) p. 6.

Steven, S., *The Poles* (New York: Macmillan, 1982).

'Surowsze kary dla spekulantów' (Harsher Penalties for Speculators), *ZW* (31 May 1984) p. 8.

Warzocha, A., 'Kurs obracania barana' (A barbecueing course), *Przegląd Tygodniowy* (31 January 1988) p. 4.

W. O., 'Umowne nie znaczy dowolne' (Agreed Upon – Not Arbitrary', *ZW* (6 April 1987) p. 2.

'Wysokie grzywny za przestępstwa skarbowe' (High Fines for Fiscal Offences), *ZW* (15 August 1987) p. 6.

Zagrodzka, D., 'Jedną nogą w wielkim świecie' (One Foot in the Grand World), *Pol.* (21 March 1981) p. 6.

Zarzecki, J., 'Z Polonią czy bez?' (With or Without Polonia?), *Pol.* (31 December 1983) p. 6.

Zieliński, J. G., *Polskie Reformy Gospodarcze* (Polish Economic Reforms) (London: Odnowa, 1974).

ZGPTS (Polish Sociological Association), 'Społeczeństwo polskie drugiej połowy lat 80-tych' (Polish society in the late 1980s), *Dwadzieścia jeden*, 4 (Warsaw: Oficyna Wydawnicza RYTM, 1987) pp. 42–67.

4 The Second Economy in Hungary

Istvan Kemeny

The Communist party has come to power twice in Hungary since the Second World War – on both occasions, courtesy of the Red Army. The first time was between 1945 and 1948. That power was swept away by the Hungarian Revolution of 1956. However, after the crushing defeat of that short-lived revolution in November 1956, Communist power was restored. But, as G. H. N. Seton-Watson has observed, 'counter-revolutions in practice never succeed for long in restoring the previous order . . . Hungarians must with reluctant gratitude acknowledge that the regime of Janos Kadar differed from that of Ernö Gerö' (Seton-Watson, 1978: 2). Thus, in tracing the origins of the second economy in modern Hungary, we must begin in 1956.

HISTORY OF HUNGARY'S SECOND (HIDDEN) ECONOMY

The crushing of the 1956 Revolution was followed by a transitional period of six to eight months (for a thorough description of this period and the following decade, see Petö and Szakács, 1985). The new leadership gathered experts and organised committees which were to prepare for extensive economic reform. In the industrial sector, the new political leadership raised factory workers' wages by approximately 20 per cent. They accepted the workers' councils' demands for the elimination of the piece rate system. Taxes on small trade and crafts were also reduced. In the agricultural sector, the new leadership abolished the hitherto compulsory delivery of agricultural produce to the state. Furthermore, by stating that they would support agricultural co-operatives and private farming equally, they resigned themselves to the dissolution of the former.

The reform efforts were short-lived. In the summer of 1957, the leadership decided that,

> there was no need for changing the institutional system and

therefore no need for reforms pushing in that direction either. On the contrary, the leadership believed that it was precisely the given institutional order that suited best its purposes (Petö and Szakács, 1985: 359).

The reasons for the policy change were the surprisingly fast consolidation of the political system and the success of 'normalisation', as evidenced by restored production levels. The leadership interpreted these developments as a sign that no further changes were required: business could be conducted as before. Moreover, the policies of the dominant Communist powers also influenced Comecon decision-making. Bauer's seminal study of economic development in six Central and East European countries identifies the Soviet 'seven year plan' and China's 'great leap' as key factors influencing economic policy throughout the East bloc (Bauer, 1981: 84).

THE COLLECTIVISATION OF AGRICULTURE

In December 1958, the Central Committee of the Hungarian party made a decision which was to engender the greatest social change in three decades: the collectivisation of farming. The impetus for that decision was, as before, inspired by the Soviet example. Hungary followed suit with China, Bulgaria, Czechoslovakia, Albania, East Germany and Rumania, in eliminating private farm-ownership and thus, an entire peasant class. As elsewhere, the Hungarian party leadership firmly held the belief that the elimination of private farm-ownership was inevitable. Only momentarily could the party, as vanguard of progress and socialism, tolerate half of its citizenry living by market forces and wanting to receive a profit for what it provided. Economic independence was perceived as going hand in hand with ideological and moral independence, and therefore was regarded as incompatible with socialist goals.

The collectivisation of agriculture put the final touches to the elimination of Hungarian civil society, a process which had begun under Communist power in 1947. Eliminated were social groups whose members were independently capable of widening their individual horizons and increasing their material position by their own efforts. These individuals had not accepted that others should determine their way of life; they had sought their own. They had had the means and the ability to avert outside interference in their own affairs, and had been accustomed to settling their shared problems, together with other members of civil society.

Collectivism could be effectively implemented because the peasantry, drawing its own conclusions from their experiences during the crushing of the 1956 Revolution, regarded open opposition as doomed to certain failure (Berend, 1983: 270). The party's use of psychological pressures, physical force, and other forms of constraint in cases where opposition was attempted further confirmed their views (Petö and Szakács, 1985: 446). Nevertheless, they did employ various forms of passive resistance. First and foremost, many withdrew from the new forms of organisation. Between 1949 and 1953, 250 000 of Hungary's 2 196 185 peasants abandoned agriculture. Subsequently, between 1959 and 1962, another 500 000 peasants followed this example.

Others withdrew themselves fully or partially from working on the collective farms. Donath suggests that from 1961 to 1964, approximately 20–25 per cent of the communal farm membership did not work on the farms, and half of the membership worked on them very little (Donath, 1977: 200–3). The incomes of communal farm members were dramatically lower than those of state-estate workers and thus many found it preferable to work elsewhere. As Donath states, 'a considerable part of the peasantry, having become members of collective farms, adopted a negative attitude' (Donath, 1977: 203).

From 1961 to 1964, crop production fell by 10 per cent as a result of this resistance. Paradoxically, communal farms owning half of Hungary's agricultural land produced 39 per cent of the country's gross production, whereas individual and household plot-holders, owning 15 per cent of the country's agricultural land, produced 42 per cent of gross production (Petö and Szakács, 1985: 467). Livestock holdings also fell. For example, by 1964, the country's cattle holdings were 30 per cent lower than in 1950 (Petö and Szakács, 1985: 471–2).

Pilfering and stealing (a form of resistance still widespread) is best described by Sozan:

> There are many well-known forms of supplementary stealing, from stealing from one's working hours – truancy – and using the time thus gained for moonlighting, to the lifting of tools, stealing grain, chemicals, fuel, animals and other goods. Even though the property of cooperative farms is guarded by eight or ten people, it is easy to get round supervision by knowing the ropes and means of corruption. This is not unlike the pre-war situation when the estate

allowed for thievery by agricultural labourers, included it in its calculations well in advance, and ignored the practice. The 'compulsion for stealing' has survived the era of hired agricultural hands. Socialism has not only sustained it, but extended it to the entire society. It became a built-in part of the whole system. Stealing (and I use this term in its broadest sense) in all its ritual, symbolic and other implications, has become an engrained element of peasant culture today, as much a part of it as, say, Maypoles or Easter eggs. Stealing these days is not done by just some people but by almost everyone. The chief accountant steals just the same as the animal-feeder who hides groats in his trousers or in her bra, or the watchman who knows full well what goods workers smuggle home, or the swine-tender who deliberately breaks the animal's leg on the trough so that members of the cooperative may buy it cheaply. ('You want a suckling? You shall have it tonight . . .') Everyone is familiar with the system. What a cooperative member finds demoralizing is not the fact that the whole system is based on stealing, but that he cannot steal enough (Sozan, 1985: 95–6, this author's translation).

These adopted policies caused food-shortages in Budapest and in provincial towns. In the villages, the shortages were so severe that it was often difficult for the inhabitants to find basic foodstuffs. By 1961, the situation had declined so drastically that Hungary (traditionally a grain-exporting country) had to import 3000 tons of wheat, and even this was not enough to meet demand (Petö and Szakács, 1985: 465–75).

The food shortage started to subside only in the latter half of the 1960s, when the government was forced to make concessions by allowing household farming plots and share-cropping. A similar situation had occurred in the Soviet Union after the first wave of collectivisation in 1929. The authorities believed these were temporary measures, and that large-scale mechanised collective production would eventually take care of the needs of the population. Like the Soviet leadership, the Hungarian leadership permitted household plots (within narrow constraints) and allowed share-cropping on a one third basis as an interim solution. But with continuing food shortages, a symbiosis of private and communal farming dominated the co-operatives (Donath, 1977: 205–7).

To a certain extent, this symbiosis catalysed a reorganisation process in civil society. Under the shadow of catastrophe, the party resigned itself to see the civil society it had crushed gaining a little strength. As the author writing under the name 'Janos Kovacs' states, the party

> recognised the aspirations of the agricultural citizenry, the largest and relatively homogeneous stratum of civil Hungary. In dealing with this stratum representing the largest socio-political force, the party recognized its aspirations of self-determination, of incomes according to performance and unlimited by state-imposed ceilings based on official living standards, its aspirations to preserve its links to its traditional activities and to satisfy increased consumer demand. Thus although civil society – its inter-enterprise relationships and social strata – disappeared in the process of socialist reorganisation, it was also recreated in this process, albeit in a somewhat altered form (Kovacs, 1978: 15–16, this author's translation).

This initial form of dual economy, based on the co-existence of collective and private farming, survived until the end of the 1960s. As the communal co-operative farms developed into large agricultural concerns organised according to the principles of state-owned manufacturing, another structure emerged. Since the 1970s, the members of agricultural co-operatives have behaved in exactly the same fashion as wage-earning workers in state-owned industrial plants. Moreover, the process of industrialisation also radically transformed the composition of the co-operatives' labour force. As Juhász and Magyar (1984: 187–94) state, an exchange of expertise, experience, and cultural patterns occurred between the co-operatives, industry and other non-agricultural occupations, with the co-operatives being the most open institutions on the labour market.

Over the course of the 1970s, share-cropping disappeared and plot farming was to some extent overtaken by small-scale agricultural concerns. As Juhász and Magyar observe:

> [v]arious social strata, previously excluded from peasant society, became involved in farming and its collateral way of life. Industrial and low-grade white-collar employees living in villages or urban suburbs entered the traditionally peasant market-world at a time when the peasant class in the traditional sense had ceased to exist (1984: 193–4).

According to their estimate, two thirds of small agricultural producers are external workers or white-collar employees. On the other hand, Harcsa (1984) estimates that only 15 per cent of active, privately owned small farms belong to the peasants in co-operatives.

The decline of the peasant class has not, however, meant the end of peasant culture. According to Juhász and Magyar, peasant culture has 'become market-oriented and more susceptible to technical innovations, and at the same time several elements of this culture, of peasant behaviour patterns, have spread among the non-peasant population even in the cities' (1984: 194). They argue that modern features such as co-operation organised through personal contacts, the system of mutual services, the personal character of goods-exchange and the traditional work-exchange in house-building practices are rooted in peasant traditions.

THE ECONOMIC REFORMS OF 1968

A number of compelling factors forced the Hungarian party leadership to initiate economic reforms. Chief among these were energy shortages, the lack of raw materials, and labour shortages (Csikós-Nagy, 1983). The reserves of the Soviet bloc economy which squandered its resources were beginning to be exhausted. Already by 1963 (and certainly by 1964) it had become clear that the reform plans which had been worked out by György Peter and others in 1953–4 during Imre Nagy's premiership had to be reconsidered. Reform committees were formed, and in May 1966 the Central Committee passed a resolution outlining the principles of reform. Administrative direction was to be replaced by economic methods. The detail of the Central Plan was no longer required and the controlled economy was to replace the command economy. The market was to be consumer oriented, and consumers were to be free to choose between national and imported goods. Provisions to protect against monopolies were envisioned, and collective participation in the management of enterprise was to be guaranteed to workers.

The actual programme of reforms introduced in 1968, however, was less comprehensive. Collective participation was dropped, and the state's export monopoly remained intact. But within the spirit of the reforms was still a commitment to the self-reliance of individual enterprises, to competition, and to an alignment between the central planning process and the actual market conditions. Promises to eliminate shortages, increase (in reality, to create) export capability, and to raise labour productivity were also retained.

In reality, these goals have not been fulfilled. Hungarian enterprises are as dependent in the 1980s as they were in 1968. Competition between enterprises does not occur, and monopolistic situations remain. Market adjustment was not realised because the establishment of the prerequisite capital labour market had not been foreseen. The significant decisions are still made by the central machinery (Tardos, 1985: 1297; Antal, 1985: 356). And shortages remain, especially in quality goods and services such as university and high-school placement, telephones, health care facilities, spare parts, raw material and labour. In the world market, Hungary's competitiveness has declined since the beginning of the 1970s.

The reforms have abolished compulsory planning orders and currently, enterprises are governed by price, budget and credit regulations. But this simply means that instead of bargaining about planning targets, the authorities are bargaining about regulations.

THE EMERGENCE OF THE SECOND (HIDDEN) ECONOMY

The aim of the reforms was to revive the first economy. Yet in that, they failed. One effect which was not envisioned was the establishment of the second, or hidden, economy.

This flexible, creative, and unforeseen system is best exemplified by the development of secondary plants in industrial co-operatives, which operated from 1968 until they were blocked in 1972 under Soviet pressure (see Rupp, 1983). In 1967, a reform which allowed for the migration of labour paved the way for such ventures, which quickly mushroomed in and around Budapest. It all started when highly skilled workers, such as craftsmen, technicians and engineers, negotiated the establishment of joint secondary plants with their local co-operatives. Under this form of semi-private enterprise, the entrepreneur who managed the secondary plant independently was expected to hand over 50 per cent (and later 60 per cent) of his net income to the co-operative.

The secondary plants, operating in their semi-private form, are classic examples of innovation within a rigid central planning system. Central planning – when operating properly – is bound to preclude innovation. Nevertheless, innovation does take place in systems operating under the central planning principles – yet, as Rupp argues, only at a *sub-institutional* level (1983: 3–6).

Very little is written about the autonomous and private daily decisions of millions of individuals, which in fact come to shape and transform East European economies. As Rupp argues, central planning is really 'just the tip of the iceberg' (Rupp, 1983: 4) which blocks the view of how the live forces of society effect changes. More precisely, it gives the false impression that those changes are the exclusive results of central planning. The party and the central planning offices are mighty, but not almighty. They introduce reforms and implement political changes because they are forced to do so. Rupp argues that in the case of the secondary plants, the harsh economic reality facing many deficit-ridden co-operatives was the reason that they embraced the concept of semi-privatisation. Their introduction was not ideologically considered, instead the central planning office had to rationalise those decisions, by pretending that they had been arrived at independently of society's economic concerns.

Soviet-modelled economies are always imbalanced, their bureaucratic structures are rigid, and neither individuals nor groups have the means to voice their interests. Curiously, under these conditions the autonomous decisions of private individuals are more unpredictable and carry considerably further reaching consequences than similar decisions in the West. In a country where the rule of law does not apply, private individuals are forced to get around the law and to shape their country's life in a non-institutionalised way, always adjusting to the political changes of the moment. This makes peoples' lives difficult, and at the same time hinders the government's ability to control the way things are done.

The significance of 'sub-institutional forces' is given even more emphasis by Zsille (1980). He distinguishes two societies: a hierarchic one of bureaucratic structure ('high structure') and a subordinate civil society ('low structure'). Between these two societies there exists some kind of division of labour. The hierarchic society performs the political and state-managerial roles and functions, including the local extensions and strongholds of étatist bureaucracy, management of state-owned enterprises, and economic governing bodies and authorities which supervise and control small firms and their organisations. The economic function of the high structure is thus the commandeering of the economy: economic policy. But as far as the economic life of society is concerned – production in the strict sense – that task is performed by the subordinate civil society: by small firms, by the private and co-operative sectors and, finally, by those various organic units which operate semi-autonomously within state-owned enterprises and – just like individual small firms – are governed equally by inner black-market forces and by official supervision. The key to the position and behaviour of each social stratum is this: to what extent, and with what chances, is it linked to these horizontal and vertical structures? The diversity of social statuses derives basically from the fact that Hungarian society is a dichotomous system consisting of a heterogenous and decentralised world of economy, labour and culture – within the 'deep society' – and, an overlying and centralising official or 'high society', with a homogenising technology and capability to wield power in politics, management and ideology.

The latter strives towards total control over society, towards changing its dichotomy into a straightforward superordination. Since it is unable to achieve this – and this inability is always manifested in claiming to be 'liberal' and in actually practising what amounts to (borrowing the market term) 'black' liberalism – the 'high structure' also fosters the most pervasive and organic lesion of the societal psyche: schizophrenia.

There exists, even among the personnel working under state-management and control, a considerable number of people who have a real stake in productivity. They become more autonomous and mobile at lower levels of the hierarchy, towards the production line, towards smaller firms, co-operatives and private enterprises. These are the people who either reach outside the sphere of planned economy or operate within its institutional system of semi-official or unofficial activities. They are able to establish prices which differ from the state-controlled, sub-value prices, and thereby create 'free' markets. This is the terrain of more economic independence, or at least of aspirations to achieve it.

The spaces thus created, existing in the crevices, underworld, or outside of the official economy, are the grounds for activities, organisational forms and movements striving to change the centrally planned, declared, and dictated order. These are the grounds where the country's real economic life is acted out. The world of small-scale firms and workshops without and within the large industrial corporations, the world of the co-operatives – institutional or non-institutional – engender the spontaneous reorganisation process of national economy, the unofficial, inverted redistribution. This is the hidden economy. It embraces those economic actions which are undeclared and concealed, of which the statistics and revenue offices have no knowledge. But this official 'no knowledge' is in fact quite knowing. The establishment cannot help knowing when it is a common topic in everybody's conversation.

These hidden activities can be classified according to whether they are only partly or completely concealed. Let us take for example a craftsman who declares officially that he works alone with one apprentice or none. In reality, he may have help. Highly skilled workers may show up at his place to work, popping in from a factory maintenance shop after work to put in a couple of hours. Our craftsman would clearly declare only half of the work done in his shop that he himself actually did, but not the other half, done by his secret assistants. His economic activity is thus partly hidden. But his assistants conceal their moonlighting activity entirely. Another example is a co-operative, which takes part in a modern corn-producing programme and grows corn on several patches. If it wants to get anything out of it, the co-operative will not declare all its produce. It will base its production figures on the strip with the worst average production. Declaring this meagre amount, it can keep part of the excess for its members.

From a different point of view, the participants of the hidden economy may be divided into two categories according to how they appear in official statistics, whether as officially independent or as workers or employers. But the importance is really whether or not their activity increases national output. The craftsman's secret assistant, for example, does increase it. So does the plot-owner who produces purple onions and all those who breed pigs or chickens on their small farms or grow tomatoes or cabbages. These small strips of land are in fact the most important elements of the hidden economy. Almost as important are the foremen and the bricklayers who build workers' private houses or the owner-occupied communal houses for the middle class. The building of these two types of houses alone supplies a considerable part of the annual national produce. But of course these cannot be declared either, not with 2500 *forints* paid out in daily wages.

The really important factor in the hidden economy is not the bribery, nor the 'selling from under the counter', nor the tip system, but that economy's impact upon and contribution to national output. Hungary could subsist without it – at a poverty level – but the little extras which Hungarians have enjoyed in the past fifteen years are due to this very productive sector of the economy.

The hidden economy has caused an upheaval in the ownership of production in Hungary. In the early stages of socialism, both big capital and small owner-producer capital was nationalised. Eventual-

ly, it appeared that only two kinds of people were facing each other:
the leaders of the state and the wage-workers or salaried employees
of the state. One could say that socialism succeeded in proletarianis-
ing the workers, by putting a small group of exclusive 'owners' on one
side, and wage-workers on the other. The party achieved this by
depriving people of the right to change their workplace at will, and by
creating a centrally planned economy. The result of this was an
irrational economic system.

During Imre Nagy's leadership and the 1956 Revolution, Hungarian economists advised that the proletarianisation process was
complete and irreversible. They argued that the people should be
given back the right to change their workplace, and that market-
competition should replace the central plan system (this concept,
known as market socialism, was later adopted by Czech economists
during the Prague Spring). But the development of the hidden
economy has made both their diagnosis and their proposed therapy
invalid. The worker who grows purple onions or tomatoes on his
family plot for market is at the same time likely to be a proletarian,
working for a state factory. He is not only an owner of small
property, but also a small-scale entrepreneur, who considers his
expenses and expected profit very carefully. The same analysis can be
applied to craftsmen and their moonlighting workers. The typical
Hungarian worker is thus a paradox: a wage earner or proletarian on
the one hand, and on the other, a small-scale producer who settles
the price of his work and his other investments in the market.

The ownership situation has changed within factories as well, after
the reintroduction of the piece rate system in 1958. Although the
leadership spoke of setting production quotas by 'scientific' methods,
what was really meant was that quotas would be set by the plan,
whether set beforehand, or subsequently revised or corrected later.
As it stands, the quotas differ from worker to worker, depending
upon his expertise, his affiliation to the factory, his social weight and
prestige, and his membership and status in the Communist party. In
determining how these production quotas are set, one is faced with a
picture of chaos and discord. On the one hand, the factory leaders
want to increase the intensity of labour to reach higher production
levels. On the other, the workers want to supply extra production
only in exchange for extra wages.

Oedipus could kill his father only because his parents wanted to
defend themselves against the fulfilment of the prophecy. In real life,

it often happens that something comes to pass precisely because of someone's need to defend against it. Hungary's leaders fear that the workers do not work hard enough; yet despite their efforts to extract more from the workers, the only result is that the workers want to decrease their intensity of labour.

The factory managers stand in the middle. They can keep their power and relatively privileged position only by following central instructions and trying to raise the intensity of labour. But they cannot afford to go too far, for they must secure the co-operation of their workers if they are to meet the centrally planned production target and deliver the goods as ordered. The potential discord between the managers and the workers is also counterbalanced by a rational common interest – secure production – which requires that workers can count on specific wages, and management can count on specific output. Factory conflicts result therefore in a new, negotiated balance each time production quotas are set.

Whether in the factory, in private plot production, seasonal work, or moonlighting, all elements are carefully weighed by workers. Their survival depends on precise calculation and the wise allocation of their labour. Western labour sociologists call this instrumental behaviour, where work is regarded as a means to an end. Yet the Hungarian worker is not merely a *homo oeconomicus*. There is pleasure, prestige, social status, and security in work well done. Skills are often respected within the workplace community, by both workers and managers, and thus when economic calculation dictates that a job should not be done too well, or not well at all, feelings of loss and sacrifice may be very acute. Nonetheless, although factories and equipment are legally owned by the state, there is scope for bargaining and negotiation. But the battles over the proper utilisation of capital goods are fought not so much between the economic management and the workers as between the state and the workers.

In capitalist systems, the capitalists do not enjoy the right of unlimited disposal of their capital goods. They have to pay high taxes, which is tantamount to the restriction of ownership. Moreover, they have to observe many state regulations, and in addition, reckon with the trade unions. Under Hungarian socialism, state-ownership is, in principle, unlimited. But in reality it is restricted by the workers' hidden class struggle. Thus in factories, we observe the limited private ownership of capitalism *versus* the limited state ownership of so-called socialism.

THE SOCIAL IMPLICATIONS OF THE HIDDEN ECONOMY

The hidden economy has also changed the interrelationships of different social strata and groups to the state. For example, in the 1950s, the income and consumer inequalities reflected quite faithfully the hierarchy defined by the Communist party: the higher the status of an individual, the more access he or she had to consumer goods. Higher status normally yielded higher salaries. But more important than the actual income was the access to a whole scale of extra benefits: almost rent-free accommodation in the most elegant part of town, free use of official cars and drivers, vacations at exclusive spots, trips abroad, and appliances which actually worked. These benefits were assigned. Money could not buy them: they simply were not for sale. The degree of inequalities among individuals was set by the state, as sole distributor of income and consumer goods.

The development of the hidden economy has upset this order. First of all, it has affected incomes. The state is no longer the sole provider of high incomes, as one may now earn just as much on the market. The numerous complaints about it which appear in the press are symptomatic of this state of affairs. In one such article, for example, an individual recounts with pride his many achievements in serving the state, then expresses a lament about seeing fellow engineers and other professionals, who have developed careers independent of the state, doing much better materially than he. The consumer situation has also changed. Privileges, special concession shops, and similar arrangements still exist, but the party machinery has ceased to be the sole point of access to quality products or Western goods.

The hidden economy has fostered a greater degree of independence in some individuals. Because of the hidden economy, one may obtain a higher than average income, a flat, a car, and other valuable consumer goods without – or even in spite of – the state. One does not have to submit to the humiliating treatment within the state economy. The power of the state over the people has been decreased.

In 1947–8, the Hungarian Communist party nationalised the country's economic resources and consumption patterns, and wanted to extend itself into people's lives, and to absorb the whole of society. This it was not able to do completely, and during the eighteen months of Imre Nagy's premiership, nationalisation was stopped and dismantled. It could be argued that during this period, society discharged the state from its pores, and started its battle against it.

In 1955, the Communist party once again attempted to nationalise, but this simply set off the revolution which swept away the state. The crushing of the 1956 Revolution was again followed by an attempt to nationalise, which as we have seen, was successful in certain fields such as agriculture. But the nationalisation of the society was beyond the state's powers. The 1956 Revolution had created a nation (in a modern sense) from a society which was formerly so divided that Rakosi was able to rely on its extremely fractured nature as the basis of his totalitarian state.

At the same time as the state was performing its nationalisation, society embarked on its 'de-state-ification'. The first stage was the norm- and overtime-game in the factories and passive resistance, which resulted in the dual economy, in rural areas. The second stage has been the development of the hidden economy. This has gradually become the main instrument of de-state-ification. The diverse groups and strata of Hungarian society are making an effort to get back what the state had taken away from them; the hidden economy is thus a new economy, created without the state by the people. They make investments without the state, they invest their labour without the state's patronage. The state thus owns only a part of the country's resources; the other part is owned by private individuals.

THE ECONOMIC REFORMS OF 1982

On 1 January 1982, government regulations were published permitting new economic organisations. Two new organisations created through these regulations may seem to be relevant to the topic of the hidden economy, but in actual fact are not. The first of these is much highlighted these days: the economic working pool within a state enterprise (VGMK – *vallati gazdasagi munkaközösség*). The other is the specialised co-operative groups (*szövetkezeti szakcsoport*). At the end of 1985 there were 20 265 VGMKs with 200 578 members and 2613 *szövetkezeti szakcsoports* with 81 830 members (Statistical Yearbook, 1985: 340).

In the case of the VGMKs, the state-owned enterprise organises according to its own needs some of its employees into a working pool and contracts this team to perform specific, relatively well-paid extra work. The contract is always advantageous to the workers chosen for the pool because it provides higher income for extra work. While the average worker earned 5000–7000 *forints* monthly in 1986, VGMK members earned 15 000–20 000. This advantage does not, however, alter the fact that the nature of the VGMK members' activities is simply extra work done in overtime for higher pay, and that it is always performed for their employer, the state-owned enterprise. The VGMKs are thus in reality simply overtime-brigades and have nothing to do with any imaginary autonomy, enterprise or the private sector. Moreover, VGMKs are particularly convenient means for dividing and taming workers, since it is obvious that non-conformists will not be afforded such advantageous positions. As to the second type of new organisations, the co-operatives, they are co-operatives in name only (with the exception of *kisszövetkezet(s)* 'small co-operatives'). In reality, their structure is that of a state-owned enterprise, and it is likely that the specialised groups formed by them operate similarly to the VGMKs.

Unlike these overtime-brigades, some additional new organisations do fall within a 'quasi-private' sector. These are specialised economic groups formed by private individuals – GMKs (*gazdasagi munkaközösség(s)*), the civilian legal associations – PJTs (*polgari jogi tarsasag(s)*), small co-operatives (*kisszövetkezet(s)*) and the contractually rented small-scale trade- and catering-businesses. At the end of 1985, there were 20 265 GMKs with 60 452 members; 758 small co-operatives with 34 000 members, and 11 747 contractual businesses (Statisztikai Evkonyv, 1985).

I use the term 'quasi-private' to describe this sector because the overwhelming majority of members belonging to these new small organisations have kept their state-employment and pursue their GMK or PJT membership only in their free time, or as part-time activity. By the end of 1985, out of the 60 452 GMK membership, only 18 975 had changed their previous employment for private sector positions. All factors considered, it is highly unlikely that a great many people will choose to become self-employed or independent in the future. By doing so, they would lose their material security. The sharp turns characterising Hungarian economic policies are well known to its citizens, and venturing into total economic independence would involve considerable personal risk. Istvan Matko (1987) cites the example of some ten young engineers who formed a GMK and undertook to manufacture component-parts which state-enterprise had always been importing from abroad. They sold their cars, their coloured TV sets, raised loans from friends and usurers, and started working day and night in a borrowed garage. After the second year, one of their most important buyers became insolvent. As a result, the GMK could not obtain loans and buy material and was unable to deliver its orders. The court ruled that the GMK was to pay reparations in full and each engineer's private property was included in their liability.

The second and equally important consideration is that GMKs and PJTs have virtually no capital. According to available data, the private capital invested by entrepreneurs is minimal, with on average only 2000 *forints* per member. This capital is usually part of their starting capital (Sütö, 1986). Theoretically, they could acquire capital from three sources. They could start with nothing, earning, investing, earning more, investing more and finally becoming entrepreneurs of solid capital. Yet this possibility is fictitious because its realisation would require quite a different state of affairs and atmosphere in the country. The second possibility is also illusory. This would consist of Western capital being invested in small Hungarian enterprises on a partnership basis. Even if we disregard the numerous legal obstacles designed to constrain GMKs and PJTs in particular, Western capitalists are hindered in free movement by innumerable obligations. More importantly, the overall system of Hungary renders this possibility unrealistic. The third possibility – namely, that large enterprises provide small ventures with part of their capital – seems more feasible. But in order to realise this possibility, radical structural changes would have to be implemented.

The recent study, *Turning Point and Reform* (Antal *et al.*, 1986) points out, quite rightly, the dual nature of small enterprises in Hungary. It states:

> The overwhelming majority of small enterprises are dependent not only on the market, and this dual dependency generates contradictions. Only one quarter of the more than half a million small-entrepreneurs depend for their livelihood solely on the success of their enterprises. As for the rest, their enterprise means simply hard extra work to earn more while standing on the firm ground of regular employment. Since the majority of small enterprises is simply labour-market-enterprise and is absent in both the community- and the capital-market, it follows that small enterprises *do not represent significant challenge, competition or a chance of revival in the rigid economic structure*. Their dual existence and dual mentality are based not only on outlook, but on the consequences of environment and regulations as well . . .
>
> Success in the market will not lead them to growth and will not attract resources from other sectors to their ventures. *The present*

small enterprises do not offer lasting prospects to their members . . .
Small-scale entrepreneurs always travel on the steps of the train of
the national economy (they can step down or be pushed down any
time) . . . On account of their isolation, they can be, and are used
for supporting the traditional industrial structure (as in the case of
small-scale enterprises supporting their state-owned parent
company) and often become themselves parasites, living off big-
enterprise-monopolies (1986: 23–4) (all italics in original).

CONCLUSIONS

On 1 January 1968, a promising development was started in Hungary.
Although the reforms introduced were ambiguous and in many key
aspects (such as foreign trade, restructuring, capital- and labour-
markets) lacking rigour, they nevertheless gave some impetus to the
economy. The counter-reforms implemented between 1972 and 1978
reversed that tendency. Yet the standard of living did not decline in
those six years, due to two factors. First, loans from the West, used
partly for unprofitable investments, were also used in part for
consumer goods for the population. Between 1979 and 1984 administrative restrictions were introduced in both directions but nothing was
done for economic restructuring. As a result of the restrictions, real
wages decreased by 10 to 15 per cent. For the majority of the
population this was, however, counter-balanced by the ever-
increasing extra work they performed in the legal, semi-legal or
illegal sectors. In other words, while the decrease in the net output of
the first economy was compensated by private activities, it did not
result in its general vitalisation. In 1985, the government decreed a
'dynamisation' programme. This resulted in such a steep economic
decline that private activities could no longer compensate for it.

It is conceivable, in theory, that the impending catastrophe will
compel the Hungarian government to change direction. I am writing
these lines at the end of August 1987 and the programme of
stabilisation and revitalisation will be discussed in the Hungarian
parliament in fifteen days. There are some people who hope that this
programme will bestow equal rights to the single operative sector in
the Hungarian economy, and that it will open the way to private
individuals to invest their savings in small enterprises (which is at
present forbidden). Some hope it will free the way for unhindered
circulation of capital between state-owned enterprises, co-operatives

and small enterprises (not possible at present), give foreign capitalists a chance of free capital influx into small enterprises and allow small enterprises to turn themselves into share-holding companies. The author of this study expects, instead, general, non-committal promises and, as far as practice is concerned, the introduction of a tax-system which will result in the country's already poor economic production sinking even lower, its commodity supply declining even sharper and its social crisis becoming deeper.

REFERENCES

Antal, L., *Gazdaságirányitási es Penzügyi rendszerünk a reform utjan* (*Our Economic Management and Financial System on the Road of Reforms*) (Budapest: Közgazdasági es Jogi Könyvkiadó, 1985).

Antal, L., Csillag, I., Lengyel, L., Matolcsy, G., *Fordulat és reform* (*Turning Point and Reform*) (Budapest, 1986).

Bauer, T., *Tervgazdaság, beruházás, ciklusok* (*Centrally Planned Economy, Investments, Cycles*) (Budapest: Közgazdasági és Jogi Könyvkiadó, 1981).

Berend, I., *Gazdasági útkeresés 1956–1965* (*Searching for Economic Solutions 1956–1965*) (Budapest: Magvetö, 1983).

Csikós-Nagy, B., Interview in *Társadalmi Szemle* (February 1983).

Donath, F., *Reform és forradalom* (*Reform and Revolution*) (Budapest: Akadémiai Kiado, 1977).

Harcsa, I., 'Mezőgaz dasági kistermelés, életkörülmények, élet-mód', *Társadalomkutatás* no. 3–4 (1984).

Juhász, P. and B. Magyar, 'Néhány megjegyzés a lengyel és a magyar kistermelö helyzetéröl a hetvenes években' ('Some Remarks Concerning the Situation of the Polish and Hungarian Small-Scale Producers in the Seventies'), Medvetánc no. 2–3 (1984).

Kovacs, J., 'A szabadság egy rejtett dimenziója', *Magyar Füzetek* (Paris, 1978).

Laky, T., 'Eloszlott mitoszok, tétova szándékok' ('Lost Myths, Hesitant Intentions'), *Valóság* (July 1987).

Matko, I., 'Mitől féltsük a magyar szocializmust?', *Kritika* (July 1987).

Petö, I. and S. Szakacs, *A hazai gazdaság négy évtizedének története: 1954–1985: I. Az ujjáépités és a tervutasitásos irányitás idöszaka, 1945–1968* (*The History of Four Decades of Hungarian Economy: 1945–1985, Vol. I: The Period of Rebuilding and Centrally Planned Economy*) (Budapest: Közgazdasági és Jogi Könyvkiadó, 1985).

Rupp, K., *Entrepreneurs in Red: Structure and Organizational Innovation in the Centrally Planned Economy* (Albany, NY: State University of New York Press, 1983).

Seton-Watson, G. H. N., 'Introduction' in B. K. Király and P. Jonás (eds), *The Hungarian Revolution of 1956 in Retrospect* (Boulder: East European Monographs (40), 1978).

68 Hungary

Sozan, M., *A hatar két oldalán* (*On Two Sides of the Border*) (Paris: IUS, 1985).

Statistical Yearbook 1985 (Hungarian Central Statistical Office, 1986).

Statisztikai Évkönyv 1985 (Budapest, 1986).

Sütő, D., 'Kisvállalkozói jövedelemszabályozás' ('Income-Regulations for Small Enterprises'), *Figyelő* 27 (November 1986).

Tardos, M., 'A szabályozott piac kialakitásának feltételei' ('Preconditions for a Regulated Market'), *Közgazdasági Szemle* (November 1985).

Zsille, Z., 'Fekete ókonómia', *Magyar Füzetek* no. 6 (1980).

5 The Second Economy in Romania

Horst Brezinski and Paul Petersen[1]

INTRODUCTION

An analysis of Romania's economic situation of the early 1980s, despite the poor and relatively unreliable statistical information available (Pissulla, 1984: 122; Jackson, 1986a: 512) reveals that the Romanian standard of living has been drastically declining and appears to be the lowest among the Eastern European CMEA countries. Unlike Poland, where the population has openly reacted against similar developments, the Romanians have chosen to remain passive and have sought to develop privatism instead (Sampson, 1986b: 2ff). Various explanations of this attitude have been put forward: competition and suspicion between Romania's major ethnic groups; the lack of political collaboration between intellectuals and workers (unlike Poland); individualistic orientation and cultural influences on political consciousness (Kideckel, 1986: 3); and the existence of an omnipresent second economy. Of these explanations, the latter is the most important and logical one.

The historical experience of the Romanian people further explains the declining political engagement of the society, and sheds light on the roots of the second economy. For more than 1000 years the formation of an independent Romanian state was prevented by foreign powers. The Romanian people and culture could survive only by a so-called 'retreat from history'. People developed a deep attitude of distrust towards the institutions of government. The strong separation between the ruling class and ordinary citizens gave rise to corruption and bribery, which were seen as the informal means to achieve one's aspirations. With the foundation of an independent Romanian nation during the nineteenth century, these behavioural patterns did not vanish. On the contrary, this very behaviour promoted eventually the rise of some type of a second economy.

In order to understand the operation of the present Romanian

69

second economy, a brief overview of the development of the first (official) Romanian post-war economy seems appropriate.

THE DEVELOPMENT OF THE ROMANIAN POST-WAR ECONOMY

After the Second World War, Romania gradually introduced the communist political order and simultaneously developed a Soviet-type economic system. In 1950, the period of post-war reconstruction came to an end (Turnock, 1986: 160). Industrial output had regained pre-war levels, and agricultural output had reached 70 per cent of the 1938 amount (Lhomel, 1986b: 115). With the first five-year plan (from 1951–5) the country set out for rapid industrialisation on the basis of the Stalinist model of the Soviet economy. Romania thus concentrated on industrial investment and in most years put up to 50 per cent of the funds into industry, seriously neglecting the previously dominant sectors of agriculture and housing. Moreover, 70 to 80 per cent of all industrial investments focused on four sectors: electricity and fuel, metallurgy, engineering, and chemicals (Turnock, 1986: 161).

This economic strategy involved considerable changes in the employment structure: the share of those employed in agriculture diminished from 74.7 per cent in 1950 to 28.9 per cent in 1985. During the same period, industrial employment increased from 12 per cent in 1950 to 36.8 per cent in 1985. This changing employment structure was accompanied by a new ratio of rural and urban populations. While 76.6 per cent of the population lived in the countryside and 23.4 per cent in towns in 1948, in 1985 these percentages had changed to 46.9 and 53.1 per cent respectively. Prior to the Second World War, industry produced 30 per cent of the national income and agriculture 38 per cent. In 1985, industry contributed 63.3 per cent and agriculture 16.2 per cent. In addition, the Romanian leadership's decision to follow a Stalinist growth pattern of rapid industrialisation led to high rates of investment and to a gross neglect of consumer preferences (Bethkenhagen, 1981: 237). In 1950, the share of group *A* (producer goods production) in the total industrial gross production was 52.9 per cent; that of group *B* (consumer goods industry) amounted to 47.1 per cent. The respective shares for 1984 of 74.6 per cent versus 25.4 per cent underline the tendency to neglect the consumers.

This economic strategy was implemented without making major changes in the economic system of central planning. Institutional changes in the late 1960s and early 1970s (Lhomel, 1986b: 121), as well as the introduction of the New Economic and Financial Mechanism in 1979 (supposedly to function on the principles of 'self-financing' and 'self-management') were of little influence upon the operation of the centrally planned economic system. The marked deterioration of economic conditions in the 1980s, evident also in the rationing of consumer goods (bread, meat, sugar, cooking oil and petrol), was caused by factors inherent in the economic system of central planning and the Romanian way of socialism. In the 1970s, Romanian economic strategy concentrated on engineering, machine tool and petrochemical industries. In view of the structural changes on the world market, this turned out to be a mistake. Moreover, disproportionately high investments went into grandiose and costly projects. In the absence of professionalism at practically all managerial levels, any sound economic proposals were disregarded. All too frequently, politicians interfered with the most detailed economic decisions. The general principle became 'red over expert'.

Romania's hierarchical command economy showed a poorer performance than other Soviet-type economies. Operational information did not reflect reality and, in any case, did not reach decision-makers. Managerial autonomy was undesired, and economic errors were the consequence. The disregard of consumer preferences and the general decline in the standard of living did not make for incentives to co-operate. A severe balance of payments crisis at the beginning of the 1980s – though to some extent caused by external factors (Jackson, 1986b: 46f) – added to the general economic deterioration.

THE DEVELOPMENT OF SECOND ECONOMY ACTIVITIES

In general, the second economy activities in socialist countries can be divided into four categories (see the Introduction by Łoś to this volume). The first type, the legal second economy inside the first economy, does not exist in Romania because the party leadership is hostile to private economic activities within the state economy framework. In the following we will discuss the three prevalent types.

Legal Second Economy Activities Paralleling the First Economy

The most important activities are the private agricultural activities. In spite of the land reform that took place after the Second World War and of the collectivisation of the agricultural sector (which was officially completed in 1962), there still remained a number of private farmers. Private farming was accepted in areas where agricultural potential was poor (Ghermani, 1984: 262) and not suitable for co-operatives. The average size of private farms is less than 3 hectares. The share of private farming in total agricultural land (9.5 per cent in 1985) has remained practically unchanged since the 1970s.

Apart from private farming, agricultural co-operatives' members were granted private plots for growing their own vegetables, grain and raising livestock. Household plots have a maximum size of 0.125 hectare per person or 0.3 hectare per family. Their share in total agricultural land has remained constant (more than 6 per cent) since

Table 5.1   The share of private livestock, private meat production and other agricultural products between 1970 and 1985 (percentages)

Commodity	1970	1975	1980	1985
Cattle	45.2	43.2	38.5	40.0
Cows	53.6	50.1	45.5	47.0
Pigs	36.5	27.3	27.8	28.1
Sows	24.8	21.6	22.3	18.5
Sheep	44.0	45.9	43.1	50.5
Goats	99.4	99.8	99.7	99.0
Meat, total	49.2	45.9	42.5	48.5
Beef	41.5	41.9	44.7	49.4
Pork	43.4	39.7	32.7	39.6
Mutton and goat	82.5	74.8	74.2	...
Poultry	76.0	59.2	47.0	55.4
Milk	54.4	57.3	56.6	60.2
Eggs	75.8	58.8	60.0	57.5
Wool	44.1	42.9	42.8	52.8
Honey	78.7	85.5	90.9	86.8
Grain, total	12.5	12.2	13.9	24.7
Corn	18.4	19.6	23.9	35.8
Potatoes	49.9	52.1	58.4	59.3
Vegetables	31.8	42.8	41.7	40.2
Fruits	67.1	56.3	62.3	62.8

Source: Schinke 1983; Statisticheskij Ezhegodnik Stran Chlenov SEV, various years, Anuarul Statistic al Republicii Socialiste România, various years (authors' calculations).

the 1970s. The contribution of private farming, including household plot production, amounted in 1980 to 42 per cent of the total value of overall private gross agricultural production (Schinke, 1982: 23). Although the private sector's share in agricultural land (meadows, vineyards and orchards excepted) is relatively small, its share in livestock and agricultural production is very significant (see Table 5.1). As well, the yield per hectare has increased much faster than in the socialist sector (*Anuarul* . . . , 1970–85). This observation also holds true for the milk yield per cow (see *Statisticheskij* . . . , 1960–85). Yet, as mechanisation remains very limited in private farming and cannot officially be applied to household plots, required labour input is very high and constitutes an obstacle to a legal increase of productivity.

There are two other areas in which private property and activities are legal and officially accepted: services and construction. After the Second World War, private service units provided 90 per cent of all services (Rekowski and Wiśniewski, 1985: 305). By 1960 the private service sector had been nearly abolished and contributed only 1 per cent of all services. The number of independent craftsmen declined from 124 501 in 1955 to 32 923 in 1970 (Schönfeld, 1977: 309). While during the 1960s these units were not allowed to hire additional workers, the deficiency of state services has eventually led to some liberalisation. In the 1970s, private craftsmen were allowed to have apprentices again. The widening gap between supply and demand has forced the Romanian government to liberalise further their policies which, in the spring of 1980, led to the contracting out of service enterprises to individuals, who were allowed to employ up to three persons (Pissulla, 1983: 281). Still, official reports indicate that these private units contribute less than 1 per cent to the national income.

The second sector in which private investments are allowed is housing. From 1950–75 the share of private investment in housing never dropped below 45 per cent. It rose in 1975 to 59.3 per cent, but has subsequently declined, reaching only 10.9 per cent in 1985. New private construction in urban areas appears negligible. In rural areas, however, 59.7 per cent of all new constructions in 1984 were privately financed. The housing decline is mainly due to the threat of the *usufruct* restriction on houses (Leonhardt, 1978: 118). At present, individuals may possess one house or apartment plus one holiday house/flat. But there are overtures to reduce even this amount of private property allowed in order to make more housing space available for the population at large.

Further, the legal second economy consists of some other relatively minor activities tolerated by the state. Paid tutoring of pupils or students by professors at fees several times above the official pay per hour is permissible. Such activities of course indirectly improve the quality of the educational system, while absorbing socialist sector inputs only minimally. On the other hand, they undermine the official ideological concept by providing only those who can afford additional tuition with access to a better education and potential future privileges. Such social inequalities are likely to increase. It appears noteworthy that the privileged élite make ample use of such preferential opportunities. This explains why the state generally tolerates these activities.

The Illegal Second Economy Inside the First Economy

This category encompasses any underground production within the socialist enterprises. According to informal accounts by Romanian emigrés, it has reached a considerable dimension. Other phenomena in this category are: illegal redistributive activities (such as the theft of time, raw materials, semi-finished and finished products from the socialist sector);[2] the sale of train and bus tickets without turning the revenues over to the state (with profits shared between passenger and conductor); under-the-counter sales in exchange for extra money or services rendered by the buyer; and bribery to obtain desired goods and services rendered by the first economy.

The Illegal Second Economy Paralleling the First Economy

This type involves the private agricultural output which escapes the official network of distribution – that is, sales to state agencies and sales on the state regulated 'free' farmers' markets. The number of animals on private farms and household plots and meat production from these sectors suggest that, between 1980 and 1984, a substantial proportion of private meat production went into the underground channels of the Romanian economy. Assuming that production and distribution factors remained unchanged during this period, it can be concluded that probably 23.5 per cent of the production of beef and 5.5 per cent of pork went into the black market (Brezinski, and Petersen, 1987: 20). This amounts to more than 10 per cent of the personal meat consumption of the Romanian population (Jackson, 1986a: 530).

Trading convertible currency in the black market also plays a major role in the economy. Foreign currency is needed by the population to pay for faster processing of the emigration application, or to obtain goods from hard-currency shops. Unauthorised private non-agricultural production, on the other hand, is very limited as there is hardly any large registered private handicraft sector which could serve as a basis for such activities.

The range of second economy activities consists of a great variety of fields in which individuals may engage. However, the difficulty of collecting complete sets of statistical data makes a full and precise quantitative assessment impossible. The legal second economy activities can thus only be estimated to amount to 10 per cent of national income, whereas the illegal activities probably amount to an additional 10 per cent. In total, the second economy, therefore, amounts to more than 20 per cent of the national income, and to about 35–40 per cent of the official income of the Romanian population. These figures are gross estimates. Yet, the officially recorded private agricultural production proves that the second economy has been growing since 1980. This growth becomes evident when taking into account that the real income of the population rose by 5.1 per cent in 1983, by 5.5 per cent in 1984 and by 4.0 per cent in 1985 while the turnover of retail trade increased by only 0.5 per cent in 1983, by 4.8 per cent in 1984 and 1.8 per cent in 1985 (Pissulla, 1986: 188f). As the official supply of food and other consumer goods deteriorated continuously (Lhomel, 1986a: 21), people were literally driven into the second economy which, in contrast to the rest of the economy, was not stagnating at all.

The regional structure of the second economy shows rural and urban differences. Rural second economy activities are mainly related to agriculture. Consequently, there is a large legal agricultural second economy paralleling the first economy (see Table 5.1), as well as an illegal agricultural second economy paralleling the first economy which has been flourishing since the beginning of food rationing and strict controls in 1981. The urban second economy is characterised by an illegal second economy inside the first economy and an illegal second economy paralleling the first economy. Illegal private production within state enterprises and the unauthorised services offered in trades, repairs and education, as well as bribery in health services, play a significant role. The urban second economy is thus a predominantly illegal one, which does not only add to output but also has a strong distributive character.

Factors Explaining the Existence and the Rise of the Second Economy

General Systemic Causes
One of the main causes of the second economy is the insufficient supply of goods and labour. This shortage becomes apparent whenever the first economy is unable to produce the quantity or quality of goods and services demanded, or whenever distribution does not function properly. In Romania, this applies especially to consumer goods and services. This situation was in part caused by the leadership's decision to follow the growth pattern of rapid industrialisation which led to a high rate of investment and to a gross neglect of consumer preferences. The consumer goods industry, trade and services were disregarded. Consequently, wages in these two sectors are the lowest of all which, in turn, explains the inclinations among employees to sell goods under the counter.

The adoption and maintenance of the organisational model of central economic planning and management also contributed to the severe imbalances between supply and demand. Consequently, vertical channels of co-ordination still dominate, but are ineffective because of costs and inefficiencies of transmitting information to higher levels. Much of the information may be lost, distorted or obstructed on its way up the hierarchy. On the other hand, the lower level 'enterprises' are flooded by information from above. The result is a general mismanagement in the socialist sector. This is further aggravated by the frequent incompetence among Romanian industry managers, who are often chosen simply because of their political loyalty. As a result, operational plans become inconsistent and can be improved only if managers commit 'benign' plan violations to ensure that overall plan targets are achieved and the bonus secured (Brezinski, 1985: 365). Such practice is indeed condoned. Although all decisions are prescribed by the plan officially, it is well recognised that they have to be improvised somehow unofficially. This method leaves autonomy to the managers and high ranking bureaucrats who have no difficulty concealing a behaviour which may deviate from the laws and aims of the political and economic leadership. Punishment, if ever inflicted, is regarded to be of little bearing as long as the party leadership core benefits from the deviating behaviour.

Moreover, the Romanian economy is characterised by a lack of competition among enterprises, the absence of enterprise failure (bankruptcy) and a distorted price system which does not reflect scarcity and changing conditions of supply and demand. In the latter instance, a permanent monetary oversupply (in view of the shortage of goods and services) leaves an excess of funds in the hands of certain parts of the population. This creates an inadequate allocation of resources and a permanent imbalance in various markets.

Contrary to its ideological dogma, the Romanian political leadership was forced to tolerate private ownership and markets to achieve and safeguard a minimum supply of goods and services. It thus allowed a tiny private service sector and a relatively large private agricultural sector to exist. This led to the establishment of a 'free' farmers' market in which prices are state-regulated.

Since the socialist society and economic policy were not introduced by majority vote but forced on the citizens, a widespread disrespect for and indifference toward state institutions and socialist property prevail. This attitude has led to double moral standards: socialist property is regarded as anonymous property. Not stealing from the socialist sector is seen as a sign of ignorance, while the misappropriation of private property is vehemently condemned by the population. This moral stance is strengthened by a traditional distrust of and lack of confidence in the state and all formal organisations (Schöpflin, 1984: 391). The corruptive behaviour of party functionaries is perceived as the justification of the individual value system. The citizens do not feel a reciprocity between their contributions to the state (such as 'voluntary' work for the community) and the services provided by the state (Haslinger, 1985: 310ff). This also applies to the wage policy, which has steadily reflected real wage increases far below the officially proclaimed increases of labour productivity (Shafir, 1985: 106). The citizens are well aware of the privileges enjoyed by the high ranking politicians, party secretaries, members of the police and armed forces[3] as well as medical doctors, and realise that these benefits are not the result of the individuals' real and true efforts but of their power and monopolistic positions. The ordinary citizens fully know that a fair reward for their efforts can be achieved only in the second economy. Thus, where possible, they tend to reduce their active participation in the first economy (Voigt and Meck, 1984: 15).

Despite the rigid Romanian system of central planning and management, its small legalised private sector in agriculture leaves room for autonomous decision-making. As these decisions may deviate from the aims of the political leadership, state authorities implement a system of controls and sanctions.

Private agricultural producers have to keep a record of their output (*carnetul de producator*), which is controlled by the mayor of the village and by the police. Non-fulfilment of planned sales to the state is subject to sanctions. Livestock is counted at the beginning of each year. Private transports are controlled by the police; so are the prices in 'free' farmers' markets. Since the farmers have to pay lump sum taxes for their lots and the permission to sell on markets, tax policy no longer is an instrument to control private activities.

In the case of illegal activities, the urban second economy is controlled through various mechanisms: workers' committees exercise control in factories and so do the police. Possible sanctions may vary in the extreme, from fines, reduced fringe benefits (holidays, housing, and so on), demotion, expulsion and hard labour or even capital punishment in cases of serious criminal acts. In 1987, revised anti-corruption legislation, originally enacted in 1968 and reformulated in 1973 and 1979, was directed against any violations of socialist 'morality' and 'justice'. The new version penalises all forms of work not officially sanctioned. This version was more rigid than the preceding one, proving the government's inability to exercise effective control in the past. Nevertheless, it still appears easy to evade many of the imposed controls and regulations. Corruption and bribing are convenient and frequently used instruments in the performance of illegal second economy activities.

These general systemic factors explain the very existence of the second economy as a 'natural' phenomenon in socialist countries in general, and in Romania in particular. Although they contribute to the perpetuation of this phenomenon, they do not necessarily explain the recent growth of this second economy. The development of Romania's situation since the end of the 1970s and the policy adopted by the Romanian party leadership can provide insights to this growth.

Causes of the Recent Growth of Romania's Second Economy

The economic crisis in Romania at the beginning of the 1980s gave rise to growing state interest in the private sector. In order to provide a more adequate supply of meat in the national market, and to be able to keep meat exports high to pay off foreign debts, the

Romanian government enacted decrees to abolish maximum numbers of livestock in the private sector (Schinke, 1983: 56). This was an
extension of the policy to increase private production practised in the
past (in 1966 and 1976, livestock increases were decreed as well; see
Eckart, 1982: 174). To prevent undue economic growth or wealth
among the rural population, however, the peasant markets were
placed under stricter control from 1981 on. These measures discour-
aged private farmers from selling in the peasant markets (Lhomel,
1984: 191) in which maximum prices were set. At the same time, state
agencies bought at higher prices to stimulate sales to them. While the
black-market prices for agricultural products remained several times
higher than the official prices (for example, 1 kg of pork which costs
30 *Lei* in state stores may cost 100 *Lei* on the black market), the
intensified supervision by state inspectors caused private suppliers to
face reduced profits. Consequently, interest in official private production declined and the general supply situation deteriorated. In
autumn 1981, the government began rationing bread, cooking oil,
sugar, meat and petrol, but this did not guarantee the availability of
these products for all. Urbanites were forced to go to rural areas to
buy from the farmers directly. The underground economy began to
grow. Real income cuts, in 1982, of more than 7 per cent (Fink and
Tuitz, 1984: 257) and price increases for food of more than 35 per
cent on average, did not shorten the queues. Thus a decree on local
food self-sufficiency, under which permanent residents are allowed to
buy food only in their town, was enacted. But, since the official food
supply in some regions did not provide even for subsistence, black-
market consumption and speculation increased (Shafir, 1985: 117).
The relatively small number of private producers who were able to
supply the market could not invest the full amount of profits and were
also unable to spend their money for consumption (Sampson, 1983:
68). Consequently, private production did not add substantially to
the state-planned level of production.

In 1983 and the beginning of 1984, meat rations had to be cut by 40
per cent and 15 per cent respectively (Pissulla, 1985: 171). When this
led to a greater engagement in underground economy activities, the
government had to enact a new food programme in 1984. Private
producers were forced to keep at least one cow, five sheep or two
goats, one to two pigs, ten hens, 50 to 60 chicken for meat
production, five to six stock of fowl, and 10 to 15 rabbits. It
prescribed also the amount of household plot land for grain (5 acres),
vegetables (5 acres), corn (10–15 acres) and sugar beets (5 acres)

production. Farmers not meeting these prescriptions would be expropriated. The state agencies also detailed the quotas of agricultural products which had to be sold to the state (Ghermani, 1984: 268). Only the excess could be sold on the 'free' peasant market. These measures attempted to abolish true private production based on individual enterprise (Wädekin, 1986: 4). *Usufruct* on land was thus seriously restricted. Nevertheless, the regulations, repressive measures and the unsatisfied demand of townspeople resulted in an increase in the quantities of production and in the prices in the rural black market. The real income of the urban population deteriorated, and forced them to look for opportunities to engage in the second economy in order to compensate. Former villagers now living in the cities revived contact with their old relations. Friends and kinship ties regained importance, as urbanites sought to find ways to economise in their black market consumption. The élite could continue to secure consumption privileges through new access to special stores and so forth (Duchêne, 1984: 147). Ordinary citizens, on the other hand, were resolved to establish country ties, realising that these kinds of 'connections' were the only ones that could buy something for them (Sampson, 1986a: 49).

A more rigid law enforcement and severe (even capital) punishment of black marketeers (Pissula, 1984: 124f) did not help to contain the trend of the growing illegal second economy. Paradoxically, government policy in the 1980s influenced the structure of second economy activities: illegal second economy activities gained ground.

CONCLUSIONS

This analysis of the Romanian second economy shows the dilemma with which all socialist societies and economies are confronted. On one hand, legal second economy activities in agriculture, the trades and services have become a necessity because the socialist economy is unable to plan and manage effectively all activities in an economy characterised by a high degree of division of labour. Market relations exist as long as decision-makers have some autonomy, and as long as there are private property rights. Individual incentives prove to be stronger than collectivised ones. Second economy activities thus contribute largely to output. On the other hand, second economy activities tend to produce, perpetuate and strengthen a type of social stratification which is in open contradiction to socialist concepts and ideologies.

The Romanian party leader Ceausescu openly proclaimed his intention to abolish any form of second economy (*Neue Zürcher Zeitung*, 1987). Yet he fully knows that the present second economy in Romania is not the social mollifier which it is in the economies of the West: it is a necessity for the majority of the Romanian population to survive; it stabilises society.

The social stratification created by the official policies towards the second economy shows that the *nomenklatura* and the higher ranks in the armed forces, security police, party and state administration, and the managers of commercial and industrial enterprises benefit from the second economy in its various forms. But others benefit, too. Rural people produce badly needed food or procure items wanted in the black market. Urban people who are able to render services and produce consumer goods have found a new way to make ends meet. Unlike the élite, however, workers have to engage in the second economy in order to survive. Because of the difficulty in securing some of the basic benefits in the process of rising inequalities created by the second economy they are, ultimately, the losers. Besides being deprived economically, they persist in holding a deep distrust of all official institutions. Social distinctions have been exacerbated by the second economy and eventually 'society has degenerated into competing bands of interconnected networks' (Sampson, 1986b: 12). As a result, the Romanian population has developed a cult of privacy. The majority of the population has an egoistic feeling of *sauve qui peut*. The interest in the great ideal of creating a socialist society for the welfare and good of the total population seems to have vanished.

Given these disastrous consequences of the Romanian socialist economic policy, the official Romanian way of responding to the second economy appears misguided. Ceausescu intends to cope with it by abolishing all legal private production and individual economic autonomy. However, what he and his leadership in reality have been able to achieve so far has been a paralysis of the first economy, a growing underground economy, and rising societal contradictions.

NOTES

1.   The authors are indebted to Hermann Fink for helpful comments on an earlier draft.

2. To some extent, these activities explain the better performance of private agriculture. The higher yield of milk of privately owned cows is commonly explained in Romania by the fact that the cow is being milked in the private stable, but fed on the socialist premises.
3. 'Privileges enjoyed by the *nomenklatura* or communist ruling class: extra housing space, chauffeured cars, vacations in exclusive villas and preferential treatment for children' (Turnock, 1986: 276).

REFERENCES

Anuarul Statistic al Republicii Socialiste România (various years).
Bethkenhagen, J., 'Rumänien', in J. Bethkenhagan *et al.*, *DDR und Osteuropa, Wirtschaftssystem, Wirtschaftspolitik, Lehensstandard* (Opladen: Leske, 1981) pp. 237–46.
Brezinski, H., 'The Second Economy in the Soviet Union and its Implication for Economic Policy', in W. Gärtner and A. Wenig (eds), *The Economics of the Shadow Economy* (Berlin: Springer, 1985 pp. 362–75.
Brezinski, H. and P. Petersen, 'Die Parallelwirtschaft in Rumänien – ein dynamischer Sektor', *Südosteuropa*, XXXVI(5) forthcoming (1987).
Duchêne, G., 'L'économie non officielle socialiste: une interprétation théorique', in E. Archambault and X. Greffe (eds), *Les économies non-officielles* (Paris: Editions La Découverte, 1984).
Eckart, K., *Zur Agrarstruktur in den Ländern Ostmittel-europas* (Wuppertal: Wuppertaler Geographische Studien Heft, 3, 1982).
Fink, G. and G. Tuitz, 'Rumäniens Wirtschaft in der Krise', in *Südosteuropa*, XXXIII (1984) pp. 249–60.
Ghermani, D., 'Rumäniens angeschlagene Agrarwirtschaft I und II', in *Südosteuropa*, XXXIII (1984) pp. 201–11 and 261–70.
Haslinger, F., 'Reciprocity, Loyalty and the Growth of the Underground Economy: A Theoretical Note', in *Europäische Zeitschrift für Politische Okonomie*, III (1985) pp. 309–23.
Jackson, M. R., 'Romania's Debt Crisis: Its Causes and Consequences', in *East European Economies: Slow Growth in the 1980s*, III (1986a) pp. 489–502. (Compilation of Papers, Joint Economic Committee, US Congress, Washington, DC: US Government Printing Office.)
Jackson, M. R., 'Inflation und Depression: Der Preis des rumänischen Nationalismus', in *Europäische Rundschau*, XIV (4) (1986b) pp. 45–58.
Kideckel, D. A., 'Prestige and Political Consciousness in Contemporary Romania', revised paper given at the 85th annual meeting of the American Anthropological Association, Philadelphia (1986).
Leonhardt, P., 'Die neue Entwicklung des individuellen Grundeigentums, in Rumänien', in *Recht in Ost und West* (1978) pp. 110–18.
Lhomel, E., 'Roumanie', in *L'URSS et l'Europe de l'Est en 1983–84* (Notes et Etudes Documentaires, 4767) (Paris: La Documentation Française, 1984) pp. 179–97.
Lhomel, E., 'Roumanie: une économie verrouillée', in *Problèmes Economiques*, 1975 (1986a) pp. 16–21.

Lhomel, E., 'Roumanie', in *Le courrier des pays de l'Est*, 309–11 (1986b) pp. 100–30.

Neue Zürcher Zeitung, 'Rumänien – ein osteuropäischer Sonderfall', Zürich, 1./2.3. (1987).

Pissulla, P., 'Rumänien', in H.-H. Höhmann (ed.), *Die Wirtschaft Osteuropas und der VR China zu Beginn der achtziger Jahre* (Stuttgart: Kohlhammer, 1983) pp. 249–93.

Pissulla, P., 'Rumänien 1983/84 – Leichte gesamtwirtschaftliche Belebung bei fortgesetztem Restriktionskurs', in K. Bolz (ed.), *Die wirtschaftliche Entwicklung in den sozialistischen Ländern Osteuropas zur Jahreswende 1983/84* (Hamburg: Hanseatisches Weltwirtschaftsarchiv, 1984) pp. 117–76.

Pissulla, P., 'Widersprüchliche Ergebnisse: Globalziele erreicht, aber Detailpläne nicht erfüllt', in K. Bolz (ed.), *Die wirtschaftliche Entwicklung in den sozialistischen Ländern Osteuropas zur Jahreswende 1984/85* (Hamburg: Hanseatisches Weltwirtschaftsarchiv, 1985) pp. 163–213.

Pissulla, P., 'Rumänien 1985/86 – Wenig Grund zu wirtschaftlichen Optimismus', in K. Bolz (ed.), *Die wirtschaftliche Entwicklung in den sozialistischen Ländern Osteuropas zur Jahreswende 1985/86* (Hamburg: Hanseatisches Weltwirtschaftsarchiv, 1986) pp. 155–200.

Rekowski, M. and F. Wiśniewski, 'Small and Medium Sized Firms in Poland and other Socialist Countries. Experiences of Development Policy', in *Small Business in the Entrepreneurial Era* (Montreal, 1985) pp. 302–19.

Sampson, S. L., 'Rich Families and Poor Collectives: An Anthropological Approach to Romania's "Second Economy"', *Bidrag til Öststatsforskning*, 2 (1983) pp. 44–77.

Sampson, S. L., 'The Informal Sector in Eastern Europe', *Telos*, 66 (1986a) pp. 44–66.

Sampson, S. L., 'Society without the State in Romania: The Rise of Public Man?', paper submitted to the Conference entitled 'After the Fall: Post Ceausescu Romania at the End of the Twentieth Century', Lincoln and Omaha, University of Nebraska (25–28 October 1986b).

Schinke, E., *Der Anteil der privaten Landwirtschaft an der Agrarproduktion in den RGW-Ländern* (Berlin: Duncker & Humblot, 1983).

Schmutzler, G. E., 'Land und Forstwirtschaft', in K.-D. Grothusen (ed.), *Südosteuropa-Handbuch – Rumänien*, vol. II (Göttingen: Vandenhoek & Ruprecht, 1977) pp. 322–48.

Schönfeld, R., 'Industrie und gewerbliche Wirtschaft', in K.-D. Grothusen (ed.), *Südosteuropa-Handbuch – Rumänien*, vol. II (Göttingen: Vandenhoek & Ruprecht, 1977) pp. 295–322.

Schöpflin, G., 'Corruption, Informalism, Irregularity in Eastern Europe: A Political Analysis', in *Südosteuropa* (1984).

Shafir, M., *Romania – Politics, Economics and Society* (London: Frances Pinter, 1985).

Statistisches Bundesamt Wiesbaden, *Länderbericht Rumänien 1986* (Stuttgart: Kohlhammer, 1986).

Statisticheskij Ezhegodnik Stran Chlenov SEV (various years).

Turnock, D., *The Romanian Economy in the Twentieth Century*. (London: Croom Helm, 1986).

Voigt, D. and S. Meck, 'Leistungsprinzip und Gesellschaftssystem', in D. Voigt (ed.), *Die Gesellschaft der DDR*, (Berlin: Duncker & Humblot, 1984) pp. 11–45.

Wädekin, K. E., *Private Agriculture in Socialist Countries: Implications for the USSR* (manuscript) 1986.

6 Unofficial Economic Activities in Yugoslavia

Ivo Bićanić

INTRODUCTION

There is no special reason to suppose that Yugoslavs are more ingenious or imaginative than the citizens of any other country. Yet, certainly their extensive participation in the unofficial economy reflects a set of circumstances which has extended their creative capabilities in this sphere to the limits. The most important features contributing to the growth of the unofficial economy are: the underlying, long-term growth pattern of the economy and its present level of development; the nature and implementation of its associated labour paradigm; and, the impact of the economic crises of the 1980s.

In this study, I will document the increasing, structural dependence of the official economy on unofficial activities, and argue that the unofficial economy has helped Yugoslavia to weather the crisis. Without such informal accommodations, what is presently the deepest, longest and harshest economic crisis of its 67-year history would have been even more severe.

The unofficial economy has remarkably emerged without stimulating any significant economic reforms, and without creating any excessive social tensions. Županov (1984) hypothesises that the unofficial economy has developed peacefully because the power élite and the employed have tacitly agreed to permit this form of development. Politicians and administrators will turn a blind eye to the unofficial activities of enterprise managers and workers – provided that the overall power structure is not questioned. I will argue further that unofficial economic activities have become deeply ingrained in the functioning of the socialised sector, and involve all levels of Yugoslav society.

THE NATURE OF THE UNOFFICIAL ECONOMY

The Growth and Pattern of the Economy

Since its creation in 1918, Yugoslavia has evolved from a primarily agricultural and peasant economy to a dual economy, characterised by the co-existence of modern industry with traditional agricultural and artisan activities. This change in pattern has been achieved through modest, long-term growth rates. From 1923 to 1939, the average annual growth rate was 1.8 per cent (Stajić, 1959). From 1948 to 1985 (in 1972 prices), the average annual growth rate was 5.3 per cent (*The Statistical Yearbook of Yugoslavia*, 1986). Despite this growth, Yugoslavia has remained the penultimate developed European country, with only Albania trailing behind it. Its northern regions have remained significantly more developed than its southern ones. Observers such as Bogunović (1986) argue that these regional differences are increasing.

Size and Scope of the Unofficial Economy

In any given country, the level of economic development is a major influence on the form and activities of the unofficial economy, including whether the unofficial economy will become a predominantly monetary exchange economy. Using monetary measures reflecting a heavy bias to highly developed forms of economic organisation, Kukar and Simončič (1984) suggest that a significant increase in the size and scope of Yugoslavia's unofficial economy have occurred since the 1960s. They estimate that in 1961, the unofficial economy was equal to 4–8 per cent of the official economy. They suggest that by 1971, this percentage had risen to 12–16 per cent, and by 1981, to 23–7 per cent (Kukar and Simončič, 1984: 102). Yet non-monetary unofficial activities are also important. Maroević (1984), suggests that this non-monetary, unofficial activity is widespread among mixed households, where one family member is employed in the socialised sector and the other family members are engaged in private agricultural production. As over one third of all Yugoslav households are mixed households, their contribution to the unofficial economy is significant.

Indeed, the official economy's traditional dependence upon the mixed household form is an important economic factor leading to official tolerance of the unofficial economy. Regardless of the costs and benefits of industrialisation, the official economy has had to adapt to the dual nature of the economy. For example, the state freely allows households to sell their small and irregular agricultural surpluses through unofficial channels. Labour exchanges among households are also tolerated.

The mixed household structure has an extensive impact upon enterprise production. Maroević (1984: 45) notes that in a 1979 study of 179 enterprises, 23 per cent of the workers reported using sick-leave to obtain time off to work in the fields during peak agricultural periods. The managers of 72 per cent of the enterprises polled noted serious production disruptions during the agricultural season. In Vojvodina, Yugoslavia's richest agricultural region, a local enterprise was unable to raise overtime requirements or reschedule shifts because more than 60 per cent of its employees were engaged in the unofficial economy (*Ekonomska politika*, 3 August, 1986). In a recent study (see Bićanić, I., 1987: 329), 25 per cent of the mixed households surveyed admitted moonlighting. Interestingly, moonlighting was preferably carried out for a commodity or labour exchange rather than for money, perhaps reflecting the more traditional, peasant base of such informal exchanges.

The historical propensity of Yugoslavs to migrate is also an important long-term characteristic contributing to the development of the unofficial economy (Mirković, 1958; Kolar-Dimitrijević, 1976). Since the 1960s, two distinct migration patterns have emerged: external migration to developed, capitalist European countries (especially West Germany, see Baučič, 1985) and internal migration from the least developed regions of Yugoslavia to its north-west. Migrations are the pillars for two distinct kinds of unofficial economic activities; the foreign currency black market and unofficial, casual labour exchanges.

Since the 1950s, when Yugoslavs were permitted to travel again, a lively unofficial market in foreign currency has developed. The sources for this market are the remittances of Yugoslav workers abroad, and tourism. The size of workers' remittances is difficult to estimate, in particular since the proportion of official postal or bank transfers has diminished, due to the reduced numbers of workers abroad in the 1980s, new restrictions on the terms of savings in Yugoslav accounts introduced in 1983, and changes to the German tax codes in 1987. With respect to tourism, officials estimate that

between half a billion and 1 billion dollars flow unofficially to
Yugoslavia, compared to the official tourism inflow of 1.3 billion
dollars (*Vjesnik*, February 1987). Car (1984: 2) estimates that the
unofficial flow of foreign currency spent by tourists is equal to one
third of the registered inflow. Increasingly, currency is carried
perfectly legally into the country as cash, then exchanged on the
unofficial market. The exchange rate on the unofficial market is
usually 10 to 15 per cent higher than the official one, although the
National Bank estimates that the unofficial rates are only 5 to 10 per
cent above the official rate (*Vjesnik*, February and March 1987). The
exchange margin varies with the 'free market' conditions of supply
and demand; the rate is lower when supply is great, such as during the
tourist season. When supply is limited, the rate rises. For example,
when supply fell sharply in 1987, due to changes in the German tax
system, the margin was raised to 35 per cent (*Vjesnik*, April 1987).

Yugoslavs regard foreign currency deposits as desirable because
the interest rate on such deposits is maintained by the dinar's floating
devaluations.[1] In comparison, the rate of interest on dinar deposits is
below the rate of inflation, and therefore national accounts yield only
a negative real rate of interest. Foreign currency deposits are also
attractive assets during the periodic efforts by officials to mop up
currency holdings. Officials may offer preferential bank loans, or
permission to purchase imported consumer goods, cars and spare
parts to those willing to pay in foreign currency.

Other goods, especially high-priced items such as real estate and
livestock, may be available only with foreign currency. For example,
large scale transactions, such as property sales, are conducted
routinely in German marks. According to an official report in
Croatia, a square metre of land on the Adriatic coast commands
200 DM (*Delegatski Vjesnik*, June 1986). Sales are usually made in
two contracts, one bearing the true price and the other quoting a
lower price for taxation and registration purposes.

Goods in short supply domestically, such as spare parts, building
materials, clothes, shoes, and food can be purchased through shop-
ping trips abroad, providing the consumer has access to foreign
currency. Purchases made abroad are usually overlooked by customs
officials.

It is important to note that most of the foreign currency deposited
is acquired illegally. According to the law, Yugoslav citizens may
hold foreign currency deposits only if they have worked abroad, have
received contributions from abroad, or have saved per diems from

official travel abroad. The source of the deposit, however, is rarely scrutinised. Consequently, foreign currency deposits also serve as a mechanism to launder black-market currency exchanges.

Urban housing shortages, created by internal migrations, have also given rise to an intricate set of unofficial activities to solve this burgeoning problem. In virtually all Yugoslav cities there are many instances where houses are built unlawfully on green belt land, or are built to larger specifications than is officially permitted. An even greater number of houses are built in industrial zones without permits. A 1985 report of the housing situation in Zagreb suggests that 8400 houses had been built on socialised land without permits (*Vjesnik*, 10 June 1985). In Croatia, over 60 000 houses on private land and 16 000 on socialised land have been built in this manner (*Vjesnik*, 3 November 1985). As the price paid by urban authorities to peasant owners of land adjacent to urban areas is low, peasants prefer to sell their land privately. Although the private sale is legal, the new property owners cannot obtain permits necessary to build legal structures on their land, as new urban dwellings must be held in social, not private, ownership. Therefore, after the perfectly legal sale of land, their only option is to build an illegal house on it (*Ekonomska politika*, 31 March 1986: 24).

Most Yugoslav towns have some neighbourhoods in which the houses were built overnight without any permits or lawful provision for electricity or sewage. In 1986 in Dalmatia, the local electricity enterprise requested officials to legalise such residences, so that utility charges could be introduced and the stealing of electricity reduced. Indeed, the authorities eventually bowed to reality by issuing permits and re-zoning the affected areas to defuse the social tensions that had been created.

The Self-Management Paradigm, and its Role in Unofficial Economic Activities

Since the early 1970s, Yugoslavia has adopted a policy of self-managed market socialism which, in its own right, is a cause of unofficial economic activities. Three concepts are important in understanding the interplay between the practice of self-management and the unofficial economy: social-ownership, economising through agreements, and the legitimisation process.

In Yugoslavia, social ownership has become a main cornerstone of economic policy, clearly differentiating its economic system from both state socialism and capitalism. The problems of social ownership are well known in legal and economic theory, and are apparent in the case of Yugoslavia. Unclear property relations cause difficulties in carrying out investments involving more than one enterprise, joint ventures with foreign capital, and with respect to bankruptcy procedures.

Ambiguous property relations appear to have a direct relationship with stealing from the enterprise, by blue and white collar workers alike. Petty stealing, for example, seems widespread. The employed tend to steal tools and equipment for their own use, or to sell. In a poll of workers in five Osijek enterprises, 20 per cent viewed stealing as widespread; 38 per cent thought there was a moderate amount of stealing, and 42 per cent thought there was little. Filipović (1986) achieved similar results in a national survey of employed adults. Davidović's preliminary results of an extensive research project suggest that petty stealing has become a way of life (reported in *NIN*, 26 April 1987: 28–31). The so-called privatisation of social ownership was ranked second among the negative characteristics the employed perceived about their work environment. This finding replicates the results of a study conducted in 1983 (quoted in Bićanić, I., 1987: 335). Moreover, it would appear that petty stealing has increased as the economic crisis of the 1980s deepened, resulting in a general decline in morale among the employed (*NIN*, 26 April 1987: 28–31).

The concept of economising by consensus is the second cornerstone of Yugoslavia's associated labour paradigm. It is designed to circumvent the conflicting interests which normally arise in market trading. It requires the opposing forces to reach, by consensus, a self-managing agreement. In addition to the legal ambiguities involved in the application of this concept, it does not lead to efficient decision-making (Mencinger, 1986 and Pusić, 1986). The ideologically constructed model, based on *a priori* premises, differs significantly from real life. Under this legally protected and inflexible model, it has proved impossible in Yugoslavia to operate enterprises efficiently or implement sound economic policies:

> Suspended and irrelevant systemic laws embodying rules of behaviour were superseded by other rules which enable the economy to operate . . . [A]dministrating became the rule in the real economy (Mencinger, 1986: 140).

Under the current situation, the official economy could best be described as an *ad hoc*, administrating economy operating in a non-market environment. However, an economy which cannot operate by its own rules and laws has to revert to unofficial economic activities. As R. Bićanić succinctly states: 'The economics of over-lord led to the economics of under-ground' (Bićanić, R., 1972).

The Economic Crisis of the 1980s

At the end of the 1970s the world debt problem, created by increases in oil prices and rising inflation, served as an external trigger plunging the Yugoslav economy into an internally generated crisis. This crisis has continued well into the 1980s and, excepting the Second World War, has involved the greatest welfare loss in the country's 60-year history (see Bićanić, I., 1986).

To illustrate its serious impact, some macroeconomic aggregates can be mentioned. The rate of inflation in the 1980s has risen steadily, standing at over 100 per cent in 1986. The gross national product has grown at a very low rate: from 1981 to 1985, on average, it increased only 0.6 per cent annually. During the same period, the *per capita* product fell by 0.3 per cent annually. The rate of productivity growth fell, and rising capital coefficients further increased inefficiency. Exports have not kept pace with essential imports and debt repayment (even after a debt rescheduling in 1983).

Above all, the crisis has created an enormous welfare problem. During the early 1980s, unemployment rose to over 1.1 million. In the less developed areas, the rates were over 35 per cent. From 1981 to 1985, real wages fell by 4.3 per cent annually, with an extreme drop of 10 per cent in 1983. As a result, 1987 wages are equivalent to those in 1960. The incidence of poverty-related diseases, such as tuberculosis and intestinal illness, also rose. Public expectations about the economy fell dramatically. Sirotić (1986: 3) reports that in the 1970s, 15 per cent of the population surveyed expected a fall in real income every year; in 1982, that percentage had climbed to 50 per cent. Moreover, 60 per cent of the population did not consider their official income sufficient for covering their expenses (Sirotić, 1986).

Labour incentives also fell, economic inequality declined, and popular egalitarianism increased (*Ekonomska politika*, 4 March 1985: 24–6). Intra-enterprise differentials were even further reduced from previously low levels (Glas, 1987).

The economic crisis alone would appear to have provided a natural incentive for the population to engage in unofficial economic activities. Yet their participation was further induced by the state's introduction of incompetent and counter-productive economic policy measures. For example, the introduction of fluctuating interest rates for saving deposits resulted ultimately in rates below the level of inflation, which accelerated the dinar's unpredictable, yet inevitably downward float. Promised wage and price controls were not implemented, and citizens were unprotected from falling wages and real price increases. This unstable climate fostered social unrest and social tension, as evidenced by the greater number of strikes, decreased savings, reduced foreign currency remittances by workers abroad, fewer labour incentives, and the declining expectations of this period.

Faced with an uncertain economic environment, the increasingly impoverished population resorted to the unofficial economy in order to exist. Mehulić (1986: 21) demonstrates that 22 per cent of the population expected to participate in unofficial economic activities in order to make ends meet. Social relationships were also restructured. Maroević (1985) shows that family ties between first generation urban dwellers and their rural relatives were strengthened by the crisis, as urbanite dependency on this informal source of foodstuffs increased.

Work discipline also fell, and pilfering, loitering and moonlighting during working hours increased. A recent survey of the adult

Table 6.1   Negative features of the immediate working environment as perceived by the adult population

Negative feature	%
Privileges of individuals and groups	55
Privatisation of social ownership	43
Bribery and Corruption	36
Loitering and avoiding work	34
Illegality	28
Moonlighting during office hours	26
Disorder and chaos	23
Apathy and political indifference	8
Other	2
Doesn't know	9
No negative freatures	8

Source: Kroflin-Fišer (1985: 54).

Note: The totals add up to more than 100 per cent since some of the polled listed more than one choice.

population's perception of negative features in their work environment identified the following concerns set out in Table 6.1.

Unofficial Economic Activities in the Socialised Sector

It is not only the citizenry who have turned to the unofficial economy during the crisis: the socialised sector has done so as well. This is the result of an increasingly administrated economy, and should not come as a surprise, considering that the Social Accounting Service found that 40 per cent of Yugoslavia's regional laws are not in agreement with the federal Constitution (*Ekonomska Politika*, 9 September 1985 and 13 April 1987).

Although unofficial economic activities probably exist in all economies, the involvement of the state officials in this sector is more widespread in socialist economies than in other forms of economic organisation. Enterprise managers, politicians, and administrators resort to unofficial economic methods to enable an overadministrated, overregulated and inefficient economy to function. Indeed, it can be argued that if the letter of the law were obeyed, the official economy would cease to function altogether.

The key actors work in concert. Enterprise managers resort to unofficial and illegal activities in order to ensure uninterrupted production. Politicians support unofficial activities as a means of diffusing potential tensions (especially strikes), and to ensure that economic decision-making remains regionalised. Administrators maintain their own system of control by ignoring the unofficial activities of which they are aware. Managers are more highly regarded if they bargain skilfully with the administrators. Politicians are more likely to receive political support provided they make deals favourable to the perceived interests of their regions. And administrators can continue to operate under the illusion that administrating allows the economy to function smoothly.

Unofficial activities are especially prominent in foreign trade, due to Yugoslavia's problems with an overvalued currency (Škegro, 1986), its high import dependency (Babić, 1984), its large foreign trade deficit (Bajt, 1986; Mencinger, 1987) and its large unresolved foreign debt (Mencinger, 1987).

The administration has worked out a complicated system of export subsidies, foreign currency repatriation procedures, and import licences to regulate foreign trade (a description of this system, post-1986, is found in Čičin-Šain, 1987). Import rights are most frequently vulnerable to unofficial usage. Imports are regulated in two ways, through the issue of licences and through the distribution of foreign currency. Licences are issued by a system of priorities and commodity lists through which exporters receive priority treatment. Foreign currency is similarly distributed by priority formulas based upon the net import value of enterprises. This cumbersome system creates various kinds of shortages, and numerous ways have evolved to avoid the bottlenecks which are created.

Apart from influence peddling, the most significant unofficial activities in this area are the trading of import foreign currency rights, postponing repatriation of export earnings, and smuggling. The trading of import and foreign currency rights are routinely carried out among enterprises which have been administratively determined net exporters of raw materials and tourism, and enterprises which do not have such status. The premium for such fictitious contracts can be as much as twice the value of the foreign currency.

Enterprises with net export status also import and resell scarce goods to other enterprises. This activity assists enterprise managers with a means of overcoming supply shortages caused by administrative inefficiencies. Prior to the passage of a new foreign trade law in 1986, foreign currency deals in the socialised sector were robed in the mantle of the 'self-management pooling of labour and resources'. Popularly referred to as *sticung* (*Ekonomska politika*, 20 May 1985), these deals involved illegal trade in foreign currency, trading at a 'grey' rate of exchange, and inappropriate licences.

It has been common for enterprise managers to smuggle vital spare parts into the country, and for customs officials to collaborate in this activity. In the press one can frequently read comments such as: 'the customs official was, luckily, a reasonable man ... and let me smuggle the tools in my pocket' (*Ekonomska politika*, 1 June 1987: 29).

The repatriation of export earnings represents another type of unofficial economic activity. For example, the daily *Vjesnik* (19 June 1986) reported that 129 of 169 enterprises audited by the foreign trade controller in January and February of 1986 did not repatriate their export earnings within the prescribed time frame. During 1985, 1119 of 1508 enterprises similarly audited also failed to repatriate their export earnings. Enterprises are generally reluctant to repatriate export earnings because they receive only an equivalent amount in overvalued dinars and thereby lose access to foreign currency. On the other hand, the administration gains control of the foreign currency, which it can dispose of as it sees fit.

Other less well documented unofficial activities relating to personnel policies, bank loans, and investments are also worthy of note. Although data on these aspects are scarce, they are considered indisputable features of the economy – even by the state and the party (see the 1982 'blue print' for survival in the Long-term Programme of Economic Stabilisation, 1983). As the president of the Constitutional Court claimed in 1987 (*Ekonomska politika*, 13 April 1987), business law is most frequently broken by politicians and political institutions.

Unofficial activities in personnel policy are the result of failures to reconcile the party's leading role in decision-making with the concept of equality of opportunity embodied in the ideal of a 'civil society', the concept of self-determination embedded in the 'workers' self-management' structure, and the protection of social interests. Yugoslavia's baffling election system for government officials and enterprise managers provides ample opportunities for this form of unofficial behaviour. For example, the candidates for enterprise management must usually be vetted at the local government level. In effect, therefore, it is the local political élites who have ultimate power to make personnel policy decisions. These 'kitchen cabinets' attempt to portray a mantle of legality by formalising their activities through the communal personnel co-ordination committees. However, these committees are not entirely legitimate – in Croatia, in fact, they have been declared illegal by the Constitutional Court (*Vjesnik*, 1 February 1987: 5). Notwithstanding this ruling, unofficial influence peddling remains firmly entrenched in personnel policy decision-making.

Decision-making regarding investments is also an especially important dimension of the unofficial economy. During the late 1970s, the economy experienced an investment bubble (Perišin, 1980). Yet the actual process of investment decision-making during that period has remained hidden from public scrutiny except in a few prominent cases of investment failure. In these cases politicians, acting through unofficial channels, influenced the decision-making process and prolonged the secrecy of the failures. Such was the case of the ferro-nickel plant in Macedonia (*Danas*, 178, 16 July 1985: 26), the steelworks in Serbia (*NIN*, 9 September 1987), the aluminium plants in Croatia (*Danas*, 244, 21 October 1986: 13–16) and the 'Agrokomerc' food processing plant in Bosnia (*Danas*, 293, 29 September 1987; *NIN*, 30 August 1987); and *Time*, 28 September 1987).

Table 6.2   Citizens of Yugoslavia found guilty of criminal offences against the

	1976	1977	1978	1979
Total no. of convictions for offences against the economy	8002	7406	6613	6643
(% in brackets)	(7)	(–)	(7.0)	(7.0)
Proportion women (%)	8	8.8	8.3	9.8
Proportion 'blue collar' workers[2]	28.5	29.0	32.2	36.1
Proportion 'white collar' workers[3]	3.3	3.9	3.9	4.9
Poportion managers	0.5	0.3	0.4	0.4
Proportion employed in the private sector, and members of their families[4]	49.2	54.4	43.1	36.1

Source: Excerpted from the *Statistical Yearbook of Yugoslavia*, various years.

Notes:
1. The official statistics report on ten kinds of criminal offences which are further broken down by sex, age and occupation of the convicts.
2. 'Blue collar' workers are those employed in mining, industry, crafts, transport and productive services.

The Bosnian case is perhaps best documented. It concerned the financing of investment through the issuance of promissory notes, which were then repaid by new promissory notes. This method of raising funds was backed by prominent politicians, including the federal vice-president. He was forced to resign because of his involvement, as were other republic politicians, including the controller of the currency market. These officials had also suppressed public announcements about the problem (*Vjesnik*, 18 September 1987: 4). The unofficial pressure to keep this operation discreet went so far as having the enterprise manager store the bank stamp needed to prepare promissory notes in his office (*Vjesnik*, 6 October 1987: 5). Needless to say, the bank had to close its doors as well.

The issue of these promissory notes without backing is illegal according to Yugoslav law. This activity is usually referred to as 'grey money printing'. With an administratively run banking system and a relatively tight monetary policy during the 1980s, investors frequently resorted to grey money printing to acquire finance. Grey money printing has been used to relieve solvency problems, cover balance sheet loss, and to raise wages during strikes.

The press has also reported that the Social Accounting Service is economy from 1976 to 1986[1]

1980	1981	1982	1983	1984	1985	1986
7803	10 108	12 291	12 410	13 125	12 798	14 220
(7.9)	(10.3)	(11.8)	(11.5)	(11.6)	(11.9)	(12.9)
11.7	14.4	14.0	13.7	13.8	15.9	15.0
40.4	39.4	37.9	41.8	43.1	41.6	39.9
6.9	9.1	9.2	8.1	8.1	10.4	9.7
0.3	0.3	0.2	0.3	0.15	0.4	0.26
27.4	23.6	21.5	22.1	22.8	21.0	23.3

3. 'White collar' workers are those employed in administrative, financial, and security related jobs.
4. This includes peasants, owners of transport and similar vehicles, restaurant and shop owners, and those of small private firms employing up to the maximum 6 workers.

finding an increasing number of cases involving financial malpractice in inter-enterprise payments. In 1986, 154 410 cases were discovered (*Vjesnik*, 20 August 1987: 4). In every case investigated, it was discovered that politicians had been aware of 'grey money printing' activities and frequently endorsed it. Yet, the Social Accounting Service did not report any of the enterprises for financial ill-discipline. In one instance, even the police were involved in the cover-up (*Danas*, 292, 22 September 1987: 20).

Such informal arrangements have had a significant influence on Yugoslavia's economic development. Petrin (1986) demonstrates that in Yugoslavia there is a clear bias towards large-scale enterprise development, which operates irrespective of market conditions. In turn, this bias is tied to the reflexive, *ad hoc* administrating in the economy, and the inevitable unofficial economic activities. Obviously, the high reliance of the socialised sector upon unofficial economic activities is not officially part of Yugoslavia's 'self-managing socialism' paradigm. Yet investigation of such activities have remained hidden from public scrutiny, except on the two occasions described above concerning corrupt foreign trade practices, and the 'grey money' printing scandals in Bosnia and Croatia.

The extent to which unofficial economic activities have been structurally incorporated into Yugoslav society is also evident in conviction statistics for criminal offences against the economy. As Table 6.2 demonstrates, from 1976 to 1986 convictions for offences against the economy have risen significantly. There has been a steady increase in the proportion of 'blue collar' workers convicted of unofficial economic activities. Concurrently, the proportion of convictions against members of the private sector and peasants dropped steadily.

Interestingly, the proportion of managers convicted during the same period remained virtually unchanged. A slight point of discontinuity is evident across all rows in Table 6.2, beginning in 1982. This change is due to the economic crisis and the resulting increase in unofficial economic activities, and not to any changes in law enforcement. Post-1982, miners and industrial workers emerge as the dominant group convicted. The proportion of women and white collar workers convicted has also risen since 1981, while the proportion of private sector workers convicted has stabilised.

CONCLUSION

Although only limited data are available to describe Yugoslavia's unofficial economy, it is evident that the economic crisis of the 1980s spawned an increase in such activities. I have argued that this increase did not by-pass the socialised sector. Enterprise managers, politicians, and bureaucrats participated in unofficial activities. Yugoslavia's structural dependence on such activities has grown, and consequently government tolerance for such involvement has increased.

This recalls the words of Fran Supilo, a Croatian statesmen from the early twentieth century who said: 'fish smell from the head downwards but are cleaned in the opposite direction'.

NOTE

1.   Moreover, prior to 1983, the interest on foreign currency deposits was paid in foreign currency. As of 1983, this practice applies only to accounts held by Yugoslavs residing abroad.

REFERENCES

Alessandrini, S. and B. Dallago, *The Unofficial Economy* (Aldershot: Gower, 1987).

Babić, M., 'Uvozna zavisnost jugoslavenske privrede u razdoblju 1973–1983', *Vojnić* (1984).

Bajt, A., *Alternativna ekonomska politika* (Zagreb: Globus, 1986).

Baučić, I., 'Yugoslav citizens temporarily working and residing abroad according to the 1981 population census', *Yugoslav Survey*, XXVI (1) (1985) pp. 3–16.

Berend, I. and K. Borchardt (eds), *The Impact of the Depression of the 1930s and its Relevance for the Contemporary World* (Budapest: Academy Research Center, 1986).

Bićanić, I., 'Some General Comparisons of the Impact of the Two World Crises of the Twentieth Century on the Yugoslav Economy', in I. Berend and K. Borchardt (eds), *The Impact of the Depression of the 1930s and its Relevance for the Contemporary World* (Budapest: Academy Research Center, 1986).

Bićanić, I., 'The Impact of the Unofficial Economy on Economic Inequality in Yugoslavia', in S. Alessandrini and B. Dallago, *The Unofficial Economy* (Aldershot: Gower, 1987).

Bićanić, R., *Turning Points in Economic Development* (The Hague: Mouton, 1972).

Bogunović, A., *Regionalna komponenta u razvoju SFRJ Jugoslavije i SR Hrvatske* (Zagreb: Liber, 1986).

Car, K., *Devizni turistički priliv u 1983 i metodologija njegovog istraživanja i utvrdjivanja*, Turizam, XXXII (2) (1984) pp. 2–11.

Čičin-Šain, A. (ed.), *Doing Business with Yugoslavia* (Belgrade: Savezna privredna komora, 1987).

Ćubrilović, V. (ed.), *Svetska ekonomska kriza 1929–1934 godine i njen odraz u zemljama jugoistočne Evrope*, vol. V (Belgrade: Posebno izdanje Balkanoloskog instituta, 1976).

Danas (178) 16 July 1985; (244) 21 October 1986; (292) 22 September 1987; (293) 29 September 1987.

Delegatski Vjesnik, June 1986.

Ekonomska politika, 4 March, 20 May, 9 September 1985; 31 March, 3 August, 1986; 13 April, 1 June 1987.

Jerovšek, J., M. Kos, S. Maričić, J. Mencinger, T. Petrin, E. Pusić, V. Rus, and J. Županov, *Kriza, Blokade i Perspektive* (Zagreb: Globus, 1986).

Filipović, B., 'Kako zaposleni doživljaju društvena izdvajanja i individualna prisvajanja', *TRIN* (3) (1986) pp. 117–20.

Glas, M., 'Karakteristike kompleksne raspodjele ličnih dohodaka i drugih prihoda radničkih gradskih domaćinstava u Sloveniji', *Jugoslovensko bankarstvo*, XVII (2) (1987) pp. 39–55.

Kolar-Dimitrijević, Z., 'Djelovanje Velike ekonomske krize na migraciona kretanja jugoslavenskih naroda', V. Ćubrilović (ed.), *Svetska ekonomska kriza 1929–1934 godine i njen odraz u zemljama jugoistočne Evrope*, vol. V (Belgrade: Posebno izdanje Balkanološkog instituta, 1976).

100   *Yugoslavia*

Kroflin-Fišer, N., 'Jugoslavensko privredno i društveno danas i sutra', *TRIN*, (3) (1985) pp. 52–8.
Kukar, S., and M. Simončič, *Obseg sive ekonomije in tendencije v njenem razvoju v Jugoslaviji* (mimeo) (Ljubljana: Institut za Ekonomska raziskovanja, 1984).
'Long-term Programme of Economic Stabilization', *Yugoslav Survey*, XXIV (4) (1983) pp. 3–26.
Maroević, T., 'Nedostatnost prihoda – koliko i kako nam opada životni standard', *TRIN*, (3) (1984) pp. 19–30.
Maroević, T., 'Koliko smo u prosjeku prosječni', *TRIN*, (1–2) (1985) pp. 19–34.
Mehulić, B., 'Poteškoće domaćinstva u podmirivanju troškova stanovanja', *TRIN*, (2) (1986) pp. 17–22.
Mencinger, J., 'Granice razvoja "dogovorne" ekonomije ili determinante uspješnosti u slijedećim godinama', published in J. Jerovšek *et al., Kriza, Blokade i Perspektive* (Zagreb: Globus, 1986).
Mencinger, J., Dužnički teret i privredni rast, *Jugoslovensko bankarstvo*, XVII (10) (1987) pp. 3–9.
Mirković, M., *Ekonomska historija Jugoslavije* (Zagreb: Ekonomski pregled, 1958).
NIN, 26 April, 30 August, 9 September 1987.
Perišin, M., 'Statistička kretanja investicija u osnovna sredstva po socijalističkim republikama i pokrajinama za razdoblje 1952–1977', *Ekonomski pregled*, XXXI (1–2) (1980) pp. 39–56.
Petrin, T., 'Kriza male privrede', in J. Jerovšek *et al., Kriza, Blokade i Perspektive* (Zagreb: Globus, 1986).
Pusić, E., 'Kriza pravnog sistema', in J. Jerovšek *et al, Kriza, Blokade i Perspektive* (Zagreb: Globus, 1986).
Sirotić, S., 'Što ove godine kazuju ocjene uvjeta života', *TRIN*, (3) (1986) pp. 3–10.
Škegro, B., 'Efektivni tečaj dinara: koncepti, promjene, učinci', in Vojnić, M. (ed.), *Aktuelni problemi privrednih kretanja i ekonomske politike Jugoslavije* (Zagreb: Informator, 1986).
Stajić, S., '*Nacionalni dohodak Jugoslavije 1929–1939 u stalnim i tekućim cenama*' (Belgrade: Ekonomski institut NR Srbije, 1959).
Time, 28 September 1987.
Vjesnik, 10 June, 3 November 1985.
Vjesnik, 19 June 1986.
Vjesnik, 1 February, March, April, 20 August, 18 September, 6 October 1987.
Vojnić, D., *Aktuelni problemi privrednih kretanja i ekonomske politike Jugoslavije* (Zagreb: Informator, 1984).
Vojnić, D. (ed.), *Aktuelni problemi privrednih kretanja i ekonomske politike Jugoslavije* (Zagreb: Informator, 1986).
Vojnovic, M., 'Kradja kao oblik protesta', *Privreda*, (6) (1986).
Županov, J., 'Opadanje standarda i društvena stabilnost, *TRIN*, (3) (1984) pp. 7–18.

7 The Cuban Second Economy in Perspective

Raymond J. Michalowski and
Marjorie S. Zatz

INTRODUCTION

He was in his early twenties. Relaxed and playful, he swapped cigarettes and *chistes* with the three 'norteamericanos' who had wandered into that rural town of muddy surf and rocky shoreline on Cuba's leeward coast.[1] He said he served with the Cuban air force in Angola, was proud of his country, and would not leave it for the United States. Yet, with a trace of wistfulness, he told us how fortunate everyone was in the United States to be able to have everything they wanted. He was sceptical of our comment that there were homeless people and people without adequate medical care in the United States.

He had come to consciousness after socialist provisions were already established parts of Cuban life; after rationing, after socialised health care, after subsidised housing and universal public education. He took these social services for granted: they were just the background hum of his world. If his poor, developing nation provided these things he assumed that everyone in the United States certainly must have them too, along with the latest stereo equipment, designer jeans, and all the other markers of modernity. Considerably healthier, better educated, and with more opportunities than his rural counterparts of the pre-revolutionary generation, he was also aware of a world of material possibilities beyond his grasp but within the range of his desires.

This young man seems emblematic of contemporary Cuba, a personification of the dialectical relationship between socialism and second economy in Cuba. It is this dialectical relationship, set in its historical context, that is the focus of our inquiry. The analysis presented here is based on scholarly research published both in the US and in Cuba, and on our own data gathered during three research trips between June 1985 and February 1987. It should be noted that

101

as a result of the US economic blockade of Cuba, US citizens and scholars have had relatively limited access to Cuban books, newspapers, and journals, and few opportunities to conduct independent research in Cuba. Thus, while our work is an attempt to fill this gap, the scarcity of information in the United States regarding post-revolutionary Cuba renders our analysis suggestive rather than definitive.

ON THE CONCEPT OF SECOND ECONOMY

The concept of a 'second economy' is a heuristically useful device that encompasses the linkages between a variety of informal, counter-ideological, or illegal economic relations. As it applies to our analysis of Cuba, the concept of a second economy is conditioned by several other theoretical propositions.

First, 'second economy' does not reference a radical separation between 'first' and 'second' economies. A nation's economy is the sum total of economic transactions that take place within, or which have a bearing on, a nation-state.[2] While transactions contrary to official ideology may be permitted and regulated, and others may be unregulated and illegal, they are all part of a single economic system. Unless we recognise the articulations between first and second economies, the dialectical relationship between them tends to recede from view. One cannot understand, for example, the role of organised crime as a form of second economy in the United States without recognising the ways in which it is a necessary adjunct to the above-ground capitalist economy as, among other things, a mechanism to control labour activism and a source of finance capital for many businesses in the competitive sector (Chambliss, 1982; Henry, 1985; Jester, 1974).

Second, the term 'second economy' does not refer to a simple dichotomy between 'first' and 'second' economies. Informal and unregulated relations of production and distribution take a variety of forms in any society. In the United States, for example, trade in contraband items such as cocaine or heroine, unrecorded, 'cash-only' wage-labour, and an underground, untaxed, barter-economy each represent a distinct set of 'second economy' relations (Henry, 1985).

Third, the 'second economy' is not necessarily 'secondary' in people's daily lives. While this is not the case in Cuba, there are both capitalist and socialist nations where for a majority of the population the second economy is the first and primary provider of both jobs and the commodities of daily life (Portes and Sassen-Koob, 1987; Sricharatchanya, 1984; Vargas Llosa, 1987).

Fourth, we take the theoretical standpoint that economic relations – whether planned, or 'free', second or first – are not 'natural' responses to invariable economic laws. Since Adam Smith, liberal economic thought has tended to invest economic behaviour with qualities of naturalness and autonomy from the social world. However, if we assume economic laws to be universal, they are useless for explaining variations between economic systems. Variables cannot be explained by constants. Economic relations are fundamentally social relations. As Hoebel (1973: 58) notes, while valued material exists in all societies, it is social processes 'which create the circumstances that make property out of it'. An economy is first of all a set of socially produced rules for the production, distribution, and exchange of items of culturally determined value. This is not to say that modern economies do not at times appear to behave *as if* they were responding to hidden natural laws. These laws, however, are not the products of nature. They are culturally and politically established meanings of such things as property, value, and desire.

In state societies, whether capitalist or socialist, political power defines the rights of property. In Lindblom's (1977: 26) words:

> Some people believe that property is the underlying source of power. But property is itself a force of authority created by government ... Property rights are consequently grants of authority made to persons and organizations, both public and private and acknowledged by other persons and organizations.

The way in which these property rights are politically constructed determines the boundaries between the first and the second economies in any state society.

This brings us to our final point. While the term 'second economy' sounds benign, many of the forms of economic exchange to which it refers are illegal. This is particularly true in Cuba where legal second economies both inside and outside the first economy are scarce. Whether illegal second economy activity is tolerated or energetically prosecuted, and whether its consequences are virulent or relatively harmless, it represents an attempt to exercise authority in property contrary to that formally granted by the state. It is from this proposition that we take our working definition of second economy: *a second economy is any established system of economic exchange based upon the exercise of authority in property beyond that allowed by law and/or contrary to dominant ideology.*

TOWARD A CENTRALLY PLANNED ECONOMY IN CUBA

Fidel Castro and the July 26th Movement came to power with three concrete economic goals in mind: (i) agrarian reform, (ii) economic independence, and (iii) increased material quality, particularly in the areas of food, housing and health care. These goals grew out of the revolution's philosophical orientation, which blended Marti's (1972, 1985) political theory, Sandino's concept of popular front, liberal humanism, conventional economic wisdom regarding import-substitution, and classical notions of the 'rights of man' [sic] into its own distinct agenda.[3] Pursuit of the social and economic goals integral to this philosophy quickly led the revolution into conflict with US interests, local élites and a significant portion of the Cuban middle class.

Conflicts between Cuban and foreign interests – particularly US interests – are not new. Cuba historically has been economically dependent on other nations. Cuba was a Spanish colony from 1492 until 1898, at which point it became a neo-colony of the United States.[4] Nationalistic attempts to wrest control of Cuba's economy from foreign hands were typically unsuccessful, and frequently resulted in more, rather than fewer, limitations on Cuba's economic and political autonomy (Thomas, 1971). The ouster of Spain from Cuba, for instance, resulted not in economic freedom, but in the eventual domination of every sector of the Cuban economy by US capital. The US position regarding Cuba, as articulated by John Quincy Adams, had long been that Cuba represented 'an apple that had to fall by gravity into the hands of the United States' (Bourne, 1986: 27). As part of this policy after the defeat of Spain, the United States required that Cuba include the Platt Amendment in its constitution. Only then would the United States withdraw its troops from the island – troops that had been sent to 'aid' the revolution even though the Cuban revolutionaries had opposed this form of 'aid'.

The Platt Amendment authorised US military intervention whenever the US government judged that 'lives, property, or individual freedom was endangered', and was invoked to authorise intervention on several occasions (see Gellman, 1973; Hagedorn,

1920; Thomas, 1971). Under the protection of the Platt Amendment, by 1920 US investors had acquired ownership of two-thirds of all arable land in Cuba as well as control of key components of the economic infrastructure (Arnault, 1962; Dumont, 1970; Thomas, 1971). In order to sustain this economic domination, the US government helped create and maintain dictatorships such as those of Machado and Batista. Though often brutal and corrupt toward Cubans, these dictators were supportive of and compliant with the interests of US financiers, including those whose business was gambling and prostitution (Chambliss, 1987; Edelstein, 1981).

Segments of the Cuban economy benefited from the influx of US capital as increased exports fuelled modest economic growth (Williams, 1972: 2). These gains, however, were sectoral and uneven. Although the urban middle class enjoyed some improvement in standards of living, the agricultural proletariat that comprised more than half of the Cuban population continued to live in extreme poverty. It is estimated that by the time of the revolution the poorest 20 per cent of the Cuban population received between 2 to 6 per cent of the national income. The wealthiest 20 per cent, in contrast, consumed 55 per cent of all income (Brundenius, 1981: 142). This inequality translated into concrete societal problems such as widespread malnourishment among the poor, high rates of infant mortality and illiteracy, and widespread illness and death due to communicable diseases that would have been preventable with a minimum of public health services (Balari, 1985: 30, 203–4; Viera, 1987: 52–61; Zeitlan and Scheer, 1963: 15–19).

As a start to addressing such problems, in May 1959 the revolutionary government passed the First Law of Agrarian Reform prohibiting farms of over 1000 acres. This move generated a storm of opposition in a US economic and political community already nervous about the implications of the Cuban revolution. From that time on, the theme of 'communism in Cuba' appeared regularly in the US media (Scheer and Zeitlin, 1964: 319). Since most of Cuba's best agricultural land was owned by US corporations such as United Fruit, the King Ranch, and the Pingtree Ranch, any meaningful agrarian reform would inevitably threaten the interests of powerful sectors of US capital. Consequently, a tolerant approach toward Cuba by the US government was highly unlikely.

In addition to threatening US interests, the First Law of Agrarian Reform had significant internal consequences. The law was shaped by the belief that land devoted to export crops needed to be retained in large parcels. The history of dependent development had made Cuba reliant on sugar and tobacco exports. If all of the former plantation lands were redistributed as small peasant plots, the government feared export production would fall due to negative economies of scale and because cane fields would be replanted for subsistence production. Under the agrarian reform the government retained many of the larger plantations as state-run farms.

Another portion of the confiscated land was redistributed to landless peasants, and today approximately 40 per cent of Cuba's agricultural land is privately owned, either in the form of small private holdings or peasant co-operatives. To promote the development of co-operatives, the government provided incentives such as machinery, building materials, and even on-premises schools. The revolutionary government, however, specifically eschewed any form of forced collectivisation. The Cuban constitution specifically provides the right to private ownership of farm land and farm equipment, and peasants who combine their land into co-operatives retain collective ownership of the property. This private ownership is not contradictory to official Cuban ideology; the Cuban revolution is deeply rooted in and committed to the rural population. Accordingly, and in contrast to the Soviet Union and much of Eastern Europe, Cuba's revolutionary government historically has given priority to meeting the desires and improving the lives of rural dwellers rather than of those in urban areas.

Since the earliest days of agrarian reform, the revolutionary government has promoted the mechanisation of sugar and tobacco production, and a reasonable allocation of land between subsistence and cash-crop cultivation. As the new government pursued its goal of providing for both domestic consumption and foreign export, it quickly became responsible for planning production in the most critical sector of the economy. In practice, the Cuban government directly plans the production of state farms, and directs the production of private farmers and co-operatives by setting quotas and official prices.

Another important step toward a centrally planned economy came in the form of sweeping nationalisations of foreign-owned businesses. In June 1960 the Texaco, Shell, and Esso refineries in Cuba refused to process crude oil Cuba had obtained from the Soviet Union at prices lower than crude from the Gulf of Mexico. On 29 and 30 June, the Cuban government nationalised the refineries. In retaliation, on 6 July the US government cancelled the last shipment of 700 000 tons of sugar under its import agreement with Cuba. The following day the Cuban government seized 800 million of the remaining 1.1 billion dollars of US owned assets in Cuba, including sugar factories, mines, electrical power facilities, and transportation companies (*New York Times*, 1960a, 1960b). By the end of this tumultuous week the Cuban government was responsible for organising the non-agrarian sector of the economy. In the words of Blas Roca (1961: 101), '[T]he nationalization of these firms, whose value is estimated at roughly some 600 million pesos, decisively increases the weight of government property in the national economy'. This situation necessitated that the government begin to organise and centrally plan the newly state-controlled economic infrastructure.

THE SECOND ECONOMY AND THE TRANSITION TO SOCIALISM IN CUBA

A central goal of the Cuban revolution was to reduce gross material inequities – and, in particular, to alleviate inequalities in food distribution. The struggle to achieve this latter goal reveals the internal contradiction between social justice as understood by the revolutionary leaders and what were then the existing grants of authority in property.

In 1951, a World Bank team estimated that malnourishment touched 30 to 40 per cent of the urban population, and 60 per cent of rural dwellers in Cuba (International Bank for Reconstruction and Development, 1951: 442). According to a study conducted by the Catholic University in the 1950s, 98 per cent of Cuba's rural population never ate eggs, 96 per cent never ate meat, and 89 per cent never drank milk (Balari, 1985: 30). These conditions were the direct result of market strategies for agricultural exports that included leaving large tracts of fertile land uncultivated when world market prices warranted (Funtenallas, 1976: 417–18). The consequences were inadequate domestic food production and a high level of import dependency. Since the élite, the middle class and the organised segments of the urban proletariat could outbid the poor in the market competition for food, market pricing meant hunger and malnutrition for cash-poor Cubans, particularly the peasants. It is estimated that poor families frequently were required to spend over two thirds of their income merely to obtain a bare subsistence diet (Benjamin *et al.*, 1984: 3).

In May 1959, the Cuban government sought to limit the authority of merchants to sell at a market price by establishing ceilings on the prices of many basic food items. It also set maximum profit margins for both wholesale and retail trade in food (O'Connor, 1970: 269). The price and profit ceilings, however, proved unenforceable in the face of a highly decentralised system of small merchants, many of whom refused to surrender authority over the property under their control. In response, in 1960 the Cuban government nationalised the wholesale food industry and confiscated nearly 8000 retail food stores accused of hoarding and speculation. The government's attempts to transfer authority in property from the private sector to itself precipitated a contest over the definition of legitimate economic practice. Rejecting government imposed reductions of their authority in property, many merchants continued to hoard supplies in order to sell them to those able and willing to pay black-market prices (Benjamin *et al.*, 1984: 23).

By August 1961 the problem was so widespread that Fidel Castro labelled speculators 'the number one enemy of the revolution' (Castro, 1961: 160). Faced with a continuation of the traditional system of food rationing *by income* that would leave the poorer and malnourished sectors of Cuban society little better off than before the revolution, the government withdrew all grants of authority in property from the private sector retail trade in food. In March 1962 the government established the National Board for the Distribution of Foodstuffs, the first step toward creating a nationwide food rationing system (Collins and Benjamin, 1985: 68). The government, in effect, transferred the authority in property that had belonged to the private sector food industry to itself.

Following the establishment of a food rationing system, the Cuban government placed many durable commodities such as clothing and household goods under rationing although private businesses still operated in the production, transportation and retailing of a number of non-food items. By 1967 – eight years after the revolutionary triumph – some 55 000 private businesses were still operating in Cuba (Sutherland, 1969: 99). As part of the Revolutionary Offensive in 1968, however, these remaining vestiges of large- and medium-scale private enterprises were nationalised, completing the socialisation of the Cuban economy.

The initial setting of price and profit ceilings and the confiscation of the property of violators were piecemeal and sometimes haphazard attempts to deal with distortions in access to food. Rather than being part of a predetermined plan to create a socialist state, these changes were situationally-provoked responses to the difficulty of achieving the revolution's vision that 'Humanism is freedom with bread' (Castro, 1959/1986). Thus, 'second economy' activities such as hoarding and black-marketeering were not simply *responses* to the problems or inefficiencies of a centrally-planned first economy. The socialist consumer economy in Cuba arose and took its particular shape in a dialectic relationship with subterranean economic activities that were operating *before* central planning was instituted.

THE SECOND ECONOMY IN CUBA TODAY

The second economy in Cuba is characterised primarily by *illegal activities* inside and outside of the first economy. Legal second economy activities are limited to private farming, much of which is subsistence rather than cash crop in nature, and several thousand small-scale services such as private taxi-cabs.

There are two reasons for the limited amount of legal private enterprise in Cuba. First, the high degree of capital concentration and foreign ownership in the export and capital goods sectors prior to the revolution meant that once the government nationalised the largest landholdings and foreign investments there remained little private ownership in these areas. In conjunction with the nationalisation of domestic commodity distribution, this meant that nearly the entire economy was in government hands. The second reason is the commitment by the Cuban leadership to the concept of the 'New Socialist Person'. The ideology and practice of Cuban socialism has been characterised by a radical commitment to a society oriented around a socialist concept of civic virtue rather than around maximising the consumption of utility in private. The concepts of 'the New Socialist Person' and 'moral incentives', although promoted with greater intensity at some times than others, have never faded from the Cuban scene. In a speech in 1985, for instance, Castro (1985: 336–7) cautioned: 'We must guard against socialist formulas eroding communist consciousness . . . If someone works harder so as to earn more, that's a positive attitude, but not a communist attitude'. This ideology has historically played an important role in blocking or constraining the development of legal, private enterprise in Cuba.

ILLEGAL ACTIVITY INSIDE THE FIRST ECONOMY

Any system of concentrated power and authority produces possibilities for misuse, malfeasance, and corruption. In Cuba, illegal and quasi-legal second economy activities inside the first economy take two forms: those aimed at acquiring use value and those designed to produce exchange value. The first, and more common, form of illegal activity inside the first economy is characterised by the trading of favours among those with something to trade.

Cuba's dependence on agricultural export means that the country, like many Third World nations, has a relatively low level of industrialisation and a concomitant dependence on imports. Many of these imports, particularly capital goods, petroleum, medicine, and new technology, must be purchased with foreign currency. The priority given to these imports in the face of limited foreign currency constrains the supply of many imported consumer goods. In the domestic economy the emphasis on directing capital toward economic development or social consumption expenditures such as education and health care rather than private consumer goods further reduces the supply of consumer items. Allocation of these scarce but desired goods is typically by formal rationing, queue rationing, or merit evaluations by co-workers, rather than by market pricing.

In pre-revolutionary Cuba money was the engine of corruption. The substitution of government allocation for market allocation of scarce commodities has meant that in post-revolutionary Cuba money itself often does not confer an authority to purchase desired commodities. As a result the kinds of malfeasance and corruption that were endemic among civil servants in the pre-revolutionary era have been significantly reduced (Gellman, 1973: 164, 210; Lewis *et al.*, 1978; Salas, 1979: 498). Misuse of authority still occurs, but its form has been altered by socialism. Specifically, while outright bribery has been reduced, public officials who exercise some form of authority over desired commodities or opportunities are in a position to trade favours with one another. Salas (1979: 50) claims that officials so inclined may avail themselves of 'a network of contacts who facilitate access to services and goods, in return for the same treatment from the benefited official'.

This practice of trading favours is not unlike the established pattern of gratuities and assistance exchanged between businesses and executives in the United States. Comparing these two systems, however, highlights some important differences between socialist and capitalist organisation. First, in Cuba, exchanges of the type described above occur most often for the purpose of immediate consumption. In the US, their purpose is to insure future profitable relations. Second, while US businesses or executives are often (although not always) giving something they own or have legitimate authority to give, those who trade favours in Cuba are trading things over which they do not have official, legal authority. Third, within very broad limits, favours and gratuities are a legal part of business operations in the United States; in Cuba they are corrupt at best, and illegal at worst. One characteristic of the practice common to both systems is that it represents a world of benefits available only to those whose position in the social system gives them special access to items that can serve as trading pieces.

In some cases, official positions may be used to provide monetary benefits to family or friends rather than oneself. This practice differs somewhat from the trading of favours since its aim is less the exchange of material benefits than a mechanism to reap social benefits in the forms of prestige or satisfaction at providing for one's intimates. For example, a bookkeeper at a cement factory in Santiago de Cuba discovered that salaries were being paid for non-existent jobs, and in other cases individuals had received salaries for workdays of 24 hours or more. To keep these favours secret, the director of the cement plant fired the bookkeeper. Subsequent appeal resulted in her reinstatement, the firing of the director and sub-director of the plant, and the public presentation of Silvia Marjorie Spence, the bookkeeper, as a symbol of the newly initiated government campaign against corruption (Center for Cuban Studies, 1987: 7–8).

It is difficult to gauge the scope of such activities inside the first economy. However, the generally high standards of morality used to judge Cuban government officials, the periodic crackdowns on corruption and public criticism of officials living 'la dolce vita' (Castro, 1966: 57; 1986: 2), the influence of mass organisations, particularly local, state, and national assemblies, and the limited power of pesos as a tool for bribery suggest that corruption and misuse of government power are probably substantially less common than during the pre-revolutionary era.

ILLEGAL ACTIVITY OUTSIDE THE FIRST ECONOMY

Every law creates the opportunity for crime. At the very moment the

Cuban government nationalised retail distribution in foods and other consumer items, it expanded the opportunities for criminal markets by making formerly legal activities illegal.

Black and Grey Food Markets

Since the revolutionary government's first tentative steps to redirect food distribution by indicative pricing, a black market in foodstuffs has existed in Cuba. Black-market activities in food take a number of forms. In some cases the offences are small-scale and individualised. Some workers in state stores, for instance, will short-weight customers and sell the excess 'under the counter'. Similarly, some workers in state-run cafeterias and restaurants will serve reduced portions, creating a surplus for sale on the black market. There is also some evidence of larger operations involving more organised distribution. In these cases, the black-market foods are stolen from government food supplies destined for ordinary consumers, or in some instances the export market (Benjamin *et al.*, 1984: 48).

Black-market crimes such as those described above involve the sale of goods which the seller obtained illegally in the first place. With the institution of rationing, a 'grey market' for food also emerged. In contrast to black-market crimes, 'grey-market' activities usually involve selling or trading items that the seller possessed or acquired legally. A man or a woman with a few fruit trees or a small garden, for instance, might sell the produce to neighbours. Cubans will also sometimes sell or trade their rationed allotments of cigarettes, coffee, or foods they do not want to someone who desires more than they are entitled to under rationing. While formally illegal, this type of grey marketeering is seldom prosecuted (Benjamin *et al.*, 1984: 40).

The line between grey and black market activities is indistinct. Instead of merely trading or selling one's own coffee allocation, for instance, a small-time operator might purchase coffee allotments from a number of non-drinkers for resale on the black market. Similarly, individuals may obtain fruits or vegetables from family or friends in the countryside and then sell them rather than using the food for their own consumption. While the initial acquisition of the commodities may be legal, or at the most border on the illegal, their sale or resale for profit crosses the line between grey and black markets.

Black and Grey Markets for Durable Goods

The black market for durable commodities is less extensive than that for food. Much of this durable goods black market involves imported items, and operates through the mechanism of the currency black market. Where domestically produced goods are concerned, the durable goods black market is in many ways similar in pattern to the black market in foods.

The ration system provides a basic supply of clothing and personal items, as well as coupons which can be used for major household purchases such as refrigerators, fans, air conditioners and so forth, when they are available. Domestically produced durable goods find their way to the black market in several ways. Consumer goods may be stolen from state supplies in warehouses or stores. Some of these thefts are for resale purposes rather than personal use and may involve criminal rings with access to black-market distribution networks. This type of theft, however, did not appear to be widespread or a major concern of the law enforcement officials with whom we spoke.

Raw materials such as wood, leather and cloth that can be used to make consumer goods are also a target of theft. These offences usually are not organised, but instead involve individual artisans such as woodworkers, leatherworkers, or artists who have access to materials from state-run enterprises. In 1985, this practice led to a crackdown on the Saturday open-air market in Havana where some artisans were selling goods made with stolen materials. There is also a 'grey-to-black' market in rationed allocations of household durable goods, not unlike the one for foods where individuals may either exchange their allocation of some consumer item, or sell it to an illegal operator for later resale.

Currency Black Market

A final type of black-market activity in Cuba concerns illegal means of obtaining foreign currency, particularly US dollars. As both an inducement for tourism and as a means of obtaining additional foreign currency, the government established tourist shops in hotels in the late 1970s. These shops, which accept only foreign currency, sell a variety of domestically produced and imported items, most of which are either unavailable to Cubans or available only in limited quantities or at high prices. For those Cubans desiring items such as foreign-label designer clothes, tape players or cameras, trading *pesos* for dollars with foreign tourists at exchange rates above those set by the government is a way of obtaining the dollars necessary for purchases in the tourist stores. Officially these stores are off limits to Cuban citizens, although store clerks seldom verify the nationality of customers. Cubans with dollars will also sometimes find compliant tourists to make purchases for them in the hotel stores.

While some of the goods purchased illegally in the hotel stores are diverted to the black market, the majority are purchased for personal use. Illegal trading in foreign currency appears to be largely a crime committed by young, urban males. We saw little evidence of criminal organisation such as a trading 'turf' controlled by specific groups of youths. Illegal trade in dollars is largely confined to tourist areas such as la Rampa in Havana and the beach community of Varadero. The young people we encountered in the interior and coastal areas of Cuba, by contrast, had little interest in currency exchange. This is not simply because they lack opportunities for this crime. We found that outside of the tourist areas not only were the young people we met not interested in trading *pesos* for dollars, they were disdainful of the motives of the more urban youth who engage in money changing (Michalowski and Zatz, 1987). This is consistent with Viera's (1987) suggestion that frequent contact with affluent foreigners in Havana can promote commodity oriented and possibly criminogenic orientation among young people.

CONTROLLING BLACK MARKETS

Control of black and grey markets in Cuba is characterised more by efforts to increase officially available supplies and by ideological pressures than by arrest and conviction of violators. Steps toward increasing available supplies have been pursued in three areas. First, as Cuba recovered from the post-revolution loss of skilled technicians, reallocated some land and resources from export to domestic consumption, and became more experienced with the techniques and skills for organising co-operative farms, production grew sufficiently to allow many items to be removed from the rationing system. Between 1970 and 1980, the government was able to reduce by 50 per cent the number of basic food items controlled under rationing. Second, these increased supplies made possible the opening of 'parallel markets' in the mid-1970s. This official parallel market consists of stores or 'free' sections in stores where unrationed items are sold, or where one can buy additional quantities of rationed items. Because they are not subsidised, the parallel market prices are substantially higher than those for the same items under rationing. Parallel market stores allow for a degree of discretionary spending not possible during the early decades following the revolution. Third, a farmers' market was initiated in 1980. This particular experiment with market socialism was ended in 1986 when the market was ordered closed. Part of the reason for this closure was that some farmers were redirecting produce from government run markets to the more profitable private farmers' market. Of equal importance, however, was the fear that the farmers' market was threatening to reproduce not just the structure of capitalism, but also the egoistic consciousness of capitalists (Center for Cuban Studies, 1986; Treaster, 1987).

Ideological pressures exerted through mass organisations, particularly the neighbourhood-based Committees for the Defence of the Revolution (CDRs) are an important element in the social control of black-marketeering in Cuba. The CDRs issue ration books, decide on special allocations, and supervise the ration system in general. The most active CDR members are generally those who are most 'integrated' into the revolution and committed to its goals. While most Cubans have some contact with the black or grey markets for food, moral sanctions and peer pressure by CDR activists operate to curb the most egregious offenders.

This is not to say that criminal sanctions are not also used in the battle against black markets. The relatively low level of prosecution in comparison to other offences, however, suggests that criminal sanctions are not the foremost strategy. Penalties for black-market crimes vary significantly between those for individualised offences and those for criminal organisation. Penalties for individualised offences are typically small fines or incarceration ranging from a minimum of three months (less for juveniles) to a maximum of two years. For more organised offences, the penalties mandate incarceration from one to eight years (Grillo, 1982; Cuba, Republic of, Codigo Penal . . . , 1978).

NOTHING FAILS LIKE SUCCESS: UNDERSTANDING CUBA'S BLACK MARKET

While socialism may eliminate markets, Selucky (1979: 39) argues, it does not eliminate the market function. Instead, central planning attempts to imitate the market function. Problems in doing this, it is argued, arise for several reasons. First, central planning lacks the flexibility of free markets and is therefore less able to respond quickly to unplanned fluctuations in demand or supply. Second, effective central planning necessitates accurate data regarding anticipated supplies and expected demands. Such data are difficult to obtain even in the most developed nations (Dumont, 1970: 110).

Central planning in Cuba has clearly experienced the kinds of structural problems in organising production and in co-ordinating distribution that Selucky describes. While the Institute of Internal Demand regularly recommends modifications and substitutions, changes in long-term plans are often not possible or do not keep pace with changing popular desires. Fidel Castro (1986: 6) noted this in his address to the Third Party Congress:

> Although basic products were guaranteed, the supply to the population was unstable, there being little marketing flexibility . . . There has been an inadequate and unstable supply of consumer goods . . . aggravated by irrational distribution.

Periodic official campaigns against waste, mismanagement, bureaucratic ossification, and inferior quality by government enterprises indicate a continuing problem with economic inefficiency in Cuba's centrally-planned system. Production and distribution problems increase the likelihood of black markets by widening the gap between supply and demand for consumer goods.

These familiar observations, however, focus on the supply-side problems under socialism. There is also an important and ironic demand-side to the equation. The most obvious achievements of Cuba's socialist revolution have been reductions in hunger and poverty (Benjamin *et al.*, 1984: 3). Even a subcommittee of the US Congress (Theirot, 1982: 2) concluded that 'a highly egalitarian redistribution of income . . . has eliminated almost all malnutrition, particularly among young children'. Personally, we were impressed during our travels in both urban and rural Cuba with the fact that we saw no signs of malnourishment among children, something that we cannot say for any other Latin American nation we have seen.

Another consequence of socialist redistribution and improved health care in Cuba has been the decline in the infant mortality rate to 17 per 1000 live births – comparable to infant mortality in developed countries and far below that of most developing nations (Sivard, 1985: 38–9).[5]

Revolutionary policies aimed at reducing Cuba's endemically high rates of unemployment and narrowing the income scale more than doubled the income share of the poorest 40 per cent of the population in the first three years after the revolution (Brundenius, 1981: 148). Average wages in Cuba have risen substantially since the 1960s. In 1983 the average wage was 180 *pesos* per month, representing a 33 per cent increase over 1975 wages (Anuario Estadistico, 1984: 109; since there were no substantial increases in the state-controlled prices over the time period examined, the purchasing power of the *peso* in 1983, at least in the first economy, was approximately equivalent to that in 1975). A substantial increase in the employment of women has also contributed to expanding family incomes (Federacion de Mujeres Cubanas, n.d.). Additionally, in the heady years after the triumph of the revolution, the government instituted a broad range of free or low cost public services including education, medical care, medicine, burial, public phones, and public entertainments. Charges for public utilities such as gas, electricity and transportation were lowered, and rents were set at 10 per cent of income.

The effect of these policies was that Cubans could obtain basic or improved levels of subsistence while spending smaller proportions of their rising incomes. This growth in discretionary income quickly pushed demands for food and other commodities beyond available supplies. Those who had rarely eaten meat or dairy products now wanted to buy more than the rationed limits. Many of Cuba's poor who before the revolution could barely pay their rent now wanted to buy furniture, fans, a radio, and maybe even a television (Balari, 1985). Two years after the revolutionary triumph Fidel Castro (1961) commented that, 'Our problem is precisely that now people have work and have money . . . While production has gone up since the revolution, it hasn't caught up to the increase in purchasing power'. This contradiction was – and remains – one of the essential forces behind the black and grey markets in Cuba. Rectification of gross social inequities in countries with low levels of economic and industrial development, such as Cuba in the 1950s, is difficult to accomplish without curtailing market competition for scarce goods. Expanding non-monetary, non-competitive rights to a share of the social product increases the availability of money for discretionary consumer purchases. This, however, rapidly pushes demand beyond supply, resulting in a decline in the purchasing power of money.

The Cuban government is attempting to improve the quantity, quality and variety of foods and consumer items available through its parallel market stores. These efforts, however, are not being realised quickly enough to satisfy expanding consumer desires. In order to preserve the value of their wages – and by extension preserve the economic value of their labour – some Cubans turn to black and grey markets to meet their commodity desires. In part, Cuba's black and grey markets thus result, in a fundamentally dialectical sense, from the success of the revolution in achieving many of its goals of social justice through redistribution.

NOTES

1. *Chistes* are jokes, particularly of a teasing kind. Dr Richard Dello Bruono accompanied us on this particular trip.
2. The increasing internationalisation of economic relations has created a world in which, for most nations, economic decisions made outside their borders have significant internal repercussions. The concept of economy must thus include these international linkages in order to understand domestic problems and policies in any nation. This is particularly true for export-dependent developing nations such as Cuba.
3. See in particular: Donald Hodges (1986), Fidel Castro (1959, 1985), and Joel Edelstein (1981), for the early philosophical orientation of the 1953–9 Cuban revolution.
4. Although post-revolutionary Cuba has reduced its reliance on a single trade partner (LeoGrande, 1979), and there is no longer any foreign ownership of any property in Cuba, like many developing nations, Cuba is still reliant on a major, developed trade partner – in this case, the USSR. While this reliance constrains Cuba somewhat, Cuba is not a clone of the Soviet Union. Erisman (1985) convincingly demonstrates that Cuba frequently takes a position in international politics and in its internal policies that is contrary to that supported by the USSR. With apologies to Althusser (1971), we suggest that Cuba enjoys a 'degree of relative autonomy'.
5. See Balari (1985) for data comparing social conditions in Cuba pre- and post-revolution.

REFERENCES

Althusser, L., 'Ideology and Ideological State Apparatuses', in *Lenin and*

Philosophy and Other Essays (New York: Monthly Review Press, 1971).

Arnault, J., 'Cuba et le marxisme', *La Nouvelle Critique* (September 1962).

Balari, E. R., *Cuba–U.S.A.: Palabras Cruzadas* (La Habana: Editorial de Ciencias Sociales, 1985).

Benjamin, M., J. Collins, and M. Scott, *No Free Lunch: Food and Revolution in Cuba Today* (San Francisco: Institute for Food Development Policy, 1984).

Bourne, P. G., *Fidel: A Biography of Fidel Castro* (New York: Dodd, Mead, 1986).

Brundenius, C., *Economic Growth, Basic Needs and Income Distribution in Revolutionary Cuba* (Lund: Research Policy Institute, 1981).

Castro, F., speech before the United Nations, quoted in P. Bourne, *Fidel: A Biography of Fidel Castro* (New York: Dodd, Mead, 1959/1986) p. 209.

Castro, F., quoted in *Obra Revolucionaria*, 'Primera reunion nacional de production', 30 (1961).

Castro, F., 'Discurso de Fidel Castro en el noveno aniversario al ataque a Palacia', *Bohemia*, LVIII (1966) pp. 50–7.

Castro, F., speech to the young Communist League, in M. Taber (ed.), *Our Power Is that of the Working People: Fidel Castro Speeches*, vol. II (New York: Pathfinder, 1982) p. 336.

Castro, F., *History Will Absolve Me* (La Habana, 1984).

Castro, F., 'Main Report to Third Party Congress', *Gramma Weekly Review*, 7 (1986) pp. 2–21.

Center for Cuban Studies, 'Capitalismo No! Cuba Ends Free Market Experiment', *Cuba Update*, VII, (3–4) (1986) pp. 16–17, 33.

Chambliss, W., *On the Take* (Bloomington, In.: University of Indiana Press, 1982).

Chambliss, W., 'State Organized Crime', paper presented at the American Sociological Association Annual Meeting (Chicago) (1987).

Collins, J. and M. Benjamin, 'Cuba's Food Distribution System', in S. Halebasky and J. Kirk (eds), *Cuba: Twenty-Five Years of Revolution: 1959–1984* (New York: Praeger, 1985) pp. 62–78.

Cuba, Republic of, *Annuario Estadistico de Cuba: 1983* (La Habana: Comite Estatal de Estadistica, 1984).

Cuba, Republic of, *Codigo Penal y Los Delitos Militares* (La Habana: Departmento de Textos y Materiales Didacticos, 1978).

Dumont, R., *Cuba: Socialism and Development* (New York: Grove Press, 1970).

Edelstein, J. C., 'The Evolution of Cuban Development Strategy, 1959–1979', in H. Munoz (ed.), *From Dependency to Development: Strategies to Overcome Underdevelopment and Inequality* (Boulder, Col.: Westview Press, 1981) pp. 225–65.

Erisman, H. M., *Cuba's International Relations: The Anatomy of a Nationalistic Foreign Policy* (Boulder, Col.: Westview Press, 1985).

Federacion de Mujeres Cubanas, *La Mujer en Cuba Socialista* (La Habana: Empresa Editorial Orbe, circa 1980).

Funtenallas, C. (ed.), *United Fruit Company: Un Caso del Dominio Imperialista en Cuba* (La Habana: Editorial de Ciencias Sociales, 1976).

Gellman, I., *Roosevelt and Batista: Good Neighbor Diplomacy in Cuba,*

1933–1945 (Albequerque: University of New Mexico Press, 1973).

Grillo, J., *Los Delitos en Especie* (La Habana: Editorial Pueblo y Educacion, 1982).

Hagedorn, H., *That Human Being: Leonard Wood* (New York: Harcourt Brace & Howe, 1920).

Henry, S., 'Can the Hidden Economy Be Revolutionary? Toward a Dialectical Analysis of the Relations between Formal and Informal Economies', paper presented at the Annual Meeting of the American Society of Criminology (San Diego) (1985).

Hodges, D., *The Intellectual Foundations of the Nicaraguan Revolution* (Austin, Texas: University of Texas Press, 1986).

Hoebel, E. A., *The Law of Primitive Man* (New York: Atheneum, 1973 reprint of 1954 original).

International Bank for Reconstruction and Development, *Report on Cuba* (Baltimore: Johns Hopkins University Press, 1951).

Jester, J. C., *An Analysis of Organized Crime Infiltration of Legitimate Business* (Huntsville, Texas: Institute of Contemporary Corrections and Behavioral Sciences, 1974).

LeoGrande, W. M., 'Cuban Dependency: A Comparison of Pre-Revolutionary and Post-Revolutionary International Economic Relations', *Cuban Studies* 9 (2) (1979) pp. 1–28.

Lewis, O., R. Lewis, and S. Rigdon, *Neighbors: Living the Revolution* (Urbana, Ill.: University of Illinois Press, 1978).

Lindblom, C., *Politics and Markets* (New York: Basic Books, 1977).

Marti, J., *Antologia* (Madrid: Salva Editores, 1972).

Marti, J., *Manifiesto de Montecristi: El Partido Revolucionario Cubano a Cuba* (La Habana, Editorial Ciencias Sociales, 1985).

Michalowski, R. and M. Zatz, 'Black Dollars for Blue Jeans: The Currency Black Market in Cuba', paper presented at the Fifth Scientific Conference of the Social Sciences (University of Havana) (February 1987).

New York Times, 'Land Seizures Evaluated' (12 January 1960a) pp. 1, 11.

New York Times, 'Text of US and Cuban Statements on Seizures' (12 June 1960b) pp. 1, 10.

O'Connor, J., *The Origins of Socialism in Cuba* (Ithaca: Cornell University Press, 1970).

Portes, A. and S. Sassen-Koob, 'Making it Underground: Comparative Material On the Informal Sector in Western Market Economies', *American Journal of Sociology*, XCIII (1987) pp. 30–61.

Roca, B., *The Cuban Revolution: Report to the Eighth National Congress of the Popular Socialist Party of Cuba* (New York: New Century, 1961).

Salas, L., *Control and Deviance in Cuba* (New York: Praeger, 1979).

Scheer, R. and M. Zeitlan, *Cuba: An American Tragedy*, revised edn (New York: Grove Press, 1964).

Selucky, R., *Marxism, Socialism, and Freedom* (New York: St Martin's Press, 1979).

Sivard, R., *World Military and Social Indicators* (Washington, D.C.: World Priorities, 1985).

Sricharatchanya, S., 'The Real Market Is Black', *Far Eastern Economic Review* (17 May 1984) pp. 80, 82.

Sutherland, E., *The Youngest Revolution* (New York: Dial Press, 1969).
Szulc, T., *Fidel: A Critical Portrait* (New York: William Morrow, 1987).
Theirot, L., *Cuba Faces the Economic Realities of the 1980s*, East–West Trade Policy staff paper (Washington, D.C.: U.S. Government Printing Office, 1982).
Thomas, H., *Cuba: The Pursuit of Freedom* (New York: Harper & Row, 1971).
Treaster, J. B., 'Castro Recoils at a Hint of Wealth', *New York Times* (8 February 1987) pp. F8, F28.
Vargas Llosa, M., 'In Defense of the Black Market', *New York Times Magazine* (22 February 1987) pp. 28–31, 42, 46–7.
Viera, M., *Criminologia* (La Habana: Editorial Puebleo y Educacion, 1987).
Williams, W. A., *The Tragedy of American Diplomacy*, 2nd edn (New York: Dell, 1972).
Zeitlan, M. and R. Scheer, *Cuba: Tragedy in our Hemisphere* (New York: Grove Press, 1963).

8 The Second Economy in Nicaragua is the Second Front: Washington's Efforts to Destabilise any Succeeding American Revolution[1]

W. Gordon West

INTRODUCTION

The second economy in Nicaragua becomes empirically apparent to even the most casual visitor within a few days if not hours:

> As I leave the library to walk to lunch, there is a well-dressed elderly lady on the way down the Avenida Simon Bolivar (the main street) who keeps asking every day if I want to sell American dollars to buy some [black market] *cordobas* (Field notes, 10 March 1985).

Conceptualising, explaining, and understanding this second economy, however, is enormously more difficult than becoming aware of it. Clarifying distinctions are needed, especially regarding the use by northern economists of the term 'second economy', connoting restrictions on free labour markets (see Thompson *et al.*, 1980; Henry, 1979; Scraton and South, 1984), and the Third World 'second economy', occupied by the marginalised majority, but only occasionally analysed criminologically (Walker-Larrain, 1983: 20). Latin American criminologists now argue insistently that northern theories and concepts cannot be uncritically applied to the particularities of their continent (see, for example, Aniyar de Castro, 1979–80: 7–15; Del Olmo, 1981; Riera and Del Olmo, 1981).

First, however, given that more than half of Nicaraguan production is privately owned (Conroy, 1985), and its governing Sandinistas (FSLN) are as well described as nationalist, youth-oriented, and indeed Christian (Randall, 1983) as socialist, and in 1984 held open multiparty elections, we must note that Nicaragua does not easily fit any simplistic inclusion in this collection as a 'Marxist' state.

The Nicaraguan case regarding law, justice and the second economy cannot be understood without identifying its specificities, locating them within its substantive context of dependency within the world economy. In addition, one must consider integrating material on demography, the local marginal economy, marginal occupations and petty street crime with organised and state supported crime. The data presented in this chapter lead to the conclusion that the growth of (especially illegal) second economy activities in transitional states in the Third World cannot be understood as simply a 'flaw' of 'planned' or even 'mixed' economies, but results in large part from deliberate efforts at destabilisation by the central capitalist, so-called 'free market' economies.

THE HISTORICAL CONJUNCTURE IN NICARAGUA[2]

Somozism as Kleptocracy: The American-sponsored Banana-republic National-security-state Dictatorship as Organised Second Economy Crime

Historically, Nicaragua suffered a prototypical seigneurial *latifundism*. As with so many other Latin American republics, formal political independence from Spanish domination allowed only a short period of indigenous capitalist development in traditional import-export markets, followed in succession by the development of coffee, sugar and cotton, gold and meat exportation (Wheelock, 1974/79). The development of this agroexport economy, dependent upon large numbers of seasonally-employed migrant peasant labourers, produced a 'classic', large, impoverished landless or small-holding *campesino* class, continually driven to swell the cities' marginal economy ranks by atrocious rural conditions. And it produced a tiny landlord and business élite dependent economically and culturally on the North (Tefel, nd/1972; Barry, Wood and Preusch, 1983). These conditions possibly spawned the traditional social problems and crime integrated into a marginal economy so often discussed in the literature (petty juvenile delinquency, drunkenness, prostitution, brawling, and minor theft; for example, see Clinard and Abbott, 1973; Castro Rodriguez, 1945: 42).

But the more noteworthy, and certainly more profitable, activity has been the all-but-ignored upper class crimes, most notably those of the Somoza dictators. Starting from an unremarkable small-holding family in 1933, Anastasio Somoza Garcia parlayed control of the American established *Guardia Nacional* into presidential power. For the next half-century, the family used every conceivable governmental and military perquisite as well as opportunities for corruption, engaging in a truly remarkable criminal spree of rapacious and brutal greed. By 1979, the US government estimated his fortune at almost a billion dollars. The formally public police had become not only the private police of the Somozas, but they also had become the major criminal group in the country (see Diederich, 1981: 31), resorting to full-blown police-state terror to enforce this ignominious system of 'second economy crime' (Diederich, 1981: 300; CIDH, 1976: 35, 49, 51, 80).

Sandinism: Trying to Transform the Second Economy and Control the Black Economy While Depending upon the First and the Marginal Economies

> It happened that as we did the vigilance block by block, near here we stopped a truck from the Internal Commerce Ministry, from which was being unloaded 23 sacks of rice, which were doubtlessly contraband. The cargo was turned over to the police so they could deal with it (*Barricada*, 1 March 1985).

When the insurrection triumphed on 19 July 1979, Nicaragua was a country jubilant, but in ruin, bleeding and grieving. Revolutionary Nicaragua inherited all the problems of underdevelopment, poverty, and dependency upon an agroexport economy as described above. To these were added the disasters of the 1972 earthquake and the horrendous destruction inflicted by the *Guardia* in its dying moments: in a country of less than 3 million, half a billion dollars in damage, with gross internal production falling by 30 per cent to 1963 levels, some 50 000 killed – almost all of whom were under age 25 – 100 000 injured, 40 000 orphaned, 200 000 families homeless and 750 000 depending on food assistance. Somoza left only $3.5 million in the Treasury, and $1.6 billion debt (the highest *per capita* in Latin America) (EPICA, 1980). About three quarters of the debt incurred since 1979 has resulted from efforts to restore these losses, as well as rebuild war damages and losses from severe natural disasters (floods, etc.) (IHCA, *ENVIO*, July 1984: 7).

Underdeveloped Nicaragua found three quarters of its population composed of the urban middle class, small producers and artisans, the informal urban commercial and service sector (some 25 per cent alone), and the *campesinos* (another 33 per cent). Although the urban and rural salaried workers (composing some 6.5 per cent and 15 per cent of the population respectively) generally opposed Somozism, and supported the revolution, their few members alone necessitated building a much wider national revolutionary coalition (IHCA, *ENVIO*, July 1984: 4). It used international aid and its nationalised inheritance of the Somozas' vast holdings to reactivate the agroexport economy under a formally mixed model (with 60 per cent of the economy still privately owned, although governmentally regulated). It redistributed land (especially to co-operatives – see Stalker, 1986: 23), maintained basic real incomes through food subsidies (IHCA, *ENVIO*, July 1984: 4), inaugurated health and educational programmes, and pursued a foreign policy of non-alignment, while holding democratic multi-party general elections.

Relatively consistent Sandinista behaviour has reaffirmed their pronounced commitment to a mixed pluralistic model (FSLN, 1984). They faithfully paid debts contracted by Somoza to Western banks until the last few years, when such payments became unsustainable throughout Latin America. They invested heavily in long-term development projects involving the private sector, and supported the large-capitalist agroexport group (IHCA, *ENVIO*, July 1984: 2, 6), often at the expense of immediate payments to poorer sectors, and the political costs of restraining some forms of popular mobilisation (*ENVIO*, 1987: 21). Their pledge of maintaining a mixed economy cannot easily be dismissed as simply a transitional ploy.

It is against this social background of economic adversity, matched by political will and the reorganisation of public and private property relations, that developments more specific to the second economy must be seen.

RECONCEPTUALISING THE SECOND/MARGINAL/GREY/
HIDDEN/SHADOW BLACK ECONOMY IN NICARAGUA:
SURVIVAL, PROFIT, LARCENY AND DESTABILISATION

Criminologically, one of the most striking achievements of the
revolution has been the dramatic decline in the official rates for
ordinary crimes, such as homicide, robbery, and traditional property
crimes like theft. In contrast, there has been a dramatic increase in
'economic' crimes, investigated by the new Department of Economic
Investigations of the Sandinista Police (see Table 8.1). These include
such offences as decapitalisation, hoarding, speculation, non-
productive use of capital, etc. In seeking conceptual clarity regarding
these economic crimes, we intend to analyse these activities as
integral to survival within different class, gender, and age locations in
a transitional Third World society.

Table 8.1   Police-recorded criminal occurrences

	1980	1981	1982	1983	1984
Murder and homicide	864	390	313	320	n.a.
Robbery	10 497	4147	1435	1986	n.a.
Economic crimes	—	117	208	294	496
Total (including all crime)	38 781	22 554	10 439	8402	7500

Source: Revised from West (1986/1987); compiled from Nunez de Escorcia
(1985).

The Second/Marginal Economy

Enterprising workers have discovered that they can earn more by
selling goods than by manufacturing them. So people are drifting
out of the factories and into the markets. Only 20 000 people work
in the factories of Managua. But there are 30 000 or more
beavering away in the Eastern Market alone. The people under
most pressure in Nicaragua today are those on fixed salaries.
Government workers, for example, are on a monthly pay-scale
which stretches from 4500 *cordobas* to 28 000. But a manager in a
private firm could easily pick up 100 000 in the same period and
even a soft drinks seller on a street corner can earn 40 000 (Stalker,
1986: 13).

First, we must recognise the socially legitimated, economically essential, and formally quite legal place of the officially deprecated second/marginal economy in all Third World countries such as Nicaragua. Given the demographic explosion and lack of a regular waged urban working class (*ENVIO*, 1987: 24) families have always had to survive as best they could, through income from wage labour, maid work by the mother and with the kids selling stuff on the corner (Interviewee, 25 April 1985; see West, 1987b).

Furthermore, in the last few years of three-digit inflation not being matched by readjusted wages (*ENVIO*, 1987: 20; IHCA, *ENVIO*, July 1984: 22), Nicaragua has experienced an ingress towards its informal sector (*INIES*, 1984a: 6; Lapper, 1986: 7), particularly by technical and professional personnel (Stalker, 1986: 22; Barthos, 1987). Such a flight to the marginal sector is an enormous problem for the government and for social planners (Lapper, 1986: 7). On the other hand, it must be recognised that the existence of such a second/marginal economy has been essential to the livelihood of half the population – before as well as after the revolution.

More controversially, this second economy can also be reconceived as not simply a problem, semi-legitimate, or an embarrassing fallback but rather as a creative popular response in situations of duress. The *ENVIO* staff suggests that initially the popular sectors expected that the revolution would deliver a cornucopia of goods. When by 1982 this dream was not fulfilled, they made demands on the state sector; in the last two years they have turned to private solutions (*ENVIO*, 1987: 24). Some of these responses include meeting inflation with barter, the creation of more commercial agility, sometimes with state support (for example, through co-operative stores of the National Union of Farmers and Stockraisers (UNAG)), the demands by workers to receive more of their wages in kind, and so forth.

The Grey/Hidden Economy

Isidoro Lopen (not his real name), a mechanic by trade, moonlights on weekends as a smuggler. Most Saturdays he sets out from his home in Managua and drives northeast to *Tierra Azul*, at the war-torn center of the country. On the way out, his Fiat station wagon is jammed with plastic cups, batteries, kerosene, cigarettes and other contraband found in local markets. On the way back the load included hens, beef and lard . . . patrolling soldiers either look the other way or buy illegal goods from him (*Time*, 30 March 1987: 37).

Criminologically, we must comprehend how such legal second/ marginal economic activities can so easily shade into the formally illegal petty grey/hidden economy. Under such economic pressure, everyone can be expected to maximise their utilities to take advantage of whatever perquisites their post affords. An enormous sector of informal, small-scale merchants, often producing the goods they sell, give and accept 'bribes' simply to maintain themselves in business in an inflationary and fluid economic situation (*ENVIO*, 1987: 23, 26). Restauranteurs, for instance, feel pressured to offer free meals (or more) to both privately and state-employed soft-drink and beer deliverymen, whose supplies are crucial to their business (Field notes, 17 April 1985).

Some of these grey economy opportunities have been inadvertently developed by the government, in part through its offering some special privileges to offset the drawing power of the marginal economy described above, which are then 'abused' by the supposedly benefitting employees. Somehow, the 100 000 cards to low-priced supermarkets issued to productive sector employees grew to 350 000 (*ENVIO*, 1987: 22). Quick resale of subsidised shirts and shoes allows a small profit (Stalker, 1986: 22). One can easily imagine how one might begin to 'do a few favours for friends', which under conditions of dire necessity begin to grow to much larger proportions. Barter and small-scale corruption, of course, are not infrequent in the First World – and they are equally difficult to police and control in the Third World.

Clearly, in such an economy, one's standard of living becomes highly dependent upon access to 'economic perquisites' such as a free car, subsidised lunches for government employees, or cards to the government department stores for shoes, or – more generally – access to subsidised basic foods through government cards; or access to American dollars (Field notes, 14 April 1985).

The Shadow/Black Economy

On his 2800 acre *Hacienda Namalsi*, near the Honduran border, Alfonso Ramos had 800 acres in coffee trees. In 1980 he got credit from the National Development Bank to cover all projected production expenses. Yet it looked abandoned to a journalist visiting the hacienda in June 1981. Before the revolution, Ramos employed 200 workers; in 1981, only 27. Left unattended, the coffee trees were hard hit by the coffee blight. When coffee trees are not cared for, with weeding, fertilizers, pest control, yields are reduced for years to come. Ramos had also stripped the estate of almost all the machinery, including seven tractors, harvesters, and irrigation pumps – some taken into Honduras. And investigation revealed that he had sold the machinery, converted the money into dollars, and smuggled them out of the country (Collins, 1982: 45).

Small illegal grey market activities shade almost imperceptibly into the large-scale black ones (often legally similarly classified). Such large-scale transactions are far more lucrative, more socially disruptive, and seldom available to persons who are marginal. Of great distress to Sandinista officials has been the discovery of various types of corruption by government employees, ranging from black market 'trafficking in dollars, exorbitant payments for unusable articles, "sweetheart" commissions, transfer of merchandise to the black market, fraud, embezzlement and theft of money of international subscribers!' (*El Nuevo Diario*, 11 December 1984). Especially in the chaos immediately after the revolution, there were various corrupt actions, usually of a petty nature: a few block committee (CDS) officials became involved in collecting marriage ceremony fees, charging money for local fiestas, and distributing basic food cards, etc. (see Herrera, in *Barricada*, 11 September 1985). Doubtlessly there has also been some corruption of higher government officials. How else could some key goods such as cooking oil, sugar, rice and soaps (produced by a few government controlled factories) end up on the black market? Some are siphoned off at the factory, others leaked by officials, either for private gain, or to placate disgruntled sweet-toothed consumers (Collins, 1986: 456). As elsewhere, access to scarce and valued goods (especially those with higher value at different exchange rates or unavailable because of the American embargo) provides a temptation difficult to resist (*Time*, 30 March 1987: 37; *Maclean's*, 23 February 1987).

More seriously, many in the middle and upper classes have sought to offset inflation by hoarding dollars as hard currency. While the retail price of goods has grown 530 per cent from 1980 to 1985, the exchange rate for *cordobas* has leapt some 3619 per cent (Vilas, 1987: 14). Obviously, these kinds of black market speculation and hoarding are illegal, and on a widespread basis disrupt the economy. 'Half a billion dollars illegally left the country between mid-1980 and mid-1981' (Collins, 1982: 145). These are clearly types of second economy crime not available to those who are marginal.

Of far more important economic impact than either government employee corruption or black-marketeering in dollars have been the sustained efforts at decapitalisation and depletion of inventories (Vilas, 1987: 14). The Insurrection not only resulted in enormous material and social damage to the country's infrastructure and production, but also triggered direct decapitalisation of about three quarters of a billion dollars (US) in the 1978–84 period (IHCA, *ENVIO*, July 1984: 7). Decapitalisation cost an estimated $140 million in 1981 alone, plus $100 million lost in labour problems and strikes (often fomented by the fringe left) (National Network, 1983: 304). Vilas estimates such capital flight at more than $1.5 billion (1986: 153). For instance, about 25 per cent of the country's livestock was destroyed or removed during the Insurrection (1977–9) (IHCA, *ENVIO*, July 1984: 22); some 200 000 heads of cattle were rustled over the Honduran border. Collins recounts the types of economic destruction as including reduction of cultivated acres, laying off needed workers, selling of livestock and machinery to foreign buyers rather than to the national marketing boards, fraudulent use of governmental production loans, over-invoicing to play on the different exchange rates, inflation of fees charged by foreign firms, payment of excessive salaries, etc. (Collins, 1982: 44). Equally crucially, whereas 'under Somoza over 80 per cent of investment came from the private sector, by 1981, only 10 per cent [did]' (Collins, 1982: 145). The stance of many of the large bourgeoisie towards the new mixed economy was becoming ominously clear by their activities in the 'second economy': while many had clearly opposed Somoza, many were reluctant to relinquish Somozism!

RESPONSES TO THE SECOND ECONOMY

Economic Measures

In 1985, the newly elected Sandinista government acknowledged that the private sector agroexport-led development model had experienced major difficulties (Vilas, 1987). In spite of its commitment to a 'basic needs' economy, efforts at too rapid transformation of the old credit, labour, and marketing systems had resulted in distorting the informal peasant reproduction process (Utting, 1987). There was a fundamental policy shift towards supporting the small and middle peasantry through land redistribution, consolidation of the co-operative movement regarding credit, technical assistance, etc. and encouraging local self-sufficiency in food production. Co-operative stores in rural areas, organised by the National Union of Farmers and Stockraisers (UNAG), in addition to enhancing local supply of necessities, have also begun to buy local produce. Large-scale long-term agroexport projects were scaled down (Vilas, 1987. 16–17; *Maclean's*, 23 February 1987). Besides hiring freezes and raising basic salaries (Barthos, 1987), new measures in fiscal and monetary policy (*Barricada*, 9 February 1985) were introduced to undercut the black market by reducing the overvalued *cordoba* through a free market in currency.

From early 1982 (with expansion in 1983), ENABAS (the National Basic Food Corporation) had brought in 'guarantee cards' (for some two dozen basic products such as rice, beans, sugar, salt, laundry soap, corn, cooking oil, and gasoline) as a part of the subsidised basic product distribution. As well, it opened thousands of workplace lunchrooms and sales depots for those on fixed salaries (civil servants, industrial workers, professionals, and so on), maintained a regional quota system and a system of state-supported local stores, over half of which were privately owned (*tiendras populares*) (Stalker, 1986: 23), and established special programmes to ensure everyone's right to nutrition at affordable prices, readjusted annually in the last few years (IHCA, *ENVIO*, July 1984: 31; Vilas, 1987: 16).

Popular Action

Especially in the first few years after the triumph, various groups occasionally occupied suspected Somozista property, harassed suspected speculators, and seized properties abandoned by large land-owners, those who were clearly decapitalising, or speculating (Collins, 1982: 48ff; Vilas, 1986: 139–46).

In the control of speculation and the distribution of basic products, the reorganised country-wide, democratically-run neighbourhood block committees (*Comites de Defensa Sandinista – CDS*) have been a major element (INIES, 1984b: 26ff), each with secretaries of the defence of the economy, popular inspectors, nightwatch patrols (*Vigilancia Revolucionaria*), and so on (see West, 1987a). At the most fundamental level, the CDS have co-operated extensively with the Ministry of Internal Commerce (MICOIN) and the Sandinista police through Popular Supply Committees to co-ordinate effective and just distribution of essential consumer products through the thousands of local retail outlets, enforcing government price controls and the guarantee card system.

Moreover, weekly 'Face the People' sessions put government ministers under grilling from local groups, and local non-governmental organisations such as the CDS themselves have undertaken self-assessments which included aspects of policing corruption and the second economy (Stalker, 1986: 9; Herrera in *Barricada*, 11 September 1985). The independent daily newspaper *El Nuevo Diario* has been particularly hard on black-marketeering, even publishing reports of smugglers' licence-plate numbers.

Legal Responses

The post-revolutionary government basically operates under the 1974 Criminal Code, updated by post-revolution legislation in a very piecemeal fashion in response to immediate crises. As yet no progressive reconceptualised overview has appeared. The coalition Government Junta issued a decree in March 1980 to end decapitalisation, divestments and illegal exportation of assets, to prevent further sabotaging of the recovery of the economy. Legal measures in July 1981 included a more stringent decapitalisation law, and legislation allowing the expropriation of properties of individuals absent for more than six months. New taxes of 30–100 per cent were imposed on luxury goods imported from beyond Central America, and foreign exchange was regulated with sanctions of up to three years' imprisonment for speculation, hoarding, or disinformation. While these examples of new enactments are clearly essential in the control of the illegal second economy, they are equally tentative, exploratory and revisable attempts to combine substantive and formal justice regarding activities most elusive to reconceive, and reinforce.

Partly to encourage private enterprise and to avoid aggravating entrepreneurs, the government has only reluctantly used direct policing. By 1981 there were only 40 inspectors (Collins, 1982: 131); more recent reports indicate a tightening of enforcement, with some 50 inspectors dispatched to the *Mercado Oriental* alone (Lapper, 1986: 7; see also Barthos, 1987; *El Nuevo Diario*, 13 April 1985).

ANALYSIS AND DISCUSSION: IS THE MIXED ECONOMY FLAWED, OR IS NICARAGUA 'TOO GOOD AN EXAMPLE'?

Structural Difficulties

The Sandinistas not only inherited a country in ruin, bankrupt, and mortgaged for at least a generation, but they also inherited an economy dependent upon agricultural exports just when these products were beginning to experience serious declines in world prices, compounded by increased oil costs, and soaring interest rates (*ENVIO*, 1987: 20). While the overall economic performance of the Sandinistas in the early years of the revolution compared favourably with that of their neighbours (see Vilas, 1986: 231; Conroy, 1985: 220), the regional structural problems nonetheless remain serious.

Government Policies and Private Sector Response

From 1979, the Sandinistas aimed for a mixed economy which would be export-led, with massive investments in large-scale infrastructural projects traditionally favoured by social democrats and liberals (*ENVIO*, 1987: 30). Easy credit was given to large landowners reaping surpluses (from coffee, sugar, cotton, etc.) to be used in 'social wage' programmes (Vilas, 1987: 12), while controlling wages which had historically been so highly exploitative as to be unable themselves to reproduce the labour force without supplementary income (Vilas, 1987: 12, 19). By the mid-1980s, this began to drive workers and *campesinos* from rural employment into urban self-employment if necessary, in the marginal sector. Furthermore, the complex system of foreign exchange rates, and the maintenance of an overvalued *cordoba* (Vilas, 1987: 12) clearly fuelled black market speculation, as effective demand outran supply (Collins, 1986: 453). 'In an economy in which the government controls only 30 per cent of industrial production and 20 per cent of agricultural production, private capital investment is crucial' (Vilas, 1987: 13). Yet, despite its favoured role in this development model, the landed oligarchy has not reacted amicably. Breaking with the past and developing a new model has been difficult anywhere in the world even under the most propitious conditions (*ENVIO*, 1987: 30).

The White House's Intervention

Since President Reagan's assumption of power in 1981, the United
States administration has waged a so-called 'low-intensity' war of
attrition against Nicaragua. While the central horror of this intervention is the terrorist assault, rape, kidnapping, torture, and murder of
tens of thousands of Nicaraguans, civilians as well as military (see
West, 1986/1987), we are concerned here with the economic aggression which has affected the second economy.

First, the US military buildup in the region has been enormous
(constant manoeuvres, base-building, weapons upgrading, troop
force quadrupling, and legal and illegal military aid – see Tower
Commission, 1987). In response, whereas Nicaraguan military spending constituted only 17 per cent of the 1980 and 1981 national
budgets, the figure rose to about 50 per cent since (IHCA, *ENVIO*,
July 1984: 21). Secondly, defence costs have negatively affected many
other sectors of the economy, and the warfare has brought increasing
damage to some key coffee and cattle producing areas, as well as
seriously affecting the smaller mining, forestry, and fishing sectors
(Vilas, 1987: 13; Melrose, 1985: 38; Fitzgerald, 1987: 198). Thirdly,
there have been the international treaty-violating American cut-offs
in aid and trade (LeoGrande, 1982: 74), some explicitly targetting the
informal sector as potential recruits to the anti-government opposition (Barry, 1986: 16), even before the formal 1985 American
embargo. Fourthly, the Americans began a strategy of contriving
technical objections and political pressure against any international
loans for Nicaragua (Maxfield and Stahler-Sholk, 1985: 258–9). By
1984, the financial aggression in denied loans technically approved
amounted to about $200 million, in comparison with the $321 million
in military losses (Fitzgerald, 1987: 202). By 1986, the direct economic cost and its consequent human suffering is estimated at more
than $2.8 billion since 1981 (Tirado, in *Toronto Star*, 24 January
1987; Vergara Meneses *et al.*, 1986: 60). One of the most painful and
costly consequences of this aggression has been the displacement of
over 250 000 persons by June 1986 (Vergara Meneses *et al.*, 1986: 53),
nearly a tenth of the total population.

Although it is certainly no friend of revolutionary governments,
even the World Bank projections of investment rates, production,
balance of payments, foreign loans, and inflation indicate that
without such hostility from the United States, the Nicaraguan
economy would have had a healthy rate of growth, with a Gross

Domestic Product by 1990 some 86 per cent higher than in 1980, in contrast to the current prediction of some 15 per cent (Fitzgerald, 1987: 208–11). Inflation rates by 1985 would have been only a third of the 70 per cent experienced (Fitzgerald, 1987: 204).

Unquestionably, the United States has seriously undermined the Nicaraguan economy, not only directly through its covert–overt proxy contra guerrilla war, but also by destabilising the domestic economy, cutting bilateral aid, and subverting multilateral aid programmes, in addition to its active lobbying to disrupt Nicaraguan markets, in clear violation of the General Agreement on Trade and Tariffs (GATT) and UN international trade agreements designed to ensure the free markets it so vociferously champions. More specifically, far more than any flaws internal to the Sandinista economic strategy, these American measures would seem to be the crucial explanatory factors underlying the growth of the illegal second economy discussed above. Since neither the direct military threat nor the economic loss posed by tiny impoverished Nicaragua can explain these extreme American actions, one is left with the geo-political symbolic one: Nicaragua is just 'too good an example' (Melrose, 1985).

CONCLUSION: THE SECOND ECONOMY IS THE SECOND FRONT

This study has examined Nicaragua, a small, peripheral Third World economy in Central America, and indicated some major continuities and discontinuities from before and after its 1979 revolution. First, northern classifications do not easily fit: Nicaragua was a 'free market' economy before 1979 only in the narrowest legal sense – the family dictatorship exercised heavy central planning. Since 1979, the mixed economy model adopted prevents any easy classification of Nicaragua as Marxist. Once again, this case demonstrates the need for an indigenous Latin American criminology. Secondly, the marginal, grey, black and other economies are highly intertwined and integrated; in particular, analysing the Third World's huge legal marginal sector is crucial to developing an understanding. Traditional Marxist conceptions of *'lumpenproletariat'*, for instance, as simply the 'dangerous classes' (Marx, 1867/1967: 602) need reformulation in order to comprehend Third World marginality. Thirdly, different marginal, grey, and black economic activities are differentially available to people, depending upon their class, age, and gender. We need more research to understand the situation of the reproduction of marginality (especially regarding southern women and children) (see West, 1987b).

Fourthly, the most serious illegal economic activities seem to be those committed by persons in the wealthy private sector, and by United States' military and economic aggression. Fifthly, although the Sandinistas seem to have successfully made some moves toward economic policy improvements in establishing a 'war/survival' economy, the possibilities of government responses are limited by structural economic problems and United States' power. World interdependence has meant that crime problems at the periphery are connected to those at the centre (Tower Commission, 1987). To the extent that the second economy in Nicaragua is subordinate to the north (Vilas, 1987: 19), crime in peripheral countries must be analysed with reference to northern imperialism (see The International Court of Justice, 1986; the House–Senate Committee investigations of the Iran-Contra scandal, *New York Times*, May and June 1987).

NOTES

1. Acknowledgement is due to Dra. Vilma Nunez de Escorcia, La Comision Nacional de Promocion y Proteccion de Derechos Humanos; Peter Rivera, Lillian Hurtado Cubillo, and Rosa Maria Rodriguez of La Corte Suprema; Jim and Margaret Goff of El Centro Ecumenico Valdivieso; Judy Butler and Carlos Vilas of El Centro de Investigaciones y Documentaciones de la Costa Atlantica; Scott Evanson, Miguel Fried, and Cathy Gander of the Instituto Historico Centroamericano; David Dye of INIES and Stanford University; Nigel South of the Institute for the Study of Drug Dependency, London; Phil Scraten, Edgehill College, England; Jock Young, Middlesex Polytechnic, London; Richard Sparks, Rutgers University, New Jersey; Laureen Snider, Queen's University, Kingston, Canada; and John Clarke, the Open University, England. And personal thanks also to Eldon Bennett, Lorraine DeGras, and Cheryl, Carey and Kyle West.

   For financial support, my thanks to the Social Science and Humanities Research Council of Canada, the Centre of Criminology at the University of Toronto, and the Ontario Institute for Studies in Education; the analyses and opinions expressed herein are solely attributable to the author.

2. This section is a drastically shortened revision of material in West, 1986/1987; 1987a; 1987b forthcoming.

REFERENCES

Aniyar de Castro, L., 'Notas Sobre el Poder y el Abuso de Poder, para el Topico: Delitos y Delicuentes Fuera del Alcance de la Ley', *Capitulo Criminologico*, 7/8 (1979–80) pp. 7–15.
Barricada, various issues indicated: including May 1980; 11 June 1984; 30 March 1985.
Barry, T., *The Destabilization of Nicaragua* (New Mexico: The Inter-Hemispheric Education Resource Centre, 1986).
Barry, T., B. Wood and D. Preusch, *Dollars and Dictators* (New York: Grove Press, 1983).
Barthos, G., 'Bloom Is Off the Rose of Nicaragua's Revolution', *Toronto Star* (12 April 1987).
Castro Rodriguez, R., *Sistemas Carcelarios*, unpublished dissertation (Leon, Nicaragua: Universidad de Leon, 1945).
Central Intelligence Agency (CIA), *Manual del Combatiente por la Libertad*, reprinted in English as *The Freedom Fighter's Manual* (New York: Grove Press, n.d.).
CIDH (Comision Interamericana de Derechos Humanos), *Informe Sobre la Situacion de los Derechos Humanos en Nicaragua* (OEA doc. 16, 1976).
Clinard, M. B. and D. J. Abbott, *Crime in Developing Countries* (New York: Wiley, 1973).
Collins, J., *What Difference Could a Revolution Make? Food and Farming in the New Nicaragua* (San Francisco: Institute for Food and Development Policy, 1982).
Collins, J., 'The Food System: Expanding Demand, Sabotaged Supply', in P. Rosset and J. Vandermeer (eds), *Nicaragua: The Unfinished Revolution* (New York: Grove Press, 1986).
Conroy, M. E., 'Economic Legacy and Policies: Performance and Critique', in T. W. Walker (ed.), *Nicaragua: The First Five Years* (New York: Praeger, 1985).
Del Olmo, R., *America Latina y su Criminologia* (Mexico: Siglo XXI, 1981).
Del Olmo, R., 'Remaking Criminal Justice in Revolutionary Nicaragua', *Crime and Social Justice*, XVIII (1983).
Diederich, B., *Somoza and the Legacy of US Involvement in Central America* (London: Junction, 1981).
El Nuevo Diario, various issues indicated, including: 11 December 1984; 13 March 1985; 6 January 1985.
EPICA (Ecumenical Program for Interamerican Communication and Action), *Nicaragua: A People's Revolution* (Washington: EPICA, 1980).
ENVIO Staff, 'Slow Motion towards a Survival Economy', *Against the Current*, XI (1) (1987) pp. 20–8, vii.
Fitzgerald, E. V. K., 'An Evaluation of the Economic Costs to Nicaragua of US Aggression: 1980–1984', in R. Spalding (ed.), *The Political Economy of Revolutionary Nicaragua* (Boston: Allen & Unwin, 1987).
FSLN (Frente Sandinista de Liberacion Nacional), *Plan de Lucha del FSLN* (Managua: FSLN, 1984).
Globe and Mail (Toronto), various issues indicated, including: 21 July 1979; 9 December 1986; 30 March 1987; 31 March 1987.

Nicaragua

Henry, S., *The Hidden Economy* (London: Martin Robertson, 1979).
IHCA (Instituto Historico de Centro America), *ENVIO* various issues indicated, including 'The Right of the Poor to Defend their Unique Revolution' (Managua: Nicaragua) (July 1984).
IHCA (Instituto Historico de Centro America), *Update*, various issues indicated, including: 'Nicaragua 84: The Human and Material Costs of the War', IV: 1 (29 January 1985).
INIES (Instituto de Investigaciones Economicas y Sociales), 'Una Aproximacion al Sector Informal Urbano de Nicaragua' (Managua: INIES, 1984a).
INIES (Instituto de Investigaciones Economicas y Sociales), 'Abastecimiento y Participacion Popular' (Managua: INIES, 1984b).
INSSBI (Instituto Nicaraguense de Seguridad Social y Bienestar), *La Prostitucion en Nicaragua* (Managua: INSSBI, 1982).
INSSBI (Instituto Nicaraguense de Seguridad Social y Bienestar), *El Menor en Situacion de Riesgo* (Managua: INSSBI, 1984).
International Court of Justice, 'The Decision of the World Court', in P. Rosset and J. Vandermeer (eds), *Nicaragua: Unfinished Revolution* (New York: Grove, 1986).
Lapper, R., '"Bisnes" in Nicaragua: A New Headache for the Sandinistas', *Nacla Report on the Americas*, XX (2) (April–May 1986) pp. 8–10.
LeoGrande, W., 'The United States and the Nicaraguan Revolution', in T. W. Walker (ed.), *Nicaragua in Revolution* (New York: Praeger, 1982).
Maclean's Magazine, 'In the Shadow of War: The Battle for Nicaragua' (23 February 1987).
Marx, K., *Capital* (London: Lawrence & Wishart, 1867/1967).
Maxfield, S. and R. Stahler-Sholk, 'External Constraints', in T. W. Walker (ed.), *Nicaragua: The First Five Years* (New York: Praeger, 1985).
Melrose, D., *Nicaragua: The Threat of a Good Example?* (London: Oxfam, 1985).
Miles, S., 'The Real War: Low Intensity Conflict in Central America', *Nacla Report on the America*, XX (2) (April–May 1986) pp. 17–48.
Ministerio de Estranjero, *Informe Sobre la Agresion* (Managua: Nicaragua, 1985).
National Network, 'Atlantic Coast: Miskitu Crisis and Counterrevolution', in P. Rosset and J. Vandermeer (eds), *The Nicaragua Reader: Documents of a Revolution under Fire* (New York: Grove, 1983).
New York Times, various issues indicated.
Newsweek, various issues indicated.
Nunez de Escorcia, V., 'Justice and the Control of Crime: The Sandinist Popular Revolution', *Crime and Social Justice*, XXIII (1985).
Randall, M., *Christians in the Nicaraguan Revolution* (Vancouver: New Star, 1983).
Riera Encinoza, A. and R. del Olmo, 'The View from Latin America – Against Transnational Criminology: A Call for International Cooperation', *Crime and Social Justice*, 15 (1981) pp. 1–70.
Scraton, P. and N. South, 'The Ideological Construction of the Hidden Economy: Private Justice and Work-Related Crime', *Contemporary Crises*, XVIII (1984) pp. 1–18.

Stalker, T., 'A Journey through the New Nicaragua', *New Internationalist*, 156 (February 1986).

Sumner, C., 'Crime, Justice and Underdevelopment: Beyond Modernization Theory', in C. Sumner (ed.), *Crime, Justice and Underdevelopment* (London: Heinemann, 1982) pp. 1–39.

Tefel, A. R., *El Infierno de los Pobres* (Managua: Universidad de Centroamerica, nd/1972).

Thompson, J. R., M. Sviridoff and J. E. McElroy (Vera Institute), *Employment and Crime: A Review of Theories and Research* (Washington, D.C.: US Department of Justice, National Institute of Justice, 1980).

Time Magazine, various issues indicated, including: 30 March 1987; 2 April 1984.

Tirado, V., 'War against Contras Said to Cost $2.8 Billion', *Toronto Star* (24 January 1987).

Tower Commission (The President's Special Review Board), *The Tower Commission Report* (New York: Bantam–Times, 1987).

Utting, P., 'Domestic Supply and Food Shortages', in R. Spalding (ed.), *The Political Economy of Revolutionary Nicaragua* (Boston: Allen & Unwin, 1987).

Vergara Meneses, R., J. R. Castro and D. Barry, *Nicaragua: Pais Sitiado (Guerra de Baja Intensidad: Agresion y Sobrevivencia)* (Managua: CRIES (Coordinadora Regional de Investigaciones Economicas y Sociales), 1986).

Vilas, C. *The Sandinista Revolution: National Liberation and Social Transformation in Central America* (trans. J. Butler from: *Perfiles de la Revolucion Sandinista*) (New York: Monthly Review, 1986).

Vilas, C., '"War Sandinism"', 1979–1986', *Against the Current*, January–February, II (1) (1987) pp. 12–20.

Walker-Larrain, H., 'Marginal Youth in Chile: Deviance within a Context of Social Reproduction', *Canadian Criminology Forum*, VI (1) (1983) pp. 19–34.

West, W. G., 'El Terror Internacional en Nicaragua', *Capitulo Criminologico*, 13 (Maracaibo, Venezuela: Universidad de Zulia) (1986/1987) pp. 187–200 (reprinted in *Poder y Control* (Barcelona, Spain), 1, pp. 195–205.

West, W. G., 'Vigilancia Revolucionaria: A Nicaraguan Policing Resolution to the Contradiction between Public and Private', in C. D. Shearing and P. C. Stenning (eds), *Private Policing* (Beverly Hills: Sage, 1987a).

West, W. G., 'Marginality, Immorality, Deviance, and the Third World Young', submitted to *North/South: The Canadian Journal of Latin American and Caribbean Studies*; (forthcoming in CIDE/OISE/PIIE (eds), *Education y Trabajo: El Norte y el Sud. Education and Work: North and South* (in English, Toronto: OISE Press, and in Spanish, Santiago: CIDE/PIIE, 1987b).

Wheelock Roman, J., *Nicaragua: Imperialismo y Dictadura* (Havana: Ciencias Sociales, 1974/79).

9   The Second Economy in Socialist China

Xin Ren

INTRODUCTION

China's economic development has been the subject of much interest and scholarly attention in the West. However, rarely does research stumble on the subject of the so-called second economy or private economy, which takes on an extensive significance in the contemporary history of Chinese economic development. Since the Chinese Communist Party (CCP) started its 'socialist transition' in the pattern of relationships of production in the mid-1950s, the second economy has been officially viewed as being not only inconsistent with Marxist ideology, but also as a latent form of capitalism which is assumed to be detrimental to the communist society. However, the second economy has co-existed and survived in parallel fashion with the official, centrally planned economy for more than thirty years. The fluctuations of the second economy witnessed over this period reflect the results of various political struggles between the leftists and the rightists of the party.

In this chapter I intend to examine the second economy in socialist China from an historical perspective, with particular attention to the conflicts of the CCP's radical economic policies. I will also explore the confrontation of the second economy with Marxist ideology and the relationship between the second economy and the political élite, as well as the official control of the second economy. Through such an exploration, we can obtain a picture of the impact of the second economy on China's economic development.

THE CONCEPT OF A 'SECOND ECONOMY' IN CHINESE SOCIETY

The concept of a 'second economy' is applied to all economic activities that are officially viewed as being inconsistent with Marxist ideology and the principle of the state dominated economy (Łoś, Introduction). As it relates to China's economic system, the second economy can be broken into four categories. First, those sectors of the second economy which exist legally within the state system and comprise contractors and co-operatives under collective ownership. They operate under a contract with state-owned enterprises. These economic sectors are the participants of the centralised economic planning. Their only differences in relation to the state economy are the size of production and the form of ownership of the means of production. Although these sectors are subsidiary to state production and distribution, their collective ownership is legitimate according to the constitution. It is officially accepted as a lower form of socialist economy. In fact, the collective enterprises have often been integrated into the state economy when the size of collective production has grown too large, thereby becoming potentially competitive with the state economy.

The second sector of the second economy encompasses those illegal economic activities which occur inside the state economy, such as illegal production and distribution involving the abuse of public property and funds. In China, the party monopolises not only the entire national bureaucratic mechanism, but also all aspects of the economy, from planning of production to marketing. The monopoly is often carried out by a huge web of interpersonal relations. When the relaxed economic policy (under which both individuals and organisations are assumed to have more freedom and autonomy to make profits) was reintroduced to China, abuse of power, mismanagement and misspending of public funds for self-gain also spread. Apparently, members of the élite – who have political power – are particularly capable of engaging in private economic activities and of reaping substantial personal profits. Also, being rich and greedy is no longer regarded as a bad quality nor identified with capitalism. Naturally, the power and the greed inevitably lead the party's élite to abuse public property. When the party's bureaucrats at every level are thrust into a marketing environment, they have been known either to turn the market into an underground operation benefitting relatives and associates, or to restrict it in various ways.

There are also two other types of the second economy which exist outside of the state economy. First are those legally registered or licensed private businesses, such as handicraft workshops, family restaurants, food stalls and small poultry farms. They are discriminated against because they are viewed as ideologically inconsistent with the state economy, and consequently, suffer various economic, political, social and legal restrictions. The second type involves economic crimes such as unlicensed production and distribution, illegal trade and barter, contraband and black-market activities. Most of these types of economic crimes are committed by ordinary people. They are always the targets of official anti-economic crime campaigns.

HISTORICAL BACKGROUND OF THE SECOND ECONOMY

New Democratic Reform (1949–52)

When the CCP triumphed over the Nationalists in China in 1949, the task it faced was twofold: to create a 'socialist society', which was supposed to later move in 'transition to communism'; and to develop the Chinese economy from a backward agrarian one into a modern industrial one. In order to fulfil this twofold task, the communist party launched a campaign, the so-called 'New Democratic Reform'. It aimed to confiscate property from the bureaucratic capitalists tied to foreign interests and to form socialist industries. In the countryside, the poor peasants received land and properties once owned by rich landowners. By the end of 1952, the New Democratic Reform had resulted in great feats of economic performance. The total value of industrial production rose from 10.8 billion *yuan* in 1949 to 27.0 billion *yuan* in 1952, a rise of 150.6 per cent. Production value increased at this time by 178.6 per cent (Selden and Lippit, 1982). By then, the state had control of all major areas of the national economy, including industry, retail trade, wholesale trade and transportation (see Table 9.1).

Full-scale Socialist Transition (1953–7)

In 1953, the Central Committee of the CCP worked out general guidelines for the period of the transition to communism and the first 'Five Year Plan' for socialist construction. The general guidelines identified two long-range goals: 'the socialist industrialisation of the country, and the socialist transformation of agriculture, handicrafts and capitalist industry and commerce' (China Handbook. . . , 1984).

Table 9.1   The result of 'New Democratic Reform'

Economic sectors	1949 (%)	1950 (%)	1951 (%)	1952 (%)	1953 (%)
Industry:					
State enterprise	34.7	45.3	45.9	56.0	57.5
State-capitalists	9.5	17.8	25.4	26.9	28.5
Private enterprise	55.8	36.9	28.7	17.1	14.0
Retail trade:					
State trade	—	14.9	24.4	42.6	49.7
State-capitalists	—	0.1	0.1	0.2	0.4
Private trade	—	85.0	75.5	57.2	49.9
Wholesale trade:					
State trade	—	23.2	33.4	60.5	66.3
State-capitalists	—	0.7	1.2	3.2	4.4
Private trade	—	76.1	65.4	36.3	30.3

Source: Kraus (1982), p. 42.

The major target of the transition, apparently, was the private sector of the economy. The percentage of the private sector making up national income soon dropped sharply from 79 per cent to 7 per cent in a span of four years (China Handbook. . . , 1984). Moreover, virtually the entire labour force migrated from private to state enterprises and co-operatives during the same period (see Table 9.2). Meanwhile, there was an ideological debate between two different groups in the party on the future shape and direction of the economic system. In contradistinction to the leftist radical idea that the party's priority was to continue the socialist revolution, the rightist faction insisted on the importance of developing the national economy. To promote this goal, the latter encouraged the private economy. They soon found themselves under heavy attack by the 'anti-rightist' campaign.

The Great Leap Forward and Consolidation Phase (1958–65)

When the ideological debate on the direction and the shape of the economy was settled in favour of the radical 'leftist' (Maoist) theses, by the end of 1957, the Great Leap Forward led to the so-called co-operative movement in agriculture. In two years, 96.3 per cent of rural households had joined at least one form of the co-operative. In 1958, the people's commune, a system with three-level ownership

Table 9.2   Mobility of labour in economic structure (1949–57)

Sectors	1949 %	1952 %	1953 %	1954 %	1955 %	1956 %	1957 %
Industry and commerce:							
State	6.0	10.8	10.8	22.9	37.5	99.4	99.6
Private	94.0	89.2	89.2	77.1	62.5	0.6	0.5
Handicraft:							
Co-ops	—	3.1	3.9	13.6	26.9	91.7	90.2
Private	—	96.9	96.1	86.4	73.1	8.3	9.8
Agriculture:							
Co-ops	10.7	40.0	39.5	60.3	64.9	97.2	—
Private	89.3	60.0	60.5	39.7	35.1	2.8	—

Source: China Handbook . . . (1984) pp. 23–35.

and unitary power of administration and economy was set up throughout China (Wei and Chao, 1982). In four months, 120 million peasant households joined the commune (Prybyla, 1984). Meanwhile, the 'communist wind' (*Gongchanfeng*) swept across the country, bringing a catastrophic economic downturn.

In 1959, in order to correct the radical economic policy, the public was again reassured that 'the means of livelihood owned by members (including house, clothing, bedding and furniture) and their deposits in banks and credit cooperatives will remain their own property after they would join the commune and will always belong to them' (CCP's Document. . . , 1958). Commune members were also allowed to retain the trees that grew around their houses, the small tools, small domestic animals, and poultry. Private sideline occupations were allowed as a necessary component of the economy, on the condition that it would be at no cost to the collective work. The goods produced privately could, in principle, be sold at free markets and were not liable to taxation. In 1961, the formation of some 40 000 rural free markets was reported, at which 25 per cent of the total rural production was sold (Kraus, 1982). The correction stimulated the legal second economy in rural areas and helped the recovery from the economic depression. The second economy reappeared in both urban and rural areas with the support of rightists from the party leadership, who declared that 'as long as we increase production, we can even revert to individual enterprise; it hardly matters whether a good cat is black or white – as long as it catches mice, it is a good cat' (Den Xiao-ping). For the rightist, economic development (ideology aside) has always been the priority.

The Cultural Revolution and the Confused Phase (1966–78)

The rightist revision did not last very long. In 1966, the Great Proletarian Cultural Revolution smashed all rightist efforts to develop the national economy. The upheaval brought the national economy to the brink of collapse. Maoism pushed along an ultra-left line toward 'a larger size and a higher degree of public ownership' against the right-revisionists. Collectively-owned businesses in the urban areas were once again devastated. They were condemned both as the 'tail of capitalism' and as the 'soil that engenders the bourgeoise'. As for the private entrepreneurs and sideline producers, the ultra-leftists criticised them as 'spontaneous forces of capitalism' and condemned them as 'taking the capitalist road' and as the 'enemy of communist revolution'. The private entrepreneurs were ordered to hand over their profits and to switch to state production units. Between 1966 and 1970, more than 50 000 handicraft workers in the arts and crafts trade in Beijing were forced to suspend operations or to switch to other products. It resulted in a sharp decline in exports of the traditional art crafts (Liang, 1982).

In the rural areas, the previously allowed private plots for each peasant household were also forcibly surrendered to the communes and the free markets were completely suspended. Any activity involving private production and trade was regarded as a counter-offensive act against the revolution. The commune system was once again forced to centralise the three-level ownership into one. Under the ultra-leftist slogan 'we would rather have socialist grass than have capitalist wheat seedling', the productive echelons became totally devastated. The peasants in the enlarged productive units were no longer able to see any direct relation between their individual work effort and the collective productive results. Such political and economic turmoil lasted until 1979 when the new leadership started a process of economic reform.

The Economic Reform (Post 1979)

The new economic reform aims at (i) abolishing the commune system in rural areas in order to let individual peasants lease farmland and contract the output quotas with the government so that they will be able to make profits beyond the quotas (*People's Daily*, 5 June 1987); (ii) giving more autonomy to industrial production units in planning, production, distribution and marketing by decentralising the public ownership and separating the party's political power from management authority; and (iii) facilitating the co-existence of multi-forms of ownership of production: private and co-operative businesses, the state enterprises and foreign investors.

The reform, however, does not change the economic system. The ownership of the major means of production such as farmland, factories and mines have remained state-owned. The state only lends the right to use the property to the individuals or co-operatives. Because of the distinction between the state-owned and the non-state enterprises, the private sector (approximately 4.5 million people) still lives on the edge of society without the guaranteed benefits of housing, medical care, pensions, and job security offered by the state-owned work units. Most of these private businesses are handicrafts, simple manufacturing establishments, services provided by family workshops, restaurants, food stalls, transportation services, tailoring, and small livestock operations (raising chickens, pigs, ducks, or fish). In 1986, the total private business sales volume was estimated to be US$19 000 million, according to the State Administration for Industry and Commerce. The output of private enterprises grew by a staggering 60 per cent in that year (Baum, 1987). Yet, these private sectors count for only a small proportion of the GNP (2 per cent of industrial production and 20 per cent in service and commerce) (*People's Daily*, 5 June 1987).

However, the problem which private businesses often confront is they must endure the envy of others and keep abreast of the scrutiny of the local cadres. Otherwise, their contracts or financial loans may be arbitrarily terminated if they do not satisfy the local cadres' personal, bureaucratic, or monetary demands. If a private enterprise is too prosperous, the state may then absorb it into state-run industries in spite of the fact that the state already takes one third to one half of the profits from private enterprises in the form of state taxes. The state also sanctions regulations regarding the development of private enterprises which prohibit owners of private businesses from hiring more than three workers. Under such restrictions, the private economic sector prospers only when the central economic planners offer some scope for market forces in the socialist economy managed by the government.

The Economic Functions of the Second Economy

When the centrally planned economic model fails adequately to deliver goods and services to meet the demands of the people, it becomes necessary to have another sector functionally substituting the official one. In the area of production, it is also important to have an alternative place to turn to when the state-controlled economy does not provide sufficient co-ordination among the production units in terms of the flow of stocks to maintain production levels. In playing a role in both fields of consumption and production, the second economy often functions legally and illegally. In addition, barter is a common form of the second economy due to Chinese economic traditions and underdeveloped market mechanisms. For most rural families, sales of their products are not for cash, but rather for daily household necessities. For example, a farmer sells eggs in exchange of salt, soy sauce and sugar, and so on, or sells sesame oil to get sesame seeds for future oil production. Basically, they join the marketplace in order to meet their private consumption needs rather than to make profits. This type of second economy activity generally functions to fill the gap between the state's supplies and the people's demands.

Since individuals or collective businesses have the advantage of flexibility and diversification in operation, it is very productive and economic for state-owned enterprises to contract with individual enterprises to manufacture or repair small parts and accessories by using industrial scrap. A large portion of small, collectively owned factories in urban and rural areas are operated under contracts with state enterprises. Recently, many state-owned enterprises have even set up their own subsidiary companies under collective ownership. These collective businesses as well as individual traders and peddlers also fill the gaps between the channels of circulation of raw materials and production operated by the state-owned large enterprises.

Furthermore, the second economy plays a role as an intermediary in production supply when the formal, official supply is in shortage or marketing co-operation is frozen. For example, during the busy farm season, many agricultural supplies, such as pesticides and chemical fertiliser, might be in short supply. These shortages have caused the emergence of individual traders and dealers, who have access to stocks, or through connections, can obtain the supplies from inventory to purchase the goods through the 'back door' at the market price and sell them to the rural production teams at a profit. In some cases, they do not even need to purchase merchandise themselves; instead, they arrange a deal between supplier and purchaser. According to the law, such intermediary activity is illegal. But when the employees of state supply agencies seek not only the value of the merchandise but also an additional personal benefit, they need such intermediaries to help them to find the right customers. Of course, the intermediary not only does a favour to both supplier and purchaser but also expects to have the favour returned from both parties. The state employees exchange favours and make profits for themselves by abusing public property. Those who demand these products have two choices: either to buy the goods at a high price in order to maintain the seasonal production, or to wait for the official supply, and risk losing the entire crop if the state fails to deliver the goods on time. In order to guarantee the supplies, the buyers often have to bribe the employees of the state supply agencies. Many small businesses and enterprises completely rely on the 'back door' method to get supplies needed for survival.

IDEOLOGICAL STATUS OF THE PRIVATE ECONOMY

In Mao's thought, the economy should always be subordinated to politics. Guided by his ideal of a pure communist China he launched several political movements – such as the Great Leap Forward and the Cultural Revolution – which disregarded the Chinese economic reality. They were bound to produce disastrous economic results. Fundamentally, the fluctuations in the rates of economic growth in socialist China can be seen as a result of a confrontation of Mao Ze-dong's communist ideal with the country's economic reality (limited capital accumulation, rapid population growth, technically backward agriculture, unevenly developed industry and a low *per capita* food supply). The fluctuation of the private economy also reflects the struggle between Mao's ultra-leftists and the revisionists on the issue of what order of priority the party's mission should be: the economic development of the nation, or the continuation of the ideological revolution?

In general, the confrontation between the second economy and Maoism originated from two sources: first and foremost, the fundamental Marxist economic law, which maintains that the productive forces determine the relations of production. The relations of production must be suitable to the nature of the productive forces; although these relations are in the final instance determined by the latter, they can also contribute to the shaping of the latter. Based on this 'reaction theory', Mao Ze-dong claimed that the advanced relations of production – that is, public ownership of the means of production – would provoke the growth of the productive forces. Private ownership, as a remnant of the exploitative class, would be regarded as detrimental to socialism. Ideologically, officials attempted to convince the public that bigger is always better, and that the higher the degree of public ownership and the bigger scale of production, the better the economy would be. Mao's criterion for successful socialism was measured not by the people's living standards, but by the extent of public ownership. For this socialist goal to be met, the continual revolutionary progression of the ownership of the means of production was considered to be the first task for the CCP.

According to Mao's ideology, the proletariat's historical mission was not only to create a 'new society' but also to make 'new persons' – that is, communists. Besides physical elimination of the old political, social and economic systems, Mao Ze-dong thought that the people's consciousness must also be changed through the class struggle in order for them to adjust to socialism. Maoists strongly believed that class struggle in every field is necessary for preventing the class enemies from attacks against socialism from both political and ideological fronts. For a long period of time, the private economy was understood to represent capitalist interests and to be a potential lure toward capitalism. Such a belief can be traced back to Lenin, who said that 'small production engenders capitalism and the bourgeoisie continuously, daily, hourly, spontaneously, and on a mass scale' (Lenin, 1965). Therefore, according to Mao Ze-dong, the campaign against the private economy was no longer just an economic debate but had also become a part of the political struggle. Private economic activities no longer represented just individual interests, but were also considered to be a capitalist action against socialism. As a part of his class struggle programme Mao launched a number of ideological campaigns one after another during his regime: the 'Anti-Rightist Struggle' in 1958, the 'Socialist Education Movement' from 1961 to 1965, and the 'Great Proletarian Cultural Revolution' between 1966 and 1976.

Yet, with his death, Mao's ideal lost its popularity and the private economy has resumed under recent economic reform. However, the fear of being criticised, being labelled as a capitalist, and being taken over by the state at any time still remains among private sector entrepreneurs.

THE OFFICIAL CONTROL OF THE SECOND ECONOMY

Political Repression

Since the private economy had been officially viewed as being inconsistent with Marxist ideology, this sector experienced great political pressure, especially during the political movements against the remnants of capitalism. In Mao's leftist regime, being identified as a member of the proletarian class brought more than just the status of a first class citizen (the term 'proletariat' in Chinese means a class without any property). The way to identify a person's status was to see if he or she was poor, and liked being poor. The logic of this equated being poor with being of the proletarian class, and being or desiring to be rich with a capitalistic tendency. Therefore, someone earning an above average income (with the exception of old revolutionary cadres) was officially viewed as the target of the socialist revolution offensive. For a long period of time, the official mentality was that the poorer you were, the better person you were.

Political repression is often combined with social prejudice that affects not only individuals but also their families and their relatives. China is a homogeneous society where collective or community interests and reputation are considered more important than individual ones. During the ultra-leftist regime, individuals who engaged in private business were labelled as capitalist and were often isolated from the community. The family members and children were also implicated and discriminated against by the community because of the immediate political consideration, and the Chinese feudalist tradition that 'one criminal can implicate all relatives and associates'.

Economic and Social Discrimination

The private economy is always discriminated against to some degree by the official economic policy. For instance, private entrepreneurs cannot normally obtain loans from the banks. The state rarely supplies the necessary raw materials even to licensed private producers. Therefore, in the leftist regime, the black market becomes the most important source of supply in order to maintain production. Even now, private businesses are still vulnerable to integration or even confiscation by the state. Compared with the difficult years, the current economic reform has provided private businesses with a 'could-not-be-better' status. But it is only a product of current economic policy rather than a result of legitimacy under the law. Significantly, the 'could-not-be-better' status of private businesses is secured only by the current policy of economic reform, rather than guaranteed by the law.

Still, there are notable restrictions to the current policy. Most private entrepreneurs, rural residents and their families are not eligible for state-sponsored social welfare programmes. For example, the state provides full-coverage medical insurance to its employees, while private workers and peasants are not eligible. In the case of private workers' families, the discrimination is also extended to their children – who, for example, are ineligible to join state-sponsored day care programmes. In 1980, when the central government decided to increase the price of non-staple food in the cities, city residents who were employees of the state or collectively-owned units were given five *yuan* to supplement their monthly salaries. However, privately employed workers were not considered for this subsidy. Since social welfare benefits are distributed only through the state institutions, to their employees, the private workers are totally excluded from any social welfare scheme. They are, in effect, second class citizens.

Chinese society under the communist rulers assesses a person's status not by economic criteria but rather by his or her social affiliation. A state employee undoubtedly possesses privileges above those of a collective or private worker in terms of political status, social dignity and economic benefits. Such social mentality affects many people, especially youth. As a consequence, many young people choose to remain unemployed without any social security benefits and to wait idly for a state job offer rather than accept a position with a private business.

Penal Control

The myth that there is no crime whatsoever in socialist China is long gone. However, the scale of application of criminal law toward illegal economic activities has fluctuated depending on the 'political climate'. The perpetrators of economic crimes are always treated differently based on their political standing and privileges. Since élite criminals possess political power, removal from their position is the conventional way to punish them for wrongdoing instead of through criminal procedures. However, ordinary criminals, who do not have access to political power, are always subject to penal measures. These 'little' criminals are the targets of 'anti-crime campaigns' or crackdowns on crime. As a result of the economic reform in 1980, various forms of economic crime have rapidly spread throughout the country. This serious problem has forced the CCP's leadership to launch a campaign against economic crimes. The campaign bears dual functions which involve not only controlling the economic deviance and disorder but also removing political opponents within ongoing inner party struggles.

Economic Crime by Ordinary People

Most economic crimes committed by the ordinary people involve smuggling, illegal trading, contraband, theft, fraud, bribe-taking and corruption. According to the official report, the estimated total value of goods smuggled to China was more than twenty million *yuan* between 1980 and 1982. The total value of contraband in gold, silver and other precious metal smuggled to Hong Kong was more than US$600 million from 1980 to 1983 (O-Yang, Cua and Lei, 1984). The exchange of foreign currency in the black market has had a great impact on the decline of the exchange rate in the Bank of China, where the trade dropped 61 per cent in 1981 as against 1977, even though foreign investment and the tourist businesses doubled. According to the annual report of the Department of Industry and Commerce, from 1980 to 1981 instances of illegal trade where each case involved more than 10 000 *yuan* increased 150 per cent (O-Yang, Cua and Lei, 1984). Thefts, which involved stolen public property, comprised 80–90 per cent of the total cases prosecuted for theft. Public property most commonly stolen is gold, industrial raw materials, electronic merchandise and artifacts from the state-owned museums. These stolen goods are usually sold through two channels: (i) licensed private retail shops, or (ii) the illegal black market.

Since greed and corruption have crept back into China, mismanagement and misspending are commonplace as well. The lust for wealth and worldly possessions seems to be leading a new generation away from the socialist dream. The CCP's leadership feels that the foundation of the state controlled economy is being shaken. To restore order to the national economy, the government launched a campaign to crack down on economic crimes in early 1982. Between 1982 and 1986, thousands of cases were tried and many criminals were either sentenced to prison or executed. But the volume of economic crimes still climbed: a 55.5 per cent increase from 1985 to 1986 (*People's Daily*, 7 April 1987). Besides its ineffectiveness, the campaign, due to its very nature, has also involved serious problems of injustice. With bitter irony, people say that the worst thing is not 'committing' an economic crime but committing it 'at the wrong time', since the campaign has led to more convictions and harsher punishment than under everyday conditions.

Economic Crime among the Élite

Economic crime committed by the party élite is not new in China. It can be traced back to 'Three-Antis' (Sanfan Movement) in 1952 when hundreds of CCP's members were punished for fraud, corruption and bribe-taking (Chesneaux, 1979). Three decades later, élite economic crime has become more serious and widespread in terms of the economic power costs and the numbers of officials involved. A study by the Institute of Law of the Chinese Academy of Social Sciences has discovered that in 1982 there were a total of 22 331 economic crime cases tried at various levels of the court, among which 5243 were cases of graft, embezzlement and fraud associated with the party élite. This accounts for 23.4 per cent of the total economic crime brought to trial in 1982. In some provinces, 70 per cent of the loans from banks were illegally invested in the smuggling trade through various levels of the party's cadres who were in charge of loan application approvals (O-Yang, Cua and Lei, 1984).

Frustrated by the inner party's scandals involving economic crimes and by the loss of public confidence in the party, the new leadership of the CCP has tried to control the epidemic of economic crimes committed by its members. Since 1982, a number of criminals who are low- or mid-ranking party members have been convicted and sentenced, or even executed. The news was published in the official newspaper as a warning to others. The leadership hoped the 'show window' would convince the public that social justice had been done. One example appeared in a *People's Daily* report on 29 May 1987 which stated that the former governor of Jiangxi province had approved $6 million in US currency as a loan for his personal associate to pay a smuggling bill. As a consequence, he was convicted for abuse of power, misspending of public funds and taking a bribe. However, he was punished only by being expelled from the party and removed from his position. If he had been an ordinary citizen or even a low-rank party functionary, he would have been sentenced to prison. The Chinese have a long-standing tradition that 'criminal penalty is not applicable to senior officers'. The CCP's élite have greatly benefitted from this old feudal tradition.

By the same token, a new organ of the CCP named the 'Central Commission for Inspecting Party Discipline' was set up in 1978 (*Profiles*, 1981). Its main function is to inspect party members' conduct and to discipline their wrongdoing without going through the criminal justice system (which generates publicity). This commission has superior power and privilege over the sanctity of the law and the legal system. Frequently, those élite criminals, who are guilty of serious economic crimes are simply dismissed or punished by a transfer from one position to another. The law is imposed only to punish and deter the general public, and not the élite.

CONCLUSION

Although the second economy has significantly expanded in both urban and rural areas, it is only a product of the current economic reform policy, rather than an establishment of status of *legalis homo* (Wang and Lei, 1986; Zhang, 1986; Xie, 1986). The reform is aimed not at changing the state's command of the economic system but rather at making the sluggish centrally planned system more efficient. Thus, the CCP's new leadership intends to adopt only capitalist technology, not its private economic system (Prybyla, 1986). It is not surprising to learn that, in China, the private economy continues to be restricted under the state-controlled economic system. As the party's chief economist, Cheng Yuen, once stated, the Chinese economy is a 'cage economy'. Within the cage (the state controlled economy), the bird (the private economy) is allowed to fly freely, but the bird is forbidden to break the cage and fly away. Furthermore, for political reasons, the party's élite will never be willing to relinquish control over the economy. They know that if they do so the foundation of their political power will soon vanish. Therefore, CCP leaders face a dilemma in continuing with the reform. On the one hand, if they continue to encourage multiple forms of economic ownership, the expanded private economy will create pressure for more freedom in production, distribution, pricing and marketing. On the other hand, the CCP maintains that the 'Four Persistences' (to persist in Marxism, the Socialist Road, the Communist Leadership and the Proletarian Dictatorship) are the fundamental principles of China (Lee, 1983). These principles lead to policies and practices which seek to restrict the development of the private economy. Consequently, the conflict within the party's reform policies will force some private economic activities, such as setting market prices and free trade, to go underground in order to avoid state control. Thus, as long as the conflicting policies regarding the economic reform continue, the illegal economic activities will not be reduced.

Frustrated by the economic disputes and crimes, the party's leadership is urgently trying to establish a series of laws (the Contract Law, the Bankruptcy Law, Law of Chinese–Foreign Joint Ventures, and so on) to regulate economic activities. But, on the other hand, through the actions of the Central Commission for Inspecting Party Discipline, the party has also provided privileges to its élite by excusing their wrongdoing. The enforcement of the law is virtually standardised on a dual basis and, therefore, its legal effect is crippled. Worst of all, now that the reform in the economic system has begun to threaten the supremacy of the party (with its 44 million members) the party's early enthusiasm for reform has begun to wane. Because of the *de facto* conflicts and difficulties that the CCP confronts, there is no doubt that the market economy, in both legal and illegal forms, is still marginal and will remain the same way as long as the Chinese economy is under the domination of the centrally planned model.

REFERENCES

Baum, J., 'Working on the Edge', *The Christian Science Monitor* (29 February 1987).

CCP's Document of the Sixth Plenum of the Eighth Central Committee in Wuhan on 10 December 1958, *Communist China, 1955–1959*, Documents, I, p. 123ff.

Chesneaux, J., *China: The People's Republic, 1949–1976* (Sussex: The Harvester Press, 1979).

China Handbook Editorial Committee, *Economy: China Handbook Series* (Beijing: Foreign Languages Press, 1984).

Kraus, W., *Economic Development and Social Change in the People's Republic of China* (New York: Springer-Verlag, 1982).

Lee, E., 'Economic Reform in Post-Mao China: An Insider's View', *Bulletin of Concerned Asian Scholars*, XV (1) (1983) pp. 16–25.

Lenin, I. V., *Left-Wing Communism: An Infantile Disorder* (Beijing: The Foreign Languages Press, 1965) (in Chinese).

Liang, X., 'The Rehabilitation of Collective Enterprises in Urban Areas', in L. Wei and A. Chao, *China's Economic Reforms* (Philadelphia: University of Pennsylvania, 1982).

Łoś, M., see Introduction to this book, pp. 1–10.

O-Yang, T., Q. Cua and Y. Lei, *Serious Crimes in the Economic Field* (Beijing: Law Press, 1984) (in Chinese).

People's Daily (7 April 1987), 'Attorney General's Report to the National People's Congress, 1987' (in Chinese).

People's Daily (5 June 1987), 'No Reform, No Chinese-Style Socialism' (in Chinese).

Profiles: 'China: The Chinese Party's Inner Party Discipline and Democracy: A Preliminary Examination of Central Control Commission for Inspecting Discipline', *Asian Thought and Society*, 17 and 18 (September–November, 1981).

Prybyla, J., 'The Economic System of the People's Republic of China', *Asian Thought and Society*, IX (25) (March 1984) pp. 3–29.

Prybyla, J., 'China's Economic Experiment: From Mao to Market', *Problems of Communism*, 35 (1) (1986) pp. 21–38.

Selden, M. and V. Lippit, *The Transition to Socialism in China* (New York: M. E. Sharpe, 1982).

Wei, L. and A. Chao, *China's Economic Reforms* (Philadelphia: University of Pennsylvania Press, 1982).

Wang, Z. and F. Lei, 'On Private Cooperation in the Civil Law', *Political Science and Law* (March 1986) (Shanghai: Institute of Law, Shanghai Academy of Social Sciences, 1986) pp. 20–4 (in Chinese).

Xie, S., 'On Legal Problems of Private Economy', *Political Science and Law* (February 1986) (Shanghai: Institute of Law, Shanghai Academy of Social Sciences) pp. 28–30 (in Chinese).

Zhang, P., 'Adjusted Subject in Economic Law', *Political Science and Law* (January 1986) (Shanghai: Institute of Law, Shanghai Academy of Social Sciences, 1986) pp. 18–20 (in Chinese).

10 The Second Economy in Angola: *Esquema* and *Candonga*

Daniel dos Santos

HISTORICAL BACKGROUND

Angola won its independence in 1975, after four centuries of Portuguese colonial rule and fifteen years of liberation struggle. Prior to the Berlin Conference in 1884–5, Portugal had confined Angola to the role of slave supplier for the plantations of Brazil and other colonial markets in the Americas. The Portuguese presence in Angola during this period was assured by the King's armies, the Catholic Church, and the representatives of overseas companies involved in huge slavery transactions and small-scale trade.

The industrial revolution, which came late in Portugal, and the abolitionist movement forced Portugal to reorient its colonial needs and policies. Still interested in acquiring cheap labour, Portugal replaced slavery first with a forced labour system, and later the *contrato* (contract) system. Under this latter scheme, the colonial army would select or seize labourers from the indigenous villages and deliver them (by force if necessary) to plantation owners. The proprietors would sign a *contrato* with the colonial government for the *contratados* (the labourers). Most of the time, the *contratados* were paid less than the vital minimum. A permanent administrative body – a colonial State – was created to manage the task of dispossessing the African population of its land and redistributing it to the Portuguese settlers and the agricultural monopoly companies.

During the nineteenth century, Portuguese explorers had discovered new primary resources in Angola. Mining operations were established, and with them the full *proletarianisation* of the indigenous population commenced. Both miners and agricultural workers were integrated into a monetarised system. The Colonial Pact was redefined: besides serving as a labour reserve, Angola became a supplier

157

of agricultural goods and raw materials for metropolitan Portugal. Political turmoil in Portugal, beginning with the republican over-throw of the monarchy at the turn of the century, and culminating with the imposition of the new Constitutional Law the *Estado Novo* (the Portuguese fascist regime) in 1933, was accompanied by various attempts to integrate the Angolan colonial economy more completely into the metropolitan one. Indeed, Angola's subordination to the Portuguese economy remained intact until the end of the 1950s.

After the Second World War, and following the wave of independ-ence calls throughout Africa, nationalist political movements emerged in Angola. By 1960, a colonial war had erupted. Unable to sustain the war effort alone, Portugal opened Angola to American and European investors. This invitation was also predicated by the new industrialisation of Portugal, a condition of its integration into European markets. European integration was built on a scheme of *rent capitalism* which allowed Portuguese industrial entrepreneurs and bankers to go into partnership with international capital in a fierce competition for the exploitation of Angolan resources. The new policy thus forced the modernisation of colonial capitalism and, at the same time, the industrialisation of Angola itself. This second revision of the Colonial Pact escalated the development of the extractive industry, the mechanisation of certain agricultural sectors, and the creation of many subsidiary industries, services and banks (Torres, 1983; Meyns, 1984). On the eve of independence, Angola was among the Sub-Saharan countries[1] with the highest economic growth rates, despite its colonial status.

The decolonisation process(1974–5) following the military coup of April 1974 in Portugal was a disaster (Heimer, 1979; GPDC, 1979). Portugal was politically and economically weak, facing bankruptcy. The officers who had carried out the coup were divided by political party ideologies and interests, were not organically linked by social class. They had neither a defined policy to deal with Angolan independence, nor the resources to take charge of the *retornados* who fled Angola, taking with them money and diamonds, and leaving behind destroyed vehicles, industrial equipment and agricultural machines.[2]

On the other side, the Angolan liberation movements displayed quite different, if not opposing ideologies. They represented different fractions of the Angolan social structure, tied to distinct historical realities.[3] Building a united front seemed almost impossible. Furth-ermore, with the departure of the Portuguese army, the struggle quickly took an international turn, reflecting the growing interests of multinational capital in Angola. Through the recruitment of mercenaries and the supply of financial, technical and logistical support, the USA (Stockwell, 1978) backed the Zairean army and the National Liberation Front of Angola (FNLA) against the People's Movement for the Liberation of Angola (MPLA) which was supported by socialist countries and some Western countries such as Sweden and Norway. The National Union for Total Independence of Angola (UNITA) had the support of the remaining Portuguese settlers – and, later on, of the Republic of South Africa which invaded Angola at the same time.

The April 1975 coup in Portugal changed the nature of the liberation struggle by moving it from the rural areas to the urban centres. When MPLA took power and unilaterally proclaimed Angolan independence, it inherited a very difficult situation: not only the effects of a devastating war, but also a lack of technicians who, like the settlers, had abruptly left the country.

ON THE POLITICAL STRUCTURE

Soon after independence (May 1977), two members of MPLA's leadership, Nito Alves and José Van Dunem, attempted a bloody coup against President Agostinho Neto's leadership. The coup failed, and the repression that followed was violent, short, and directed not only at the coup supporters but against all dissenting forces, in an effort to put an end to the political factions within MPLA.

In December 1977 at its first ordinary congress, MPLA adopted a resolution to transform itself into a party 'guided by Marxism–Leninism'. The MPLA – *Partido do Trabalho* (Workers' Party) was proclaimed the political instrument of the Angolan working class, whose long-term aim was to build an alliance between workers and peasants that would serve as the basis for the transition to a people's democracy. This decision came after MPLA had gone through several internal conflicts. Of these, most important was a split, on the right led by Daniel Chipenda (an important member of MPLA's Steering Committee) and on the left, the *Active Revolt*, led by influential intellectuals (Heimer, 1979; dos Santos, 1983).

The *processo de rectificaçao* (rectification process) completed the task of creating a more homogenous and unified party, but the party was a restrictive one. Presently the membership is limited to 35 000, and prospective new members have to undergo a thorough public examination of their record. The party structure is organised through cells guided by committees. The Party Congress elects the Central Committee and the President. The Political Bureau, which is an executive body, is selected by and from the Central Committee members. Mass organisations (of youth, labour, women and children), whose leaders are usually members of the Central Committee, serve as the link between the Party and the population.

The Angolan Constitution stipulates that the party is the leading body of the political power structure. The government and the People's Assembly are the executive bodies, subordinate to the party. Due to the security difficulties caused by the war, most of the legislative work of the People's Assembly is placed with its 25 member permanent commission led by the President of the party, who is also the head of the State and the Commander-in-chief of the People's Armed Forces for the Liberation of Angola (FAPLA). Theoretically, the Party Congress is the supreme decision-making body, but in reality the Political Bureau prepares and submits decisions to the Congress for approval. The party also selects and nominates both ministers and high-ranking officials (such as the province commissioners) who are responsible to the President and the Central Committee.

Due to communication difficulties created by the war and the restrictive size of the party, the government's presence in rural areas is limited. The concentration of political decisions in the capital creates contradictions between urban (petty bourgeois, workers and marginals) and rural (especially peasants) citizens, and also among the regions. Moreover, the majority of civil servants and government bureaucrats are not members of the party. They were promoted after independence from the lower echelons of the colonial State. There is thus a gap between the policy decisions taken by the party leadership and the people who are supposed to implement them. This problem becomes even more serious if one takes into account the shortage of competent middle-level cadres – a consequence of Portuguese colonial policies and subsequent abrupt decolonisation (Hodges, 1987: 13).

According to the decisions of the 1977 and 1980 Congresses, the government is responsible for the development plan, under the party's supervision. Since independence, the main goals of the different development plans have been relatively consistent: to increase agricultural production, to support light industrial expansion linked to agriculture, and to control all economic sectors (oil, diamonds, coffee, finance, foreign trade) and public services (tele-communications, postal services, press and publishing, radio and television, education, health, housing, water and electricity) consi-dered of strategic or national importance.

According to the adopted policy, Angola should increase the amount of national revenue allocated for productive investments (accumulation) in the priority sectors, and use the export revenues to satisfy its needs in production goods and technology. This strategy implies control over private consumption, yet it would not restrain social consumption and productive investments. It also necessitates a considerable increase of the GNP, without which the Angolan State faces no other option but to seek more financial credits and – consequently – to deepen its external debt.

THE SECOND ECONOMY

The *Esquema*, the *Candonga* and the Economy

Some years ago, at a political rally in a Luanda soccer stadium, a high-ranking official stated: It does not matter what people may say. It does not matter if they think our socialism is not sufficiently scientific. The main thing is that we do have our own socialism, the *socialismo esquematico*.

Soon after independence (1975), the word *esquema* (scheme) became a popular one: in order to survive and to get essential products or services, the population have had to build their own *esquemas*. The *esquema* is a systematic arrangement which refers to the ability and capacity of an individual to build networks to solve economic problems. It demands imagination to get around the everyday difficulties of satisfying basic needs for food, clothing, transportation and housing. Although *esquemas* are linked in many cases with social class, the arrangements may be stratified and interconnected, forming a real network of people helping each other. Someone may, for example, have an *esquema* for vegetables, some-one else one for clothes, another for meat, and so on. These individuals then barter their surpluses for goods they need. The *esquema* is the real economic circuit of distribution of consumption goods.

An *esquema* is not always illegal; most of the time it simply enables people to obtain what they need. On the other hand, a *candonga* is the illegal appropriation of a product for sale on the grey or black market. The first term refers to the means of obtaining products and services, as well as a way to share them, while the second concerns the product itself and is less related to the social class than to the occupation of the *candongueiro*. The *esquema* brings people together while the *candonga* individualises the relationship. Sometimes, *candongueiros* may come together through the *esquemas* and operate in a sort of organised deviance.

But how did the Angolans get involved with the *esquema* and the *candonga*? These phenomena are not specific to socialism; they existed under colonial capitalism, the way certain other activities existed such as the black market of foreign currency and the contraband operations of petty merchants. What is really new in Angola is the widespread use of these processes in ways that are neither officially or ideologically recognised.

Researchers of Angola's economy refer to the activities of the *esquema* and *candonga* as the parallel economy or parallel sector (Meyns, 1984; Morice, 1985; Bhagavan, 1986). According to this approach, the main economy and the parallel economy follow a continuous equidistant path, specific to each; they never meet. Their only relation – other than the fact that they operate in the same society – is that they are *parallel*; one is recognised by the state, and the other is not. By referring to the parallel economy as the second economy, researchers have stressed (i) the link between the official and the unofficial economies, (ii) the complementary role of the unofficial economy, but also (iii) a subordinate role of the unofficial economy (Sauvy, 1984). Yet in Angola, the second economy is far from subordinate: unofficial activities are so important that the population devotes at least one third of its productive time to them on an everyday basis. This represents a real problem for the state's goal of developing the productive forces. Absenteeism in the official economy is very high, which causes the level of productivity in most sectors to stay drastically depressed. The two economies are thus linked with one another, and cannot be described as either separate or parallel.

The term 'second economy' is a more appropriate way of describing this kind of phenomenon in the case of Angola; yet, it does not mean the second economy plays a secondary role to the main economy. The former comprises quite distinct activities, including the illegal appropriation of the means of production and of consumption goods, contraband, the black market,[4] self-construction, illegal transportation network, domestic work, and barter. It may be viewed as a mechanism of social reproduction by which a majority of the people survive and a minority becomes wealthier (Morice, 1985: 110).

Angola's second economy is organically linked, and necessary, to the official economy. With the formation of the Angolan State, the government had to assume all kinds of responsibilities including the defence of the nation; the management of mines and the oil industry; the production of agricultural products such as coffee; the provision of health and education services; the organisation of transportation; the management of restaurants and movie houses; the distribution of electricity and water as well as the management of banks, bookstores and barbershops. All responsibilities had to be assumed with no technicians, no qualified workers, no bankers, no teachers, no entrepreneurs, no managers, and almost no doctors and nurses.

State ownership and the massive nationalisation of the Angolan economy were not the results solely of an ideological choice.[5] Its colonial heritage, the independence struggle, and the South African war of aggression have also played a role. These factors have also weakened the State's ability to reorganise the economic structure and the national market. With the exception of oil – Angola's main (and fairly well controlled) source of foreign currency – and a few other products such as tobacco, the State has been generally unable to increase agricultural or industrial production or to organise a national network of distribution. The *loja do povo* (the people's stores) were supposed to implement such a network, but were unsuccessful because of the absence of qualified managers, the government's fixed price policy, the almost total lack of inspection controls, the inadequate power distribution system, the scarcity of locally produced goods, and general mismanagement and corruption.

But one must not conclude that private property has been entirely suppressed in Angola: indeed, it is protected and guaranteed by Article 10 of the Angolan Constitution. Western multinational firms and the Angolan State have formed several joint ventures in the oil, diamonds and mining sectors (dos Santos, 1983; Mas, 1986). The main producer of tobacco is Sociedade Unificada dos Tabacos de Angola (SUTA), a company completely owned by Portuguese private capital. Small commerce is mainly private, but imports and exports are controlled by the State.

The agricultural sector is also characterised by various types of property ownership including co-operatives (peasants' associations), family-owned property, private farmers and state-owned farms. Until recently, the official policy was to create large state farms to supersede the huge private plantations abandoned by the Portuguese settlers. This policy, as the one with the *people's stores*, was a complete failure, and for identical reasons: lack of qualified people, fixed prices with no link to the agricultural market, lack of transportation, mismanagement, and corruption. Officials recognised these problems and in 1987 a new policy was introduced. The policy aimed at increasing the support for agricultural producers, especially for small farmers, co-operatives and family-owned farms. It also defined new policies for peasant families, specifically in support of women producers, improving the supply of seeds, tools and transportation, and the relaxation of price controls.

Historical, structural, and political reasons underlay the development and importance of Angola's second economy and its relation to the official economy. The incapacity of the State to reorganise the national market after independence, and the absence of economic regulatory mechanisms, produced a spontaneous movement toward the second economy. The transition from a colonial economy to an independent socialist one is thus related to the existence and the articulation of different modes of production within the Angolan economy (Heimer, 1983). The growth of the second economy is therefore necessary because it re-establishes a component within the transitional economy whose historical importance was underestimated: a free market in the capitalist sense, where prices are the result of supply and demand. Demand within the second economy is strong because of the low productivity in both agricultural and industrial production, and because of the consumers' limited access to the minimal goods which are imported officially.

The second economy in Angola is essentially related to the circulation of goods and services. When oil revenues were high, it was easier for the State to satisfy Angola's needs through imports from abroad than to solve the national production and distribution problems. Imports became a key source of supplies to the second economy, through the organisations of multiple networks of *esquemas* run by *candongueiros*. Barter, more a consequence of this situation than a cause, is also an important feature of this market. In particular, it is used as a defence mechanism for the peasants and the urban poor who cannot accumulate large amounts of *kwanzas* to purchase goods. Tobacco, beer, or other alcohol, and clothes are becoming the currency of the second market. Increasingly, official enterprises and institutions are reverting to barter, too, as currency continues to lose its value.

The official economy controls the main strategic industries and services such as oil, diamonds, mineral exploitation, coffee, cement, electricity, gas, water, transportation, banking, health and education. The provision of services places a tremendous burden on the economy, as costs to consumers do not correspond frequently with real production costs. Yet by keeping and maintaining the official value of the *kwanza*, the official economy is able to deal with its foreign counterparts within the world market. Securing co-operation and military equipment from the Soviet bloc allies is also paid for in American dollars. In 1985, the total debt of Angola was US$3.2 billion. But of this, US$2.16 billion was owed to the USSR, almost exclusively military debt. Only 10–12 per cent of the total is tied up in trade commitments (Alagiah, 1986: 75). Wages fixed by the State are extremely low compared to the real prices of the second economy. For instance, in 1987 a worker earning Kz 10 000 per month (minimum official wage is Kz 6000 per month) could buy, at the official price, four cartons of cigarettes per week for which he or she would pay Kz 800 (4 × Kz 200). A worker could sell the same cigarettes in the second market for Kz 40 000 (4 × Kz 10 000). In one week, using an *esquema* and/or a *candonga*, the worker would have made almost four times more money than acquired through a month's work in the factory.

This situation raises the question of the enormous gap between legal revenue and real revenue, because there is no relation whatsoever between the national production of wealth (second economy included) and monetary inflation; the value of goods is simply not related to the value of work. If the prices of consumption goods in the second market seem too high, once they are converted into dollars in the same market, they become identical to those in any other African country. The State pays people regardless of whether they are productive, which means that Angola cannot increase its wealth. It cannot distribute what is not produced, unless it increases its external debt. At the risk of becoming poorer and increasing its external dependence, Angola still exports raw materials and imports capital as well as consumer and industrial products from the Western capitalist countries which remain its principal economic partners: the USA, France, Portugal, Italy, West Germany, and Great Britain.

The Role of the Second Economy

In 1982, when visiting the Island of Luanda, I wanted to buy an ivory
sculpture which was priced at Kz 70 000 (approximately US$2500 at
the official exchange rate). As we did not have this amount, the
craftsman asked if we had any green bank notes with the portrait of a
man (US dollars). But as we had just the ones with a lady's portrait
(Canadian dollars), he did not accept. He then suggested a bicycle or
four bottles of whisky in exchange for the sculpture.

While pharmacies, clothing stores, shoestores as well as the central
market of Luanda were completely empty, it was no secret that
almost everything could be found in the second market, in exchange
for goods or by paying higher prices. Yet, during the very first years
of independence, the second economy was not as important as today.
How then can we explain its growing importance in the Angolan
economy?

Development is a social process by which people in society try to
build the best conditions to carry out their existence. Far from being
linear, it is a meandrous and often contradictory process through
which material and social conditions are created and wealth is
distributed to individuals and groups. Without the growth of the
production of goods and services, there is no possibility for a better
distribution of revenues and resources, nor a reduction of the
sectorial inequalities. The growth of the productive forces is not
necessary for a more equitable redistribution of existing resources, as
this is a political decision. Still, such growth remains the condition for
a greater satisfaction of the people's needs.

In theory, Angola should be one of Africa's richest countries
(Hodges, 1987: 3) due to its potential in every sector. Once the
colonial surpluses and stocks were depleted, however, shortages and
scarcity changed the face of the country and second economy
activities spread rapidly. Government officials attribute this situation
to the dramatic decrease of production caused by the war against
South Africa, UNITA and FNLA, and to the hurried flight of
Portuguese settlers and technicians. Coffee production dropped by
two-thirds, the iron industry virtually stopped and the official diamond trade was undermined by an important network of traffickers
who, with some help from the Portuguese government, transformed
Lisbon into a new black market haven for diamonds.

Unable to create the conditions to increase production, the government has shown some tolerance towards the second economy. Its

sporadic repression, however, serves as a reminder that this is not an official policy; on the contrary, it is mostly illegal. But at the same time, because the government has not been able to provide the needs of the people it hesitates to act repressively on a consistent basis. Thus, *candongueiros* are denounced continually by the mass media, but generally they are not formally prosecuted. When prosecutions do occur, the justice system, as a state body, is quite lenient. If a *candongueiro* becomes famous, he may risk prosecution. But, even if he is sentenced to prison, if he is lucky enough to have some support from customers who are well positioned in the government or party apparatus, he will be released before long. In an incident a few years ago, the police and the army took one of the open-air markets used by second economy traders in Luanda by storm, killing two persons. This repressive action launched the citizens' anger and the government was pressured to make a public apology to the people, explaining the action as petty bourgeois political error done by hurried bureaucrats without the party's knowledge.

Repression is used most heavily when second economy activities endanger the official economy – namely the state controlled production that contributes to its budget or is considered to be of strategic importance, such as diamonds, oil and tobacco. Yet even if the official press stigmatises the *candongueiro*, this label does not have a negative connotation in the popular language, because involvement in a *esquema* or a *candonga* is the norm, for the worker and peasant, as well as the private entrepreneur, state official, or party member. The buyer is also frequently a supplier, and networks are internally protected. Besides the official and formal justice system, there is a private justice that is run by the people themselves, to protect the second economy from unwanted intruders (Bhagavan, 1986; Morice, 1985).

The government and the party have attempted to counter the second economy through campaigns to increase production. They have created material incentives to boost production in the enterprises and on farms. On some occasions, they have forced people back to work. Indeed, following the workers' demands which had become more and more exacting, and the agricultural workers' decision not to return to the land (1977–8), a major crisis broke out and a very repressive Law of Discipline at the Work Place and, later, a Labour Code were enacted.

Another State response was to issue ration cards at the work place. New incentives for workers, in the form of awards in kind as well as political recognition, were also made available to workers who demonstrated exemplary performance during production campaigns. But the results of such campaigns ultimately produced the opposite effect to that which was intended: workers went to the second economy market to exchange or sell the goods they received. By the beginning of the 1980s, the situation ran out of the government's control. As state revenues were dropping with the fall of oil prices in the world market, the government had to reduce its imports of consumer goods. This left even more room for the second economy to spread.

The second economy in Angola is emerging as a capitalistic market. The State apparatus is overwhelmed by the situation: the independence struggle and the war have almost destroyed the country's economic infrastructure. The majority of Angola's wealth has been appropriated by the former colonial power and multinational firms. These problems and their consequences appear insurmountable. With an illiteracy rate of 90 per cent at the time of independence, Angola has proved poorly equipped to undertake the task of socialist reconstruction. The urban explosion, particularly in the capital, is also problematic. From 1975 to 1987, the population of the capital increased from about 450 000 to 1 200 000 (Bhagavan, 1986: 24). The vast majority live as squatters in the *musseques* (shantytowns). The population of Luanda grows faster than government action, which is always trying to catch up.

Peasants comprise, however, the vast majority of Angola's active population. They have been growing their own food for centuries, even when they became agricultural workers or miners at the end of the nineteenth century. They were capable of organising themselves to protest against their condition and to demand better pay and work conditions, as the Baixa do Kassanje massacre in the 1950s testifies. In 1974–5, when the Portuguese landowners left the country in a rush, the Angolan government nationalised the abandoned farms and the plantations to avoid disaster, but it was unable to urge all agricultural workers to work for the State, nor was it able to supply them with adequate management and transportation. Their reluctance was rooted in the memory of the exploitation they endured in the colonial era. Like modern agricultural consortia (cotton, sugar), landowners had also bought the surplus of the peasants' subsistence production, usually at a price below market value. In this way, they were able to supply the urban areas with food and export to the world markets at the expense of the peasantry. After five centuries of

Portuguese colonial capitalism and exploitation, Marxism was not surprisingly the ideology that allowed Angola's people to hope for an end to Portuguese domination. Thus politically and ideologically, the Angolan independent State, under MPLA, could not maintain the former repressive structure of agricultural production.

When the old colonial production structure disappeared, however, the whole economy collapsed. Production dropped, because no structures had been established to manage the farms, transportation or distribution. People returned to the villages and tried to survive with what was left. Today, while peasants have the resources to produce enough to supply the urban areas and to export, they produce just enough for themselves. There are two main reasons for this situation: the absence of a good system of transportation and the fact that, with no real access to consumer goods, peasants do not need money. In Angolan villages, only the barter system still holds.

More recently, private merchants have emerged in the second economy. On a small scale, they achieve what the State bureaucracy has not been able to accomplish: they exchange and buy peasant products and resell them in the urban second market. But this produce is sold at exorbitant prices. A kilogram of fish, when available, may cost Kz 130 in the state stores, while it costs Kz 500 in the second market; a kilogram of maize flour is worth Kz 25 as compared to Kz 1000 in the second market; and, five onions are priced at Kz 1000 (Bhagavan, 1987: 62). The private merchants deal directly with the consumers and suppliers. They buy from workers or poor people who spend their time in the queues at the *loja do povo*, from workers who get rewards for exemplary work, from workers and petty-bourgeois (civil servants) who steal goods from the ports and airports and from state shops, and finally from peasants who, most of the time, prefer to barter their products. Then, the same people who supply the merchants go to the second market to buy what they need – but at a price 10 to 70 times higher than the official one, usually determined by the American dollar exchange rate on the black market. Those merchants who build better *esquemas* are known as the *milionarios da kwanza*, because they are also the masters of the *candonga* and have been able to accumulate millions of *kwanzas* through their schemes. They generally get involved with the second market of consumer goods as well as with the black market of foreign currency, particularly American dollars.

Everybody builds *esquemas* or participates in the *candonga* be-cause when a person has few resources, he or she *does need* a network to be able to satisfy basic needs. As the local currency is worthless, the population has to revert to barter. Each year the National Bank has introduced 60–65 billion *kwanzas* into circulation, but this money never returns to the banks. The official economy maintains artificially the parity between the *kwanzas* and the American dollar (officially US$1 is worth Kz 30, while in the black market, the rate is 1 to 1500 or even 2000). Moreover, the inflation does not correspond to the production and consumption of goods. This gap contributes to the black market in foreign currency: the population tries to get rid of *kwanzas* for American dollars and consumer goods. At the same time, it increases with the importance of barter:

> Not only is the official exchange rate way out of whack, there is a mass of unspent and excess *kwanzas* but little to buy on the market. As a result, the value of eggs, tomatoes and oranges is measured not in *kwanzas* but in bottles of beer and packets of cigarettes (Ottaway, 1986: A18).

A large number of people in Angola deliberately use illegal actions – corruption, bribery, fraud, embezzlement and stealing – in order to sell, to buy or to barter. The party, government officials and the remaining bourgeoisie élite of the colonial era, usually involved in the second economy as buyers or as the ones who offer some protection to the *esquemas* or the *candongas* of the *milionarios da kwanza*. This protection is sometimes the only means the political and social élites possess to barter or to participate in the second market. They exchange it for foreign currency and luxury consumption goods (however, these goods are not comparable to the ostentation associated with most Third World dominant classes). Corruption is also associated with some particular economic activities such as air travel (purchase of tickets to travel abroad) and cargo shipment, port and airport zones (stealing imported goods). The political and social élites also have access to better consumer goods and supplies, both in quantity and quality, through the *lojas dos reponsaveis* (stores for high-ranking people)[6] and the *lojas francas* (free shops) where they can buy goods using foreign currency only.

To repress the *candongueiros*, the justice system would have to prosecute some of the members of the political and social élites, and would even have to face the paradox of having to accuse half the Angolan population. Unless a member of the official élite is deeply engaged with the *candongueiros* and does not respect the code of discretion and silence, the justice system will keep a discerning and tactful eye on his or her second economy activities. Its repression ranges from administrative measures which may be 'smooth' or severe. The term *queda para cima* (falling upwards) refers to the transference of an official to another position at the same level or even higher. At the other extreme, the term *queda para baixo* (falling downwards) refers to heavily punitive measures, ranging from down-grading, forced resignation and expulsion (in particular for party members and State officials) – to penal measures such as social work in the community, imprisonment (used typically in the case of diamond and cattle traffickers) or even the death penalty. Regarding the official élite, the justice system acts in a similar way as in other countries. But one does not find in Angola cases of corruption and political patronage of the magnitude witnessed in Zaire, Ivory Coast, France, the United States of America or Canada, involving ministers, corporate administrators, bankers and millions of tax payers' dollars.

Contrary to what the casual observer may think, the *milionarios da kwanza* are not part of the political and social élites that run the official economy. In fact, the *esquemas*, the *candonga* and the second economy allow the *milionarios* to hoard money or to spend it on luxury products, but rarely to accumulate capital or to create productive capital. One could define them as the economic élite of the second economy, but this does not mean they are the future bourgeoisie of Angola, as they neither invest productively in the Angolan economy, nor are presently politically motivated.

THE SECOND ECONOMY IS NECESSARY, BUT . . .

The second economy is an important feature of Angolan society. At this particular historical moment (1975–87), it is the result of specific conditions of underdevelopment, and at the same time the product of resistance to them. There is not one cause but several, generally interconnected: the Portuguese colonial heritage and the decolonisa-tion process; the continuous and insidious war against South Africa and UNITA aggressions; the dependance of the Angolan economy on multinational firms and the extent of its integration in the capitalist world economy; and the administrative, managerial and political errors of the party and the Angolan government itself. In the latter instance, it is mainly an incapacity to implement the develop-ment plans, a lack of understanding of the peasantry, and a failure to build a distribution network.

The second economy in Angola functions as a mechanism of social regulation. It restores an equilibrium in a market characterised by shortage and scarcity of consumer goods, either locally produced or imported. Through this mechanism, supply is adjusted to respond to the demand of the poorest of Angola (redistribution of revenue, goods and services). At the same time, the second economy also creates a small group of hoarders.

Considering Angolan society as a totality, the second economy cannot be studied by isolating it from other economic or social components, or by examining it exclusively from a legal point of view. Those activities of the second economy that are illegal have the same social and economic regulatory functions as the official legal ones. Law is an element of the whole process – and a crucial one, as it sets forth what is ideologically or politically unacceptable. It remains a powerful instrument of control – when it is needed. In producing a certain ideological order, the Angolan State created a certain practical disorder. The law, therefore, has played a contradictory role, as it has created a social space, defined as the condition of the institutionalisation of the second economy, by excluding certain activities from the official economy. In so doing it has integrated unofficial economic activities into the totality of the Angolan social web.

The second economy is not subordinate to the official economy because it does not operate as a supplement to, or under the rules of, the latter. The application of the law makes this interdependent articulation possible. For as long as this economic link is not sufficiently institutionalised, no significant repressive and legal actions will be taken against the workers, peasants or even the *milionarios da kwanza* unless they seriously encroach on the official economy sphere. The seminars organised by the party and the government (August and November 1987) on the definition of a New Economic Policy, and the reorganisation of leading bodies of both the party and the government in early 1987, are signs of the official recognition that the second economy has performed its essential role, and is now becoming an obstacle to the development of Angolan society. The second economy allows people to survive, but it does not increase the productive forces. The current debate also suggests that private property will play a more important role in the emerging model of Angolan transition to socialism.

NOTES

1. With the exclusion of South Africa.
2. The destruction was massive: 80 per cent of plantations belonging to European settlers were abandoned; only 40 per cent of the most important industrial enterprises were functioning, 130 bridges were destroyed; only 6000 out of 28 000 trucks registered in 1973 were in condition to function. The commercial network, mostly composed of individual enterprises, was virtually wiped out (Meyns, 1984: 125).
3. Angola as a nation is the result of European colonial disputes in Southern Africa. The ethnic composition is an important dimension of the problem, but so is the fact that its territory covers a certain number of former African States and Kingdoms whose concrete history did not disappear completely with the imposition of colonial rule.
4. The use of the term 'black economy' is quite restrictive, as it means illegal economic activities.
5. At least as regards quantity (number of enterprises which are nationalised).
6. There are three types of these stores: middle-level, high-level and upper-high-level, according to the salaries of the government, the party and the enterprise's employees.

REFERENCES

Alagiah, G., 'Angola: Struggle for Balance', *South*, 73 (November 1986) pp. 73–7.
Amselle, J.-L., 'Economie souterraine, économie sans mystère', *Futuribles*, 40 (1981) pp. 55–62.
Archambault, E. and X. Greffe (eds), *Les économies non-officielles* (Paris: Editions La Découverte, 1984).
Bhagavan, M. R., *Angola: Prospects for Socialist Industrialization* (Uppsala: Scandinavian Institute of African Studies, 1980).
Bhagavan, M. R., *Angola's Political Economy 1975–1985* (Uppsala: Scandinavian Institute of African Studies, 1986).
Castanheira, J. P., 'Angola: A guerra continua', *Supplemento de o Jornal*, 582 (1986) pp. 6–9.
Copans, J., 'Les petits métiers du Tiers-Monde', *Afrique-Asie*, 230 (1982) pp. 26–8.
de Almeida, P. R., *Historia do Colonialismo Português em Africa*, 3 vols (Lisboa, Editions Estampa, 1978, 1979).
dos Santos, D., 'Cabinda: the Politics of Oil in Angola's Enclave', in Robin Cohen (ed.), *African Islands and Enclaves* (Beverly Hills: Sage, 1983).
Ferreira, E. S., *Aspectos do colonialismo português* (Lisboa: Seara Nova, 1974).
Fletcher, P., 'Angola Recovery Course Heads towards Free Market', *Globe and Mail* (9 October 1987) p. B19.

Gabor, I. R., 'La seconde économie dans une économie socialiste: un point de vue hongrois', *Problèmes économiques*, 1720 (1981) pp. 9–15.

GPDP, *A descolonização portuguesa* (Lisboa: Instituto Democracia et Liberdade, 1979).

Heimer, F., *The Decolonization Conflict in Angola, 1974–76* (Genève: Institut Universitaire de Hautes Etudes Internationales, 1979).

Heimer, F., 'Formation sociale, développement économique et option socialiste en Angola', *Genéve-Afrique*, XVIII (1) (1980) pp. 32–43.

Heimer, F., 'Sobre a articulação dos modos de produção em Angola. Uma nota metodológica', *Análise Social*, XIX (78–78–79) (1983) pp. 1091–1100.

Hodges, T., *Angola to the 1990s: the Potential for Recovery* (London: The Economist Intelligence Unit, 1987).

Hugon, P., 'Le développement des petites activités à Antananarivo: l'exemple d'un processus involutif', *Revue Canadienne des Etudes Africaines*, 16 (2) (1982) pp. 293–312.

Mas, M., 'Une politique pétrolière faite de prudence et de réalisme', *Le Monde Diplomatique*, 393 (1986) pp. 21–2.

Mattera, P., *Off the Books. The Rise of the Underground Economy* (London: Pluto Press, 1985).

Meyns, P., 'O desenvolvimento da economia angolana a partir da independência: problemas da reconstrução nacional', *Revista Internacional de Estudos Africanos*, 2 (1984) pp. 121–61.

Morice, A., 'Commerce parallèle et troc à Luanda', *Politique Africaine*, 17 (1985) pp. 105–20.

Munslow, B. (ed.), *Africa: Problems in the Transition to Socialism* (London: Zed Press, 1986).

Ottaway, D. B., 'Angola: Two Faces of War/the Government: Crumbling Economy Reverts to Barter', *Washington Post* (28 July 1986) pp. A1, A18.

Sauvy, A., *Le travail noir et l'économie de demain* (Paris: Calmann-Lévy, 1984).

Scraton, P. and N. South, 'The Ideological Construction of the Hidden Economy: Private Justice and Work-Related Crime', *Contemporary Crises*, 8 (1984) pp. 1–18.

Stockwell, J., *In Search of Enemies: A CIA Story* (New York: W. W. Norton, 1978).

Smiley, X., 'Inside Angola', *The New York Review of Books*, XXX (2) (1983) pp. 39–45.

Sumner, C. (ed.), *Crime, Justice and Underdevelopment* (London: Heinemann, 1982).

Torres, A., 'Pacto colonial e industrialização de Angola', *Analise Social*, XIX (77–78–79) (1983) pp. 1101–19.

Wauthier, C., 'Une longue marche pour assurer le développement et conquérir la paix', *Le Monde Diplomatique*, 391 (1986) pp. 23–5.

Wolfers, M. and J. Bergerol, *Angola in the Front Line* (London: Zed Press, 1983).

11 The Second Economy in Tanzania: its Emergence and Strategies of Control

Andrew S. Z. Kiondo

INTRODUCTION

The phenomenon variously referred to as the second economy, the underground economy, and the informal economy, is neither new nor peculiar to one world region only. However, its activities, mechanisms of operation, and magnitude of entrenchment within the dominant economy differ from country to country. As Tanzi states: 'Incentives for growth of these activities increase with greater regulation of the economy, larger public sectors, and higher levels of taxation' (Tanzi, 1983: 10).

Taking only one aspect of the second economy into consideration, Tanzi further notes; that '[b]lack markets for goods have reached epidemic proportions in some highly regulated African countries, and the same is reported to be occurring in some centrally planned economies of Europe (Tanzi, 1983: 11).

This present study examines the emergence of the second economy in Tanzania and the government's attempt to contain it. The first section provides an overview of the three main historical periods in the evolution of the Tanzanian economy. The second section deals with Tanzania's economic policies since the 1970s in relation to the emergence of the second economy. The third section examines the government's response in the 1980s to the second economy. The chapter concludes with a number of proposed generalisations about the nature of the second economy in Third World countries which can be drawn from the Tanzanian experience.

A HISTORICAL OVERVIEW OF THE TANZANIAN ECONOMY

The United Republic of Tanzania was founded on 26 April 1964, when two formerly independent countries, Tanganyika and Zanzibar, were united. Both countries had a considerable history under British colonialism, Tanganyika as a British territory, and Zanzibar as a British protectorate. Although the following discussion of the evolution of the Tanzanian economy is drawn principally from Tanganyika, it is assumed that the economies which evolved under the British colonial administration were similar in both areas.

The formation and development of the Tanzanian economy exhibits three distinctive, but interrelated phases:

1. the colonial phase (1890s–early 1960s);
2. the immediate post-independence period of capitalist-oriented economic policy (1964–7); and
3. the subsequent post-independence period of socialist-oriented economic policy (1967–1980s).

The Colonial Phase: 1890s–1963

It is now generally accepted that the economic needs of the European powers were the main motivation behind colonialism in Africa. This is true of East Africa, where the indigenous population was forced to produce goods for the needs of the metropolitan economy. As stated by the British Colonial Governor to Tanganyika, Mr Cameroon:

> The first object of the government is to induce the native to become a producer directly or indirectly, that is, to produce or to assist in producing something more than the crop of local food stuffs that he requires for himself and his family (quoted in Coulson, 1982: 43).

In order to make the 'natives' produce for the market, the British colonialists needed to create a capitalist economy in Tanzania. However, the conditions under which capitalism was introduced in the colony were quite different from those in Britain: the colonial state was a conquest state, imposed on the people by force. And unlike the British capitalist state which was founded under the bourgeois liberal democratic principle of laissez-faire, the British colonial state in Tanzania was not based on any democratic principles.

The economy which evolved under colonial circumstances in Tanzania is best described by McCarthy (1982) as a bureaucratic economy. It was designed to respond to the needs and requirements of the colonial bureaucracy. Its main function was to integrate the colonised people into the world economy and to extract surplus production for the needs of the bureaucracy. For its part, the bureaucracy assumed the role of controlling and regulating all economic activities in the colony.

Government intervention in economic activities was an important aspect of the colonial economy in Tanzania. The colonial government determined where markets should be, and who should sell and buy goods. In agriculture, for example, cotton production was controlled through zoning regulations, and coffee was controlled through limiting both farmers and buyers of the crop (McCarthy, 1982: 62). In other sectors of the economy, government intervention and regulation were exacted mainly through taxation. The government overregulation of economic activities was well demonstrated by a top-level bureaucrat, who in 1933, urged an investigation on the extent to which restrictions and fees of various kinds had been imposed on trade generally. He argued convincingly:

indeed we seem . . . to be getting into the frame of mind that if anyone anywhere is making a profit we should tax him and regulate him, and enact legislation about him. And in most cases there is precious little real ground for 'control' except the bureaucratic one that control is in some way desirable in itself (McCarthy, 1982: 23).

In sum, colonialism imposed a capitalist economy in Tanzania to replace a subsistence economy; as a result, a bureaucratic economy evolved. This economy was designed to serve the external interests of the metropolitan economy as well as the domestic needs of the colonial bureaucracy. In order to meet those needs, the colonial government had to intervene heavily in the country's economic activities.

According to Tanzi's proposition quoted in the Introduction, incentives for the growth of the second economy activities increase with greater regulation of the economy, larger public sectors and higher levels of taxation. The colonial government in Tanganyika met two of the conditions – namely, greater regulation of the economy and higher levels of taxation. One factor, however, was missing: a large public sector. The colonial government only regulated the economy, it never undertook economic activities of any significance. Yet the conditions for the future development of a second economy were established right from the formation of the colonial economy. As authors such as Gould (1980) suggest, a large bureaucracy and underdevelopment are the central determinant factors of corruption, which is an important component of the second economy. These features were also present during the colonial period.

The Post-independence Period to 1967

Both Tanganyika and Zanzibar became independent from British colonial rule in the early 1960s: Tanganyika in 1961, and Zanzibar in 1963. During the early 1960s, Tanzania's economy continued to develop along the directions set by the previous colonial government. The new regime of nationalists virtually inherited the colonial bureaucracy. This bureaucracy was, at independence, dominated by non-citizens whose share in the total bureaucracy was more than 70 per cent (Smith, 1966: 62, Table XII). Even with the introduction of a policy to 'Africanise' the senior and middle grade civil service, in reality only African officials who were already within the colonial bureaucracy and sympathetic to its goals were promoted. The nature of state intervention characteristic of the colonial bureaucracy was simply passed over to the new regime. Consequently, the nature of the economy remained unchanged. Production continued in the colonial pattern, with sisal, coffee, and cotton comprising the main commodities oriented toward external markets (Clarke, 1978: 58). At the political level, however, there were some changes reflecting a nationalistic shift. The top-level political echelon (the executive and parliament) evolved into an indigenous national leadership which did have a direct stake in the economy.

The economic policy that was to evolve after independence has to be seen within the context of this political change. Essentially the policy retained the capitalist orientation during the period from 1961 to 1966. That is, despite a strong state intervention in the economy, private ownership continued to be an important principle guiding economic activities. Yet a new trend emerged during this period, as government by nationals expanded the public sector by its actual involvement in economic activities and capital formation (Rutman, 1968: 58).

This trend was entrenched by the expansion of parastatals (a parastatal is defined as an economic enterprise in which the government holds at least 50 per cent of the equity; but it could also be

defined loosely as a corporation in which the government has any
equity holding; Clarke, 1978: 99–100). In fact, the creation of
parastatals started during the colonial period, but their expansion is
associated with independence. For example, the value added by
parastatals in the country's economy rose from 2 per cent to 6.9 per
cent of total GDP in the period from 1961 to 1967. Similarly,
employment by parastatals rose from 1.4 per cent to 7.5 per cent of
total wage employment during the same period (Clarke, 1978: 63).

Post-independence Socialist-oriented Development Policy: 1967–

After six years of continuity, Tanzania decided to introduce a new
policy in February 1967. The policy was contained and elaborated in
a political declaration popularly known as the 'Arusha Declaration'.
It is also referred to as the policy of Socialism and Self-Reliance. It is
important to understand the background as well as the nature of this
policy.

In the first six years of independence, Tanzania came to grips with
the stark realities of underdevelopment: the limitations to development efforts set by the dependent nature of its colonial economic
heritage. Smith (1966: 182–3 and 354–5) and Clarke (1978: 182–4)
illustrate the country's heavy dependence on foreign financial assistance in this period. The main aid donors were Britain, West
Germany and the USA. Between 1964 and 1965 Tanzania was
involved in political disputes with these same donors. First it accused
the USA of attempting to overthrow its government. Then West
Germany withdrew its recognition of Tanzania because the latter
would not close the East German Consulate in Zanzibar soon after
the union of Tanganyika and Zanzibar. Finally, Tanzania severed
relations with Britain because the latter refused to crush the illegal
declaration of independence by Rhodesia. As a result of these
disputes, the donor countries cancelled their financial commitments
to Tanzania. Unable to attract sufficient finance capital elsewhere,
the country could not effectively implement its development plans as
initially envisaged (Clarke, 1978: 44).

These financial frustrations, among other things experienced during the first years of independence, led Tanzania to adopt a new
policy of Socialism and Self-Reliance in 1967. Tanzania's socialism
was not revolutionary for several reasons. First, it was introduced
peacefully after the ruling party TANU (Tanganyika African Nation-

al Union) adopted a declaration committing the country to pursuing socialist development policies. Secondly, the development policies so pursued did not alter the relations of production existing previously. Finally, it was not based on the Marxist principle of class struggle, but could be more aptly described as a radical brand of the movement of African socialism which swept over the continent in the 1960s. The new policy of socialism, however, aimed at curbing the development of modern capitalism. In order to do so, the government nationalised what was identified as the 'commanding heights' of the country's economy. This included all banks, major industries and plantations, import–export businesses and other important commercial firms, as well as land, and (later) major buildings. In some cases, the government simply took over major shares in firms while the owners retained the rest. In this sense, it could be said that the government went into partnership with multinational corporations.

All the nationalised firms were put under the parastatal sector which came to dominate the country's economy after 1967. Additionally, a leadership code was enacted to ban leaders from involvement in capitalist activities. 'Leaders' as officially defined included all public servants and politicians earning an official income of more than Shs 1000.00 (equivalent to approximately US $200 at that time). They were not allowed to receive more than one salary, hold financial shares or make extra income by renting their houses.

While the series of nationalisations that followed immediately after the Arusha Declaration of 1967 boosted the public sector, they by no means destroyed the private sector. In fact, the private sector continued to thrive, making the country's economy a truly mixed one. The private sector continued to fulfil a critical role particularly in agricultural production. Clarke stresses this point when he says:

> Public institutions are dominant in mining, utilities, finance, and insurance. They are very important in manufacturing and transport, but on the other hand about half [of] these sectors remain in private hands. The commerce, service, construction and agriculture sectors remain essentially private. If we look at the whole economy, the importance of public institutions is still relatively small (Clarke, 1978: 68).

As the public sector continued to expand, the nature of the country's economy and underdevelopment remained unaltered. Furthermore, the newly created parastatals continued to receive financial assistance from foreign sources (Clarke, 1978: 292–3), resulting in a further deepening of the country's financial dependence. As Barkan (1984: 33–4) starkly states: 'one indicator of the extent of Tanzanian dependency is that on a per capita basis the country has become the highest recipient of foreign aid in the world'.

The policy of Socialism and Self-Reliance was not without achievements. On the social side, the government did provide free social services such as education, health services and running water. As a result, life expectancy rose from about 35 years at independence to about 52 years in 1983, while the literacy rate rose from less than 20 per cent at independence to over 80 per cent in the 1980s (Barkan, 1984: 26–7). But these achievements were made at the cost of material economic growth (Lane, 1984: 2). Towards the end of the 1970s, Tanzania's economic performance was so poor that acute shortages of basic consumer goods occurred throughout the country. This phenomenon, together with an ever-increasing state of government intervention in the economy, gave rise to the development of a second economy. In the following section we shall discuss the relationship between Tanzania's economic policy and the emergence of the second economy.

TANZANIA'S ECONOMIC POLICY AND THE EMERGENCE OF THE SECOND ECONOMY

An examination of Tanzania's economic policy in the 1970s reveals some continuities and discontinuities from the colonial period. The colonial economic policy sustained underdevelopment and created dependency in Tanzania by constructing an economy oriented towards the external needs of the metropolitan economy. This nature of the economy continued despite changes of government and policies after independence. The colonial policy also involved bureaucratic state control and heavy regulation of economic activities. The extent of this regulation and its nature varied but its presence persisted. The colonial government also created a small public sector and a few parastatals while the socialist-oriented policies of 1967 expanded and elevated the sector into a dominant position. The major policy difference associated with the post-1967 economic phase in Tanzania is that the public sector is recognised as the official economy, whereas before 1967 priority had been given to private sector.

At the beginning of this chapter, I quoted Tanzi who identified three factors associated with the rise of second economy activities: larger public sectors, greater regulation of the economy, and higher levels of taxation. These factors, especially the last two, have been present in varying degrees in Tanzania's economy since its formation. It is true that they were intensified after 1967, but the seeds were planted during the colonial administration.

Even with the intensification of these factors, the second economy activities became significant only in the 1980s. What, then, would explain the rise and consolidation of the second economy in Tanzania? To answer this question, we have to discuss the details of the second economy itself. In a study of the emergence of the second economy in Tanzania, Maliyamkono describes the range of its activities in the following way:

> The late seventies and early eighties witnessed high inflation and rampant growth in indicators of Tanzania's second economy, including foreign exchange traffic, corruption, artificial shortaging [sic], marketeering and profiteering, . . . smuggling, building and land speculation, false reporting of income and tax evasion, withholding of goods and services – even shortages of labour, fraudulent overseas orders, illegal hunting for ivory, and outright theft of scarce commodities (Maliyamkono, 1985: 9).

What one gathers from the above list is that by the 1980s the second economy had matured. Its activities permeated all sectors of the economy, and people of all walks of life were getting involved. The activities did not take place in an isolated manner any more. Rather, they took place in a co-ordinated network supported by social and political forces. In 1983, then president Mr J. K. Nyerere was quoted as saying that racketeering in the country seemed so well established that it appeared as if the racketeers were running their own clandestine regime. Determined to destroy the second economy, the President then threatened: 'We are going to overthrow the racketeering regime, we have only one government, the government of CCM ['Chama cha Mapinduzi', meaning Revolutionary Party, which is Tanzania's ruling party–ASK]' (Maliyamkono, 1985: 13).

Activities of the second economy constitute an economy only when they are sufficiently organised to the extent of challenging the first economy. This was obviously absent in the Tanzanian economy even long after its resolution to pursue socialist policies in 1967. Nor did government regulation of the economy accompany the socialist commitment. As Helleiner notes: 'Price controls, licensing systems, quota restrictions are conspicuous by their scarcity in this aspiring socialist state, . . . duties on luxury imports are not yet at "austerity" levels and there are no prohibitions on import of such items whatsoever' (Helleiner, 1972: 188).

This phenomenon of socialism without much economic regulation did not last long, however. As the country began to suffer from various economic shocks, it became necessary to extend price controls to various consumer products. The use of price controls in Tanzania dates back to the colonial period but it was considerably expanded in mid-1970s, especially with the passage of the Price Controls Act in 1974 and the formation of the National Price Commission (Rice, 1979: 95). In fact, price control practice was first institutionalised in Tanzania by the formation of the Government Control Task Force in early 1973. At that time, the Task Force controlled about 400 commonly consumed goods produced locally. By late 1973, the number had grown to 500. Then by March 1974, 602 categories of domestically produced items and 464 groups of imported items were controlled (Rice, 1979: 96).

Towards the end of the 1970s, the Tanzanian economy plunged into insurmountable difficulties. The immediate symptom of the economic problems was the crisis of balance of payment, resulting in an acute shortage of foreign reserves. This meant that the country could no longer import sufficient spare parts and necessary inputs for industrial as well as agricultural production. Most industries began to produce at low capacity, in some cases as low as 30 per cent. This in turn meant fewer locally produced consumer goods at a time when imports were diminishing. Foreign trade had thus to be put under tight state control whereby importation of only a few necessary items was authorised.

In agriculture, complete government control was possible thanks to the mostly forceful villagisation exercise of 1974. The decision to carry out the exercise was made by the then ruling party, TANU Biennial Conference, in September 1973; by the end of 1975, the resettlement of the rural population in villages had been achieved (Coulson, 1982: 249). It is important to note that no law was enacted to force peasants to move into villages, but the mere party resolution was regarded enough to empower officials to burn houses and mistreat those who resisted (see Coulson, 1982: 250–1).

Once in villages, the peasants were not forced to produce communally but they were required to undertake farming in allocated plots in the form of bloc farming. The government thus undertook to increase agricultural production through coercion, by enforcing minimum acreage rules and other rules governing crop and agricultural husbandry (Coulson, 1982: 235). Yet the reaction of peasants was either to produce less of the government required crops or retain more for their own consumption, or dispose of their produce through black-market channels where prices were higher than the official ones. As a result, by the 1980s, overall agricultural output was declining at an alarming rate (see Lane, 1984: 10–12).

Since 1980, Tanzania's economy has been characterised by an acute chronic shortage of basic consumer goods. As a result, bureaucratic regulation over the distribution of the few available goods has become the norm. Although the public sector is bound to respond to these regulations, the private sector which thrives on the principle of 'business risk' manages to get around and operate through the activities of the second economy. As shortages and scarcities of goods continue to plague the economy, bureaucratic controls continue to multiply and activities of the second economy continue to extend their networks. The development from mere isolated activities to organised networks of an alternative economy has been made possible by the failure and total breakdown of the official economy.

Whatever the immediate cause of economic failure and breakdown, the nature of the economies of most Third World countries make them particularly vulnerable to this state. What is common to all these countries is the underdevelopment and dependent nature of their economies, which render them too fragile to withstand either internal or external pressures. What we have learned from the Tanzanian experience is that while the country changed its policy from capitalist to socialist in nature, its economy remained essentially underdeveloped, dependent and bureaucratically controlled. With such a fragile economy, the pressures of the 1980s, characterised by economic decline and the unavailability of foreign currency reserves, gave rise to the massive development of the second economy.

GOVERNMENT RESPONSE TO SECOND ECONOMY ACTIVITIES IN TANZANIA

The previous sections have dealt with the economics of the second economy. This section will focus on its politics. The main question is: how does the government regard the second economy, and how does it respond to it? To answer this question, we need to know who gets what, who gains and who loses when the second economy flourishes. To do this, we have to analyse the class structures operating within both the first and the second economies.

In this study, the second economy (unofficial, contrary to the dominant and ideologically promoted economy) is juxtaposed with the first economy (the official, dominant and ideologically promoted economy). Theoretically, in Tanzania the first economy operates under the general rubric of the public sector while the second economy is mainly associated with the private sector. In practice, however, the division is not that clear cut since the activities of the second economy may cut across both sectors.

The activities of the second economy in Tanzania are best understood if grouped into two types: legal and illegal second economy activities.

The Legal Second Economy Activities Both Within and Outside the First Economy

Those within the first economy mainly involve legal dealings between the two economies. Examples include contractual arrangements whereby private entrepreneurs are provided with tenders to supply goods to public institutions or corporations. Outside the first economy, the legal second economy operates through licensed private business. Since Tanzania's socialism provides for the nationalisation of the 'commanding heights' of the economy only, the rest may, theoretically, be included in the second economy. Yet, since these are officially recognised as having an important role to play in the economy, we shall deal with them only when they degenerate into dealings which violate the law.

The Illegal Second Economy Activities Both Within and Outside the First Economy

These are the activities that we shall mainly focus upon. They include illegal transactions between the first and second economies, unlicensed private production, black markets, smuggling, bribery, and other forms of corruption. To understand the government's reaction towards these activities, we need to understand the stratification of both economies. At this point it is helpful to view both economies as divided into three sections: upper, middle, and lower. The upper section of the first economy is occupied by top politicians, civil servants, and high-ranking directors of the parastatals. These officials constitute the ruling élite of the state. Correspondingly, the upper section of the second economy is occupied by members of the business community who have connections in the government, as well as abroad. It should be noted that on several occasions, the ruling élite have been found involved in the illegal activities of the second economy. This demonstrates that there is an interaction between the two economies which, in some instances, blurs the distinction between them. Moreover, when the government seeks to control the activities of the second economy, the upper section can be regarded as relatively safe from scrutiny: usually, top-level participants in the second economy are high-level officials of the government, or individuals with enough money to protect themselves through their connections or through bribery.

The middle section of the first economy is occupied by middle class bureaucrats, party functionaries, members of the intelligentsia, and lower-level managers of the parastatals. Although these officials do not make policies directly, they influence them greatly. The middle section of the second economy consists of individuals who are only partly successful in this economy. They may be seen as junior partners in the activities of the second economy, which is actually controlled by officials in the upper section.

Finally, the lower section of the first economy consists of the ordinary workers in the government, the party and parastatals, who are responsible for implementing the decisions reached at the top and handed to them by those in the middle. Their counterparts in the second economy are individuals who are forced into the activities of the second economy by necessity. They include the unemployed as well as low paid employees who have to augment their official incomes through the second economy.

I have noted in the previous section that Tanzania's economic problems developed into an unmanageable crisis in the late 1970s. It was at this time that unofficial economic activities developed into an economy in itself, challenging the survival of the first economy. Towards the end of 1979, it became obvious to the ordinary people that top-level officials were heavily involved in the second economy. For example, during a country-wide tour in 1979, the President was openly told that some of his top officials in a region he visited perpetrated acts of corruption. Shortly afterwards, a number of officials in the region were dismissed, including the regional commissioner (Mlimuka and Kabudi, 1986: 76–7). Such complaints against the top leadership would have been voiced in other regions as well, however after this incident, the President limited public discussions following his addresses.

This case illustrates the reaction of the government towards the illegal activities of the second economy operating within the first economy (Mlimuka and Kabudi, 1986: 78–90). The reaction was prompted by, first and foremost, the economic crisis and peoples' complaints about top leadership involvement in the second economy. The crisis, characterised by a total breakdown of the economy and widespread shortages of basic consumer goods, provoked people's complaints against corruption within the government. For its part, the government blamed the economic crisis on the activities of the second economy and responded by removing a few of its top leaders who were allegedly involved. However, this sacrifice was only cosmetic as most of those affected were shortly afterwards appointed to other public posts (Shivji, 1981: 7–8). The second economy continued to thrive, and the economic crisis continued. The government, therefore, had to look for new solutions.

The subsequently adopted strategy was initiated with the enactment of the 'Human Resources Deployment Act' in April 1983. This legislation was directed at urban dwellers who were not 'legally' employed, but rather made their living through unauthorised petty business operations. The aim of the Act was to identify and repatriate individuals engaged in second economy activities to their places of origin, where they would be required to cultivate land allocated to them (Stein, 1985: 118–19). The list of activities identified as illegal included the following unauthorised operations: shoe-shining, selling newspapers, buns, roasted cassava, and other foods in the streets; selling locally brewed beer outside of authorised premises; operating small vending stalls; car washing; special festival catering and any other petty trading which involved door to door selling (*Mfanyakazi*, Tanzania Workers' Weekly Newspaper, 24 September 1983).

Towards the end of 1983, those labelled unemployed were transported to rural areas. Two million Tanzanian shillings for each region were allocated for this exercise. However, the second economy remained unaffected by this strategy. Some of the funds ended up in private pockets due to the lack of proper accountability, and those who were resettled simply returned to the urban areas a few days later and resumed their second economy activities.

While implementation of the Human Resources Deployment Act was being carried out, yet another operation was taking place. This was the famous Anti-Economic Saboteurs Operation of 1983, also termed the 'War Against *Ulanguzi*' (the term 'Ulanguzi' refers to the activities of the second economy). It is important to note that the government declared the 'war' without first passing an act of law, as was the case with the Human Resources Deployment Act discussed above. Those arrested as a result of the operation had to be detained under the Preventive Detention Act of 1962, a law which empowers the President to detain persons conducting themselves in a manner prejudicial to the security of the state (Maliyamkono, 1985: 31). To justify this, the President had to appeal to the people, and the magistrates in particular:

> We have a problem on what to do with these people. The normal procedure would be to take them to court. However, we have not yet decided what action to take in the present circumstances. Magistrates and judges forgive us if we hesitate to take the culprits to courts of law (Maliyamkono, 1985: 31).

Consequently, towards the end of April 1983, the government drafted a bill to detain 'economic saboteurs' and rushed it through Parliament. The 'Economic Sabotage (Special Provisions) Act' of 1983 defines economic sabotage as the commission of a schedule offence, or of any act or omission which is done or omitted without lawful excuse, and for a purpose prejudicial to the economic safety or interests of Tanzania, or which is likely to damage, hinder or interfere with a necessary service or its operation. The schedule to the Act listed the following as economic sabotage offences: hoarding, possession of stolen or unlawfully acquired goods, corruption, contravention of foreign exchange control regulations, and contravention of trade and price regulation laws (see Maliyamkono, 1985: 32–5).

The National Anti-Economic Sabotage Tribunal was established to handle cases falling under the Act, yet not all cases were dealt with by this entity. Some were still handled by official bodies such as the Regional Security Committees of the ruling party, or merely by the police. Some people acquitted by the tribunals were re-arrested and detained, while in other cases the government intervened even before the trial process was completed by withdrawing charges against the accused. As Maliyamkono notes (1985: 35), more often than not these diversions appear to have been intended to remove people from prosecution rather than to ensure their punishment. Eventually by the end of April 1983, as many as 1086 persons, or nearly 25 per cent of those arrested, had been released in this manner (see Maliyamkono, 1985: 36).

The majority of those arrested under the Act belonged to the middle and lower strata of the second economy, especially petty traders operating without licences. A few of those arrested belonged to the upper echelons of the second economy; however, they were eventually released either by government intervention or by bribing officials. The release of these top-level participants prompted ordinary people to complain openly that the 'big fish' were escaping the net. By the end of 1983, the whole operation was losing momentum. As with the other initiatives, there was little real impact upon the second economy.

Other strategies were also attempted during this period. For example, a radio programme popularly known as 'Mikingamo' (scandals) was introduced in order to uncover acts of sabotage. Citizens were urged to inform Radio Tanzania of any second economy activities that they were aware of. These reports would then be publicly broadcasted in order to pre-empt the continuation of sabotage, and also to inform the police to take action. Political leaders also held rallies to explain the dangers of the second economy. However, little happened to those who were exposed. The public became disenchanted and the programme died a natural death.

A market-oriented strategy was also introduced in 1984, whereby market forces were permitted to operate and various incentives to producers and exporters were offered to encourage trading activity. Interestingly, this strategy attempted through liberalisation to reverse the direction of the regime's evolution. In Dar es Salaam, formerly empty shop shelves were immediately filled with imported goods. The number of price-controlled, locally produced commodities was reduced from over 500 to approximately 60. The prices of the deregulated items skyrocketed; clearly, liberalisation without added production was not able to balance prices. Another aspect of the liberalisation programme was privatisation, whereby former parastatal organisations, such as some estates of the Tanzania Sisal Corporation, were sold to private entrepreneurs.

Up to 1987, the impact of the liberalisation process on the second economy has been mixed. In some cases, where former illegal activities were simply legalised, black markets in consumer goods were wiped out. On the other hand, the foreign currency black market is still rampant. Although people are free to import whatever goods they need, the government does not have enough foreign currency to meet the demand. And naturally, the black market is there for those who have accumulated enough money to buy foreign currency – at whatever price. A newspaper revealed in 1987 that Tanzania was losing at least Shs 6 billion a year through gold smuggling. It indicated that gold smuggling was on the increase to provide more foreign currency with which 'to bring in goods under the trade liberalisation policy' (*Daily News, Tanzania*, 7 December 1987: 1).

CONCLUSION

What generalisations can be drawn from the Tanzanian experience? In the shift from a capitalist to a socialist-oriented society, Tanzania simply intensified some of the economic features created during the colonial period: bureaucratisation and overregulation of the economy. Yet by expanding and elevating the public sector's status as the official economy, Tanzania's social policies have differed fundamentally from the colonial ones. And, by lowering the private sector to an inferior position without solving the problems of underdevelopment and dependency, Tanzania's first economy remains fragile and vulnerable to progressive erosion by the second economy.

It would seem that, notwithstanding the importance of factors conducive to the activities of the second economy mentioned earlier (Tanzi, 1983: 10), underdevelopment, dependency and a general economic breakdown represent additional key factors to consider in Third World countries such as Tanzania. The fundamental problem which gives rise to the second economy in Third World countries is the prevalence of a weak economy within a world economy whose exchange depends on hard currency. A balance of payment crisis for these dependent economies is bound to lead to shortages of commodities and a general breakdown of the first economy. These phenomena lead to the rise of and general takeover by the second economy.

Attempts at suppressing the second economy without solving the problems of underdevelopment and dependency simply fuel its further growth. The solution seems to be more goods, and not more controls. And more goods for most Third World countries would require the creation of self-generating economies.

When suppressing the second economy without increasing production proved futile, Tanzania turned to market forces to stimulate production. It remains to be seen what political implications this will have for the ideology of the regime – that is, whether it is possible for market forces to operate within the socialist framework without affecting the socialist policies of the country. Another interesting issue would be whether the use of market forces under the conditions of underdevelopment and dependency would by itself be able to increase production and/or control the second economy. However, these developments are too recent to even attempt an answer in this chapter.

REFERENCES

Barkan, J. D. (ed.), *Politics and Public Policy in Kenya and Tanzania*, revised edn (New York: Praeger, 1984).

Clarke, W. E., *Socialist Development and Public Investment in Tanzania, 1964–73* (Toronto: University of Toronto Press, 1978).

Coulson, A., *Tanzania, A Political Economy* (London: Oxford University Press, 1982).

Daily News, Tanzania (7 December 1987) p. 1.

Gould, D. J., *Bureaucratic Corruption and Underdevelopment in the Third World: The Case of Zaire* (New York: Pergamon Press, 1980).

Helleiner, G. K., 'Socialism and Economic Development in Tanzania', *Journal of Development Studies* (1972) pp. 183–204.

Holomquist, F., 'Class Structure, Peasant Participation, and Rural Self-Help', in J. D. Barkan (ed.), *Politics and Public Policy in Kenya and Tanzania*, revised edn (New York: Praeger, 1984).

Lane, P. A., 'The State of the Tanzanian Economy: A Survey', unpublished Economic Research Bureau seminar paper, University of Dar es Salaam (1984).

Maliyamkono, T., 'Ulanguzi: Emergence of a Second Economy in Tanzania', unpublished Economic Research Bureau seminar paper, University of Dar es Salaam (1985).

McCarthy, D. M., *Colonial Bureaucracy and Creating Underdevelopment: Tanganyika, 1919–1940* (Ames, Iowa: The Iowa State University Press, 1982).

Mfanyakazi (Tanzania Workers' Weekly Newspaper) (24 September 1983).

Mlimuka, A. K. and P. J. Kabudi, 'The State and the Party', in I. G. Shivji (ed.), *The State and the Working People in Tanzania* (Dakar, Senegal: CODESRIA, 1986).

Rice, R. C., 'The Tanzania Price Control System: Theory, Practice and

Some Possible Improvements', in K. S. Kim, *et al.*, *Papers on the Political Economy of Tanzania* (London: Heinemann Education, 1979).

Rutman, G. L., *The Economy of Tanganyika* (New York: Praeger, 1968).

Shivji, I. G. (ed.), *The State and the Working People in Tanzania* (Dakar, Senegal: CODESRIA, 1986).

Shivji, I. G., 'Introduction: the State of the Constitution and the Constitution of the State in Tanzania', *Eastern Africa Law Review, A Journal of Law and Development*, 11–14 (1981) pp. 1–34.

Stein, H., 'Theories of the State in Tanzania: A Critical Assessment', *The Journal of Modern African Studies*, 23 (1) (1985) pp. 105–23.

Smith, H. E. (ed.), *Readings on Economic Development and Administration in Tanzania* (London: Oxford University Press, 1966).

Tanzi. V., 'The Underground Economy, the Causes and Consequences of this Worldwide Phenomenon', *Finance and Development, A Quarterly Publication of the International Monetary Fund and the World Bank*, 20 (4) (1983) pp. 10–13.

12 Dynamic Relationships of the First and Second Economies in Old And New Marxist States

Maria Łoś

METHODOLOGICAL CLARIFICATIONS

This final comparative essay is designed to offer a theoretical synthesis of our present knowledge on the role of the second economy in the process of Marxist development. Throughout this chapter a use is made of the information provided in the national reports contained in this book, as well as of numerous other sources. While this essay is based on an overview of ten Marxist societies, five of them are grouped as 'East European states' (the Soviet Union, Poland, Hungary, Romania and Yugoslavia) and the remaining five are classified as 'developing' or 'Third World' countries (Cuba, Nicaragua, China, Angola and Tanzania).

A qualitative, historical approach has been chosen, with numerical data serving as supporting evidence in individual reports. These data are not used in the cross-national analysis due to their limited comparability. This study has not aimed at establishing abstract correlations between variables identifiable in all political systems and economic formations and, thus, does not answer questions about the universal qualities of the human nature or about their permanent social causes. The adopted approach is closer to the Weberian model of comparative study which makes use of ideal types to permit limited generalisations about historically specific differences (see Ragin and Zaret, 1983: 731). It assumes that superficially similar effects – for example, crime or the second economy – may be produced by different processes and structural clusters, which have to be uncovered in order to explore the specific meanings and the dynamics of those effects.

The present synthesis, while grounded in concrete historical case studies, glosses over secondary differences and focuses on the construction of viable types of structural situations having the greatest explanatory power within a cross-national, but inter-systemic, context. Vast cultural differences among compared societies are not the primary object of this final chapter, which focuses on the question whether formal structural similarities are prone to lead to structurally similar, informal solutions. Yet, the preceding chapters do offer a good insight into the ways by which these processes are mediated by the distinct cultural traditions and historical past of individual societies. By necessity, this final synthesis accommodates only to a limited degree the uncovered variety of meanings and symbolic social functions of the economic practices studied.

IDEOLOGY AND THE DOMINANT (FIRST) ECONOMY

According to the definition adopted for the purpose of this study, the second economy includes all areas of economic activity which are officially viewed as inconsistent with the ideologically sanctioned dominant mode of economic organisation. The official demarcation of the nature and scope of the second economy thus depends on what is ideologically and politically constructed as the dominant economy. Despite many historical and contemporary differences among the countries included in this project, their ideological definitions of what constitutes the first and second economies appear sufficiently similar to make a claim of comparability across the nations studied. Based on a detailed analysis of the first economies of all ten countries studied, I have concluded that the following five elements constitute jointly a core definition of their official economies:

1. nationalisation of at least the 'commanding heights' of the economy – meaning banks, major industries, foreign trade and usually, commerce and land;
2. central economic planning;
3. state regulation and subordination of a highly circumscribed private sector;
4. a collectivist ideology; and
5. extensive state-administered and state-employment-related programmes of social distribution of basic goods.

It may be safely asserted that with respect to these criteria, the selected countries – despite their cross-continental locations – are more similar than any other sample which might include both Marxist and non-Marxist states despite their cultural and geographical proximity. On the other hand, it is important to note that most developing countries – starting with India in 1951 – have adopted a policy of comprehensive national planning. It has been seen – regardless of the adopted ideological and political model – as a precondition for the post-colonial restructuring of the economy, furthering of indigenous national interests, industrialisation and rational allocation of scarce resources (see Choksi, 1979; 107–10). Also, the requirements and conditions attached to foreign aid and credits have usually entailed government responsibility for rational funds allocation and management. Yet – as demonstrated by a well-researched report sponsored by the World Bank – the plan, instead of reducing the uncertainty within the economy, increases it considerably, discouraging investment and contributing to the waste of resources (Choksi, 1979: 133–4). Moreover, it tends to engender high levels of corruption related to the extensive bureaucratisation of the economy and regulation of the processes of allocation of resources, licencing, and so forth.

Importantly, planning and the governmental intervention into the economy follows rather than breaks the colonial pattern of a relatively centralised and formally steered economy. In this respect, there are clear similarities between the heritage of non-Marxist and Marxist developing societies (Alavi, 1972; Saul, 1983). However, the nature of planning is different: in the latter it is proscriptive rather than indicative, more detailed and backed by force (Choksi, 1979: 114). Furthermore, the ideological castigation of private business tends to heighten some of the general difficulties of the planned economy.

It is worth noting that the Central American and African states studied shared certain initial conditions which later influenced their post-revolutionary development. Just like departing colonial powers in Africa, the ruling families and foreign companies in the Central American countries left estates and industrial plants of the size which practically precluded their immediate private purchase by native investors. Moreover, they were often decapitalised and devastated by the fleeing owners. These circumstances have been aggravated by the fact that these countries' economies had been developed in a one-sided manner suited for the maximal exploitation of their exportable resources. Consequently, the revolutionary governments were faced with the immediate problem of securing the necessary range of imports and either a deep restructuring of the economy, or else a continuation of the earlier patterns of dependency. Finally, the urgent need to develop the new states' defence capabilities has enhanced even further the direct governmental involvement in the shaping of the economy.

It is worthy of note that not only the new Marxist states, but also the old ones – namely the Soviet Union and China – were faced at the time of their revolutions with the heritage of the traditionally strong agrarian bureaucratic state (Skocpol, 1983) and the country devastated by wars and internal conflicts. As noted by Wittfogel (1981) and Sawer (1977), and put succinctly by Westoby,

> Russian social relations, both prior to and after Peter the Great's reforms, were only superficially feudal and 'Western'; fundamentally they were shaped by relations of the state to the society characteristic of the 'asiatic mode of production', in which strong intermediate proprietors are lacking, and the centralized state has a powerful role both in extraction of the economic surplus (through taxes, etc.) and in the organization, or at least regulation, of production (Westoby, 1983: 333).

Clearly, ideological considerations have not always played the decisive role in Marxist governments' crucial policy decisions, as they have been mixed with and mediated by the perceived requirements of expediency or necessity. The co-existence of different economic formations within individual countries has also created complex ideological pressures which have shaped and modified the official ideology. Finally, the extent of the direct pressure and influence exercised by the Soviet Union has differed considerably among the five developing countries in this study and at various stages of their development.

Cuba well exemplifies the situation whereby the heavy dependence on exports seemed initially to dictate a centralised, autocratic control over production. Yet, even when the state sector's productivity proved to be much lower than that of the private sector, the ideological requirements of the transition to communism prevented a change of the adopted policy goal of full nationalisation. Thus, in the name of the class struggle, by 1968 even Cuba's retail trade was completely nationalised and state farm workers were deprived of their small plots (Eckstein, 1985: 222–4; Chapter 7 in this volume).

Of all the developing countries in this project, Cuba represents the greatest degree of economic dependency and political integration with the USSR. Its economic dependency was heightened in 1972 when Cuba joined the Council for Mutual Economic Assistance (CMEA) and further reshaped its economy to fit the Soviet model and co-ordinate its five year plans with the Soviet plan cycle (Packenham, 1986: 323). Cuba's level of dependency also appears extremely high compared with other Latin American states,[1] when measured by the standard criteria (see Packenham, 1986), such as monoculture in production (sugar); reliance on and a monocultural profile of exports (both extremely high and increasing in the case of Cuba); trade partner concentration (in 1985, 90 per cent of Cuba's exports and 84 per cent of imports involved CMEA countries: Pérez-Lopes, 1986: 20);[2] capital and debt dependency (the highest *per capita* in Latin America) and energy dependency (in the 1970s, the USSR supplied an average of 98 per cent of Cuban oil imports and used them as leverage in exercising political pressure: see Packenham, 1986: 316, 321; on the question of Cuba's dependent status, see Eckstein, 1985; LeoGrande, 1979; Mesa-Lago, 1981; Packenham, 1986; Pérez-Lopez, 1986).

Cuba's dominant economic structure resembles that of the Soviet Union in so far as the extent of nationalisation, centralisation and ideological condemnation of private property are concerned. Yet, its economic dependency and underdevelopment have precluded an emulation of the Soviet model of industrialisation. Although in the late 1970s and early 1980s some restrictions over the market activity were relaxed, the self-financing principle was promoted within the state economy and remuneration was differentiated according to the labour performed, in 1986 Cuba's Party Congress reversed this direction. This decision opened a new period of radical 'Rectification' by demanding 'more power for central planners, a clampdown on the few existing pockets of private enterprise and . . . "moral incentives" instead of material ones' ('Cuba's New Image', 1988: 36; Pérez-Lopez, 1986: 16).

At the other end of the spectrum, Nicaragua differs in many ways from the orthodox Soviet model. Its mixed economy has been officially proclaimed a permanent political choice and not just a transitory phase to be eventually superseded by a full nationalisation. Yet even in Nicaragua – just as in Angola and Tanzania – the 'commanding heights' of the economy (formerly controlled directly by Somoza) have been nationalised (Chapter 8 in this volume; Fitzgerald, 1985), the plan plays a very central role, prices are state-fixed, input supplies are strictly controlled, and the state has monopolised foreign trade and credit. The centralised market economy of Somoza has thus been replaced by a mixed economy whereby a large state sector co-exists with a significant private economy (see Chapter 8 in this volume). The small entrepreneurs are well organised and constitute a genuine interest group (Marchetti, 1985: 21) despite their internal disagreements and general dissatisfaction with the state-controlled markets and credits (Davis, 1987: 166–7, 172; Gorostiaga, 1985: 15–16). On the other hand, a host of laws has made expropriations in the countryside possible and indeed frequent (Marchetti, 1985: 23–4). Perhaps most importantly, the ideological status of the private sector in Nicaragua is still vague, and the Sandinista government is grappling with the dilemma 'how to create a climate for the private sector when the economy is to serve the logic of the majority rather than the logic of capital' (Gorostiaga, 1985: 15). A 'juxtaposed economy' where each sector follows its own internal logic is clearly ruled out and private business's higher productivity, and not its underlying ideology, are the reasons for its retention in the Sandinista model.

The role of ideology varies considerably across the sample studied. In both the African and Latin American countries examined, Marxist ideas are combined with (and normally preceded by) radical nationalist movements. The adoption of the socialist strategy of socio–economic development in both Angola and Tanzania was an outcome of party politics rather than a revolutionary process. Nevertheless, despite the preservation of a considerable private sector and the absence of the Stalinist model of heavy industrialisation, their political structures and management mechanisms within the state economy resemble greatly the respective features of the Soviet model.

In China, the Marxist–Leninist–Stalinist doctrine was followed and partially replaced by Mao's model of uninterrupted mass-revolution that was eventually succeeded in the late 1970s by a more pragmatic strategy of modernisation.[3] In Eastern Europe, only the Soviet Union and Yugoslavia had undergone independent Marxist revolutions. Yet, in all the remaining East European countries the Marxist ideology has been important as a political tool for keeping the élites in power and satisfying the pressures and requirements coming from the Soviet Union. All the European countries studied experienced a Stalinist period marked by political terror and stress on heavy industry, and – with the exception of Yugoslavia – retained the major features of the Soviet model in the post-Stalin years. Even Yugoslavia has preserved the principles of socialised ownership and central planning, albeit in a revised version based on a form of self-management and multilateral bargaining.

In sum, despite many important differences, the countries studied adhere rather faithfully to the principles of extensive nationalisation, planning, subordination of the private sector, a collectivist ideology and state programmes of distribution of essential goods mentioned earlier. Their second economies can therefore best be viewed in terms of the economic activities which are non-nationalised, not effectively subordinated to the plan, and either officially outlawed or accorded a clearly secondary status.

THE DYNAMICS OF THE MARXIST DEVELOPMENT AND THE SECOND ECONOMY

Typical Stages of Marxist Development

While this project resulted in a detailed mosaic-like picture of the second economies in ten unique countries, it also facilitated a reconstruction of a model process of Marxist economic development. Its distinct stages may not be realised in full in all the countries and not necessarily in precisely the same sequence, but appear nonetheless to be a useful indication of the real processes.[4] These typical stages are: (i) the stage of radical transformation; (ii) the monopolisation period; (iii) the reformist phase (often intermingled in a cyclical way with the monopolisation stage); and (iv) post-reformist decadence.

Based on the national reports contained in this volume as well as numerous other publications and relevant sources, it has been possible to trace a relationship between the dynamics of Marxist economic development and the evolving forms of the second economy. The following subsections thus offer some observations and theoretical generalisations about the nature of interrelations between the first and second economies at each stage of Marxist development.

The key difference between this analysis and other attempts at grasping the uniqueness of the process of socialist development lies in the inclusion of the second economy and its control in the sphere of the dynamic economic reality which imposes a certain logic of progression through several distinctive stages. The second economy is not viewed merely as a response to the problems or contradictions within the first economy; it is also believed to be an important force contributing to the successive transformations within the first economy. The relationship between the two economies is treated as the key structural dimension along which both political decisions and economic practice evolve. It is when this relationship reaches the point where a further accommodation does not offer an even short-term economic promise and the ideological limits of the reformability of the one-party Marxist system are achieved, that the stage of post-reformist decadence appears almost inevitable.

The Radical Transformation Stage

The revolutionary transformation may be either spontaneous or imposed, and it may be achieved either by peaceful, political means or through a tumultuous and violent insurrection. This stage is distinguished by high levels of national mobilisation, attempts at a crash industrialisation or radical reconstruction of the economy, intensive class struggle, vigilantism, likely mass movements of the population (for example, from countryside to the cities, forced resettlements of politically distrusted ethnic groups, and so forth). It is characterised also by displacement and atomisation, combined with and resulting from a forceful collectivisation of the society.

This first stage witnesses a radical redefinition of the second economy in the face of rapidly progressing nationalisation. The market economy and private capital – even when not fully liquidated – are castigated as representing a source of political power opposed to socialism. Their representatives are targetted in campaigns directed against class enemies. The informal, non-market household economy is also often repudiated as too individualistic, traditional and reinforcing family identification instead of collective orientation.

Among common reactions to the revolutionary attack on the private economy and market mentality are attempts at smuggling of the capital abroad, hoarding goods and resources, speculation and sabotage. Since both market and non-market forms of the non-socialistic economy had been extensive in all these countries prior to the revolution, they tended to continue, even if they became objects of persecution. For instance, contrary to common arguments that the second economy was very limited in Poland during the highly repressive Stalinist years, those who lived through that period clearly recall their heavy dependence on informally procured goods and services. These personal accounts seem to be confirmed by the fact that in the aftermath of Stalin's death and the following authorisation of small-scale private business, numerous entrepreneurs reemerged swiftly from the underground in order to register their previously illegal workshops (Åslund, 1985: 52, 58). This cannot be explained solely by the persistence of the economic habits formed under different conditions. Even more important is the persistence of the need, aggravated by the general chaos of the revolutionary period in which individual needs are usually lost sight of.

The subordination of the individual to the collective is further reinforced when the initial revolutionary zeal is extended into crash projects of industrialisation, militarisation and/or radical reorientation of the economy. Consequently, the greater its stress on economic macro-projects or militarisation, the lesser is government's concern for the individual and, therefore, the greater is the pressure towards informal or illegal methods of needs satisfaction. Moreover, the greater the tendency to impose mechanical egalitarian schemes of distribution upon previously highly diversified societies, the greater the resistance and the attraction of informal, inegalitarian, secondary redistribution (see, for example, Chapter 7 in this volume).

The extent of the second economy activities at this stage seems to depend greatly on two divergent, but often initially concurrent, factors:

- The level of positive integration of the masses, due to the creation of new job opportunities, upward mobility of whole social classes or strata, redistribution of the confiscated wealth, 'basic needs' programmes, land reform, etc.
- The level of mobilisation of the repressive neighbourhood- and workplace-based vigilantism resulting in the destruction of informal networks and of the basic trust among people, both of which are essential to the second economy operations.

While positive integration reduces the subjective need for the second economy, the repressive mobilisation limits the ability to engage in it. Despite their conflicting nature, these two political strategies have been implemented simultaneously in most of the countries studied. Their presence has been especially pronounced in the USSR, China, Cuba and Nicaragua, where they seem to have brought about – at least initially – a mitigation in more serious second economy activities. In Nicaragua, however, these factors have been combined with the preservation of a considerable private sector which has reduced the need for a fully illegal underground business.

The repressive mass mobilisation is usually backed and reinforced by a high level of internal militarisation of the society and pervasive policing by security forces employed in the struggle against class enemies. The specific form and class structure of the positive integration, on the other hand, depends greatly on historical alliances crucial to the success of the revolutionary struggle or the communist party political takeover. In the absence of a well-developed industrial proletariat in the countries studied, a popular mobilisation for the radical transformation of the society had often been achieved through such means as agrarian reforms designed to benefit landless and poor peasants; opening up industrial employment opportunities for the impoverished working class; and providing channels for lofty ideological involvement to willing segments of the intelligentsia.

In the Third World countries studied, segments of the indigenous medium-and petty-business classes also played an indispensable role in the transition period. Even when displeased with the general direction of the changes, they were usually eager to co-operate in order to secure favourable treatment under the new conditions (see for example, Gorostiaga, 1985: 16; White, 1983a: 5). Moreover, they were often opposed to the oppressive regimes that typically preceded the revolutionary change in their countries. Anti-authoritarian and national liberation movements were thus often channelled into revolutionary action founded on the strategy of national unity and involving a broad spectrum of social forces (Alavi, 1972; Prybyla, 1986: 21; Vilas, 1986: 143, 246–7; Saul, 1983; White, 1983a: 5).

In a similar vein, White has concluded – based on his comparative overview of the revolutionary socialist development in the Third World – that 'revolutionary socialism has relied on classes and strata deemed secondary to the classic socialist project, notably the peasantry and various sections of the petty bourgeoisie' (White, 1983a: 3). This strategy has had important consequences for the definition of the second economy, including the initial formal accommodation of a private sector and ideological condonation of certain forms of the entrepreneurial spirit.

To conclude, the second economy activities at the radical transformation stage of Marxist development seem to be most closely related to defensive reactions of the ideologically demoted and economically threatened classes (capitalists and rural landlords); raised aspirations of other classes; individual and collective responses

to chaos, deprivation, urban overcrowding, crude egalitarian programmes and subordination of the individual to the grand projects of
the societal reconstruction; and, finally, the survival of individual
market habits, often reinforced by the collective memory of informal
coping with foreign occupations and indigenous oppressive regimes.

The Monopolisation Period

The monopolisation stage is not merely a period of consolidation
since it often negates many of the ideological pronouncements of the
revolutionary period. This stage is characterised by the growing
monopolistic tendencies of the party-state, expansion of the
bureaucracy and of the central planning system, a tendency to create
very large economic conglomerates, and either further reduction of
the private sector or its greater regulation and co-ordination with the
planned economy. Other relevant processes include the increasingly
evident stifling effect of central planning; problems of low productivity and widespread shortages; bureaucratisation of social control
leading to social inertia and alienation; and, finally, a reduction in the
scope of the costly egalitarian social programmes and their particular-
isation based on the political and administrative discretion.

At this stage, moral incentives are found lacking and coercive
legislative measures are often introduced or reinforced in an effort to
improve work habits and stimulate productivity.[5] As well, food and
basic goods rationing programmes are likely to be introduced at this
stage to help cope with the shortages and curb speculation in state
subsidised goods. Thus, the essentially economic problems tend to be
countered by either penal or bureaucratic measures rather than by
economic reforms. The latter, when contemplated – as in the 1960s in
the Soviet Union and many East European countries – tend to be
viewed as politically threatening and, therefore, are likely to be
aborted.

Faced with the progressively monopolised and bureaucratised first
economy, the second economy responds by expanding its increasingly
routinised presence. This process has several important and highly
interrelated manifestations:

- the growth of high-level economic corruption;
- the spreading pattern of setting up illegal enterprises within the
  state economy units;

- the expansion of black markets;
- the increasing black-market involvement by the legal private sector;
- the expansion of the underground business;
- the widespread economic resistance in the countryside; and,
- the growth of a network-based informal second economy.

The high level economic corruption (or 'red-collar crime' – Łoś, 1987a) proliferates during the monopolisation phase because being 'charismatically conceived and organized . . . , Leninist parties require combat environments to preserve their organizational integrity' (Jowitt, 1983: 277). Despite their growing bureaucratisation, they do not acquire an ethos of bureaucratic impersonalism, but rather demand endless personalised tributes and privileges to confirm their supreme status. A corrupt routinisation develops that 'entails the subordination of office charisma to the incumbents' particular interests' (Jowitt, 1983: 284). According to a Polish researcher of 'clientism', the prevalence of corrupt patron–client relationships constitutes a structural element of any highly centralised and hierarchically organised system, especially if it controls economic resources:

> [A]n exuberant growth of client–patron relationships is in great measure, if not entirely, a reaction of the lower levels to excessive centralisation and inefficiency of the system. In this case, the heads of various organizations located at the lower levels of the system look for the people who occupy high positions in the power structure and who control necessary resources. Clients need from patrons, first of all, material resources that they cannot obtain in any other way in the face of the scarcities, inefficiency, and arbitrariness of the distributive system . . . money for investment . . . for schools, roads, bridges . . . Client–patron relationship helps the clients to diminish the distance between them and the decision centers and bypass the intermediary levels of the super-organization . . . There is no open market on which the resources could be presented and exchanged (Tarkowski, 1983: 503–4, 505, 516; see also Adler Lomnitz, 1988; Eisenstadt and Roninger, 1981).

Besides material rewards, higher-level officials also receive 'power rewards' consisting in 'enhancement of their influence and power through resources supplied by their clients' (Tarkowski, 1983: 510).

In addition to vertical patronage lines there also emerges a common pattern of reciprocal relations among top officials themselves.

> These closed networks of privileged cliques, alienated from the rest of society, [acquire] a feudal mentality, treating the country as their own property and the citizens as their serfs . . . These top officials seek to organize relationships in such a way that every member of the clique has an opportunity to take advantage of the resources controlled by other members . . . This leads [eventually] to the virtual reprivatisation of the state economy, but without the obligations and responsibilities normally involved in private ownership (Łoś, 1987a: 3–4; see also Katsenelinboigen, 1983; Simis, 1982 and Chapters 2, 7, 9 in this volume).

These vertical and horizontal informal links among officials thus become a part of the second economy due to their direct utilisation for private allocation, exchange and control of scarce state resources. The lack of accountability of the élite in a one-party bureaucratised state, coupled with its administrative responsibility for a non-market investment and supply policy, facilitates and provokes the arbitrary use of the state property to enhance private interests.

The illegal entrepreneurship within the state economy becomes widespread when rigid and wasteful plan-based management of the economy nullifies incentives for innovation and improvement within the official economic realm (see Chapters 2, 3, 4, 9, 10 in this volume; for the model descriptions of such enterprises see Majchrzak, 1965; Mars and Altman, 1987; Grossman, 1977; and Łoś, 1988: 189–94). The illegal opportunities for making private profit within the centralised economy result mainly from (see Introduction and Łoś, 1987b):

- mechanical allotments of materials, machines, time, and personnel according to the abstract plan;
- lack of relationship between productivity and remuneration;
- stress on the quantitative goals of the Central Plan, whereby quality is of secondary importance;
- omnipresent waste;
- widespread shortages; and,
- relative labour shortages resulting from the excessive demand for labour in the centralised economy due to the low work intensity, waste, poor organisation, and stress on the quantitative dimension of economic development (employers who do not want to lose workers but cannot offer them sufficient material incentives

may be forced to tolerate illegal economic activities by their employees; see, for example, Cassel and Cichy, 1987: 129; Gabor, 1979: 296–7; Kemeny, 1982: 352–3; Kenedi, 1982: 61).

Extensive black markets are common in all highly regulated, shortage-prone economies. Tight control of producer goods, subsidised prices and frequently rationed foodstuffs and consumer goods as well as overvalued local currency, all drive black-market prices up and entail high exchange rates for hard (convertible) currencies. Moreover, the politically suppressed inflation is likely to be displaced into the black-market area. The system of state distribution becomes highly bureaucratised at the monopolisation stage, and state controlled prices cease to bear any relation to either their 'use' value or their 'exchange value'.[6] The function of money becomes ambiguous when neither production costs nor consumer prices are based on any economic calculation.

The special importance of black markets in the societies studied is a natural result of the guiding Marxist notion of value, which assumes that no value is produced in the process of circulation (Marx, 1962: 274, 177; Solinger, 1984: 13). Accordingly, Marxist states tend to reduce the process of economic distribution to essentially administrative allocation, while traditional operations related to buying and selling are conceived as parasitic and are likely to be outlawed. While free markets attempt to re-establish a semblance of a supply–demand co-ordination mechanism, their criminalisation produces many secondary phenomena typical of any black-market operations.

A high black-market involvement by the legal private sector seems inevitable at the stage of monopolisation. The increased central regulation and attempted integration of the remaining non-nationalised economic units alienates them both politically and economically. Deprived of its necessary market base by the state's control of inputs and prices, private establishments increasingly seek alternative ways of maintaining their profit-oriented operation (see Łoś, 1988: 201–2; Åslund, 1985; and Chapters 2, 3, 8, 10, 11 in this volume).

The relationship between the state economy and the private economy is extremely complex, as each economy tries to take advantage of the other. The private sector is expected to compensate for the failures of the first economy without competing with it. Yet that sector's economic flexibility and efficiency exposes a relative failure of the small-scale state economy where 'all the ordinary efficiency problems of the command economy [are] exacerbated' (Åslund, 1985: 50). On the other hand, the private sector is often accused of a parasitic exploitation of the first economy: taking advantage of its subsidised resources, undermining official price policies, seducing skilled labour with higher wages, and focusing on non-productive tasks, like trade and services.

The illegal underground economy flourishes when conducting a fully legal private business becomes almost impossible, and offers few advantages. The conflict between the underground economy and the state economy has several aspects. Given the security offered by the state employment and the duty to work enforced through anti-parasite legislations, the working time in the illegal business is often supplementary to the regular employment (see Dallago, 1987: 151–2 for a comparison of illegal employment in the West and the East). The pressing economic need for income supplementation, coupled with the attractive wages offered by illegal enterprises, often lead to 'withholding of performance' during the regular hours, absenteeism, generally lowered productivity and easy appropriation of state tools and materials. All these factors further increase the gap between the volume of goods produced and the amount of cash available to consumers (see, for example, Cassel and Cichy, 1987: 138, 141). In an economic context which is plagued by shortage and cash balance inflation – where official efforts strive to suppress rather than increase the demand for goods – these processes must have a destabilising effect. On the other hand, the inflated black economy prices reduce somewhat the demand-boosting impact of the underground remuneration. (This effect is especially pronounced when price differentials between subsidised state prices of basic goods and inflated black-market prices create powerful incentives for a speculative diversion of state-distributed goods into the illegal circulation.)

In short, 'the underground activities increase shortage in the market of investment goods and services and only slightly attenuate shortage in the market of consumption goods and services' (Dallago, 1987: 160). While the actual consumption of goods and services is enhanced by the Underground offer so is the demand for them. Clearly, however, the underground economy plays the role of a buffer and provides short-term benefits to the troubled first economy. As long as the problems of the latter are perceived to be temporary – as is usually the case at the monopolisation stage – the policed and condemned, but *de facto* tolerated, illegal economy presents a viable surrogate for reforms within the planned economy (Cassel and Cichy,

1987: 142; Grossman, 1982: 262). Unlike the legal private business, it does not force the party-state to revise its ideological and political commitments.

The economic resistance in the countryside is related to the situation, common at the monopolisation stage, whereby a forceful collectivisation or villagisation (as, for example, in Tanzania) reverses the possible advantage gained by peasants in the initial phase of the land reform.[7] Although Nicaragua is far from being a typical case in so far as it has not fully entered the period of monopolisation, its two-stage agrarian reform well exemplifies the above-mentioned policy shifts. During the early 'anti-Somocista phase' (1979–81):

> many farms had been occupied by peasants and agricultural workers . . . [T]he lease prices of lands destined for cotton and basic grains cultivation [were reduced] . . . [T]he new lease contracts displayed a preference for the small farmers associated in cooperatives [and] medium farmers . . . [At the second stage (post-July 1981)] cooperative production has received a very strong push. Eighty three percent of the land was allocated to cooperatives and only 17 percent to individual farmers . . . In some regions the stimulus to cooperative production had to deal not only with the preference of the peasants for individual production, but also the business organization FUNDE . . . that emphasized the peasant as property owner' (Vilas, 1986, excerpts from pp. 165–7).

Policies of collectivisation tend to provoke systematic attempts at reprivatisation and de-formalisation of the peasant economy. For example, in Cuba in the late 1960s:

> [i]n constricting the activities of small farmers and in eliminating the use of private plots by workers on state farms, the government sacrificed maximum production and profit within individual units for maximum economywide export production for profit. [However,] farmers profited more from producing for the domestic market, in part because they could take advantage of a black market (Eckstein, 1985: 224; see also Rumer, 1981 and Timofeev, 1982 on the Soviet 'second agriculture' in the 1970s; Sampson, 1983 on the Romanian peasant resistance; Oi, 1985 and Selden, 1985 on rural politics in China).

Likewise, the reaction of Tanzanian peasants to the forceful villagisation and a bloc farming scheme designed to increase agricultural production through coercion 'was either to produce less of the government required crops and retain more for their own consumption or dispose their produce through black-market channels' (Kiondo, Chapter 11 in this volume).

Characteristically, the official authorisation of even tiny personal plots for state farm workers brings about a massive diversion of state resources to these family holdings. This process is exemplified by the behaviour of Cuban state farm workers who, deprived of their small plots in the 1960s, were authorised to acquire them again in the 1970s:

> [Soon] public resources intended for state farms began to be used for private gain, and farmers sold their poorest quality output to the state while reserving the best for the more profitable free markets . . . The opportunity for profits, in turn, gave rise to a new stratum of intermediaries . . . Apparently because vendors and farmers . . . siphoned off surplus that the state itself wished to appropriate, the government issued new market regulations in the early 1980s (Eckstein, 1985: 233–4).

Similar mechanisms are present in the case of Romanian peasants for whom 'the collective farm functions as both a workplace and as a resource . . . [A]n efficient collective is one which provides enough resources to maintain a well-functioning household enterprise' (Sampson, 1983: 69, 70; Chapter 5 in this volume).

These forms of resistance have several layers of meaning. They signify the traditional peasant detestation of subordination to the state. They result from practical problems associated with legally obtaining necessary supplies. They also are likely to constitute a self-defence reaction to abject exploitation. For example, talking about the situation of Soviet state farm workers (*kolkhozniks*), who have been authorised to hold small family plots in order to release the state from the duty to compensate them for their labour, Timofeev notes that

> [a] peasant family is a microcapitalistic enterprise where the head of the family is required to exploit the labor of his dependants, to obtain from the personal farm the maximum surplus value and so make up for the necessary product not received by them on the collective and state farms (Timofeev, 1982: 13).

Sampson echoes this view in his comparative essay on the second economy in the Soviet Union and Eastern Europe: 'The collective farm's personal plot system can be viewed as a form of exploitation in which the collective frees itself from the obligation of paying the peasants a decent wage' (Sampson, 1987: 128).

The rapid growth of the network-based informal second economy with complex linkages to the first and second economies and to the state bureaucracy is also characteristic of the monopolisation stage of the Marxist development. It is expressed in the preponderance of connections, back-door tactics, bureaucratic corruption and informal self-help economies. They are often employed to secure essential commodities initially pledged to be delivered to all citizens by right. These practices express also more general social attempts at informa-lisation and individualisation of the access to the bureaucracies that regulate and regiment all aspects of life. Concomitant developments involve massive informal channelling of state goods for individualised redistribution, as well as the increasing role of middlemen and small-scale speculators. Moreover, the introduction of the rationing system and awards in kind – frequent at this stage – leads inevitably to the expansion of the grey markets to counteract the mechanical, uniform systems of the controlled distribution: 'People would buy their full quotas and engage in informal trades with friends and relatives until they wound up with the items they preferred' (Eck-stein, 1985: 232 with respect to Cuba; see also Chapters 5, 7, 8 and 10 in this volume).

In turn, the realisation that shortages are not a temporary phe-nomenon leads to the expansion of the informal economy in the form of self-help and self-defence strategies adopted by individual house-holds and family-based networks. They involve tapping workplace resources, moonlighting, petty household production, family plots, barter and exchange of labour. Besides their direct economic func-tion, these forms of informal economy can also be viewed as a grassroots defence against the official stigmatisation of the whole informal social sphere as politically unworthy or subversive.

Since all these practices are generally viewed as necessary strategies of survival, the moral boundaries are usually expanded to accommodate them. A Chinese writer's comment written in 1975 could have been made about any other country included in this study:

Everybody . . . knows about the backdoor. It means using your personal connections to bribe people with money or material goods so you can get something you can't obtain through normal ways, through the 'front door' . . . it is a major part of our life. When you have scarcities and a privileged group, then you have a society full of backdoors. The backdoor can be found at the top, in government organs, in the Party, in the army, through the entire system right down to the very bottom. The general gets his marble bathtub through the backdoor, and the ordinary worker his . . . bicycle the same way. People take the backdoor for granted and do not regard using it as something disgraceful or 'antisocialist'. On the contrary, those who know how to use the backdoor are regarded as clever people, whereas those who don't are considered stupid . . . It is really an informal system for bartering and redistributing food and a few necessities of life . . . What makes the common people angry is the abuse of the Big Backdoor by higher level government, Party and army officials (Frolic, 1980: 128–30).

Likewise, Oi argues that '[t]he use of personal relationships [*quanxi* or *ganqing*] to pursue one's interests is so prevalent in China that it is "almost legal"; one's ability to use connections to go through the back door is a mark of status and intelligence' (Oi, 1985: 252; also Chapters 8, 10 in this volume). Brezinski and Petersen (Chapter 5 in this volume) also mention a comparable distortion of moral standards in Romania where citizens' feelings that they give much more to the state than they receive justify illegal ways of rectifying this situation.

Naturally, the existence of an informal economy is not unique to Marxist societies. Yet, the need for the informal economy, its structure and its ideological and legal status vary greatly across different economic systems. While in the West the need for the informal economy is concentrated more among immigrant and other minorities, low income neighbourhoods and 'post-industrial subcultures' (Gershuny, 1979; Henry, 1978; Nicholls and Dyson, 1983) in non-market economies it is vital for all social strata as a mechanism of re-allocation of resources based on the individual need and not on an anonymous plan. It is a soft infrastructure which fills the vacuum between the bureaucratic state and the individual (for interesting ethnographic studies see Adler Lomnitz, 1988; Bednarski, 1987; Pawlik, 1985; Sampson, 1983, 1986; and Wedel, 1986).

Yet, there are important similarities between informal economies of Marxist and non-Marxist developing states. Both are conditioned by such perennial and inherited phenomena as the structural effects of unequal development and urban overpopulation, accompanied by the prevalence of poverty and traditionally large segments of the population relying on the survival economy. The informal activities in non-Marxist states are often tapped by the profit-seeking formal enterprises and can be viewed as an indirect exploitation of the people involved (Portes and Sassen-Koob, 1987; Portes, 1978). Nonetheless, they allow for economic participation and active market involvement by the majority of the population and contribute to the national productive output (see Sethuraman, 1981; *CUSO Journal*, 1987). In Marxist states, on the other hand, the politicisation of the economic management, the low productivity of the plan-oriented state economy, and official control over prices and supplies engender an informal economy which is extremely time- and energy-consuming, but remains mostly redistributive and corrective. Moreover, while it provides a weapon for consumers in their dealings with both the state economy and the money-based second economy, in the process it not only subordinates them to both, but also converts friendship and other human relationships into commodities essential to the satisfaction of material needs.

These countries' informal economies are often viewed as predetermined by the cultural heritage or unique historical experience of the nations or ethnic groups concerned, be it the economic underground in Nazi-occupied Poland (see Chapter 3 in this volume); 'Balkan mentality' and a 'legacy of Ottoman domination' in the case of Romania (quoted in Sampson, 1983: 53); the czarist heritage of bureaucratic corruption in Russia; or the kin-network-based, 'honour and shame', risk-taking culture of Soviet Georgia (Mars and Altman, 1983). Yet the reference to these unique national traits does not help explicate the striking similarities in the informal economy patterns in different Marxist states, especially conspicuous during the monopolisation phase.

In most East European societies, official explanations blame rural migration for the transmission of backward social patterns to the newly industrialised cities. More profound and objective academic research have lent this interpretation some credibility. Kemeny, for example, describes the Hungarian informal economy as 'rooted in peasant traditions' (Chapter 4 in this volume), Gorostiaga refers to 'urban peasants' when he stresses that the informal economy in Nicaragua operates on similar lines to the peasant economy (1985: 20), and Sampson highlights traditional cultural values in the Soviet Union and Eastern block countries that 'prioritize primary kin affiliations over allegiance to formal institutions like workplace' and make nepotism 'a moral duty' (1987: 132). While these insights have undoubtedly some sociological value, they cannot account for the accelerated growth of the second economy in those countries where the major influx of peasants to urban centres took place at least one generation earlier. Jean Oi demonstrates that it is misleading to make superficial assumptions about intact cultural continuity in the face of a radical politico–economic change:

> There are striking similarities between . . . descriptions of the pre-1949 Chinese countryside, where personal relationships (*ganqing*) formed the 'fabric of Chinese society' and the [current situation]. It would be a mistake, however, to think that the fabric is the same. Under the collectivised agriculture, peasants have fewer opportunities to cultivate the multistranded patron–client networks . . . with the local official, the landlord, the rice merchant, the middle-men buyers, and the various peddlers. Under socialism, the sale and procurement of essential goods and services are funnelled through a single, state approved local official, team leader, or state cooperative store . . . Clientism in China is comparable to authority relations in feudal or traditional pre-market agrarian settings in that peasants are almost totally dependent upon a single élite. The type of dependence and the power of the élite . . . are significantly different, however (Oi, 1985: 263).

Clearly, each economic and political formation creates its own social responses and informal solutions, mediated but not fully determined by cultural traditions and the inherited collective psychology.

The Reformist Stage

The monopolisation stage is often interrupted by periods of a reformist activity only to be superseded by new conservative-monopolistic policies, as in the case of Lenin's NEP in the 1920s and Kosygin's 1965 planning reform in the USSR, Mao's early 1950s experiment in market-plan economy, or Cuban market-oriented reforms of the late 1970s and early 1980s. The most significant current reforms under way in the 1980s are those unfolding in China (initiated in 1979), the Soviet Union (1987) and Tanzania (1984). The 1970s belonged to Hungary and Poland, but the ill-fated Polish reforms were eventually substituted with foreign credits and imports of Western technology, and Hungary moved towards a re-centralisation of the nationalised economy in the face of the rapid expansion of the private sector (Laky, 1980).

Generally, when the period of industrial mobilisation and reconstruction is over, the question of low productivity and its organisational causes comes to the fore. The party leadership's realisation of the intrinsic limitations of the centralised command economy is likely to prompt two types of reform that attempt to introduce certain elements of market: (i) internal reforms of the state economy and/or (ii) a partial legitimisation of the second economy.

The first type of reform aims normally at a decentralisation and movement away from the detailed proscriptive planning to a more liberal, indicative planning model. The latter involves usually a version of a parametric state management whereby wages, prices, taxes and interest rates are manipulated to achieve centrally planned economic objectives (Zieliński, 1974: 66; see also Dyker, 1985 and Prybyla, 1987). Yet, even in a country so far removed from the traditional command model as Yugoslavia, the central plan remains a legally binding economic instrument (for a discussion of the model of labour-managed planned-market-economy introduced in Yugoslavia in 1976, see Choksi, 1979: 176–81; Knight, 1983: 82–106; and Prybyla, 1987: 8–12, 246–57).

The market-oriented revisions of the centrally planned model have been inspired by the so-called market-socialism model originally devised by Oskar Lange. In broad lines, this proposal called for a free-market allocation of consumer goods, while preserving the planned distribution of investment goods. According to this conception, state enterprises should react to the consumer market and seek profits. In a recent assessment of this model, Prybyla has elaborated several reasons why it has proven to be impracticable. These include: (i) the high computational costs of fixing prices of producer goods; (ii) the artificial separation of the market for consumer goods from the allocation of industrial inputs; (iii) the disregard for the importance of motivation; and (iv) the assumption that planners will always respond to threatened shortages and surplaces by adjusting prices, and that 'they will not try to foist their output preferences on consumers by determining the volume and assortment of consumer goods and by fixing appropriate prices to clear the shelves' (Prybyla, 1987: 7).

The central planning of investments is one of the key areas that ensure the state's control over the economy. Its decentralisation would threaten state priorities and economic power – and, consequently, the interests of the party hierarchy. Yet, the political management of the distribution of investment goods and input supplies undermines any attempt to introduce market mechanisms into the state economy. As Dyker notes, ministerial administrators and local party secretaries, who are judged by their skills in wrestling out the greatest share of resources, 'must make systematic use of political influence and cajolery to keep supply lines open' (Dyker, 1985: 64). Market-oriented reforms within the planned economy are thus not likely to lessen the subordination of the production to political interests, clientisms and corruption. The introduction of the profit principle at the enterprise level and focusing on sales of outputs instead of on the volume of the produced goods also offer a limited chance of reviving the economy. Sales of producer goods remain normally secured by the plan, and captive consumers in undersupplied consumer goods markets are not very fastidious. The quality of the goods may be sacrificed for the sake of profits, and – in the case of partial deregulation of prices – the consumer may be simply charged more for goods in short supply, with no attempt to improve either the quality or the volume of the output (as, for example, in Poland in the 1980s – see Landau, 1987: 178).

As far as the second economy is concerned, reforms of this type open certain new opportunities and incentives for the illegal private enterprise within the first economy. When the state economy units are free to structure their production more flexibly, they can more easily accommodate additional private lines of business. In addition, the self-financing enterprises, operating in a basically non-market context which typically entails labour shortages, are often compelled to offer extra income opportunities and other informal perquisites to their employees in order to secure their co-operation. Since any market-oriented reforms in communist countries tend to be viewed favourably by western governments and international agencies, they are often assisted by foreign credits and imports of Western technology (as in the case of the Soviet reforms in the late 1960s; Hungary and Poland in the 1970s; and China in the early 1980s). The influx of these highly desirable resources sharply increases inequality among enterprises and localities, each depending on the political clout and shrewdness of the managers and officials involved. With such high stakes, the use of illegal means and bribery becomes increasingly common, used not only to attract these new resources to the particular units of the state economy but also to divert them towards the second economy projects.

The second type of reform calls for a legitimisation of certain areas of the economically successful private activity. Yet, the continued state control over input markets and the lack of competition over output sales markets deprive this sector of viable internal regulation mechanisms. Moreover, the official laws regulating private business are not normally grounded in a coherent individualistic philosophy pertinent to this type of business and, thus, they tend to be vague, contradictory and subject to frequent changes (as evidenced in preceding chapters in this volume). They attempt to preserve the private sector's secondary status, keep its development in check and integrate it economically into the overall, planned system. Consequently, the promotion of the market mentality on the one hand, and doubtful and volatile benefits of launching a legal private business on the other, enhance rather than diminish the interest in the illegal private entrepreneurship. Legal private enterprises may, however, be conveniently used as fronts for these operations.

Mixed reactions to new Soviet legislation, on individual enterprise (for information on this law, see *Izvestia*, 30 April 1987: 6 and 9 September 1987: 3) and quasi-private co-operatives (for the text of the law see *Pravda*, 8 June 1987: 4–7) which constitute a part of Mikhail Gorbachev's reform programme well illustrate the problems resulting from the unclear ideological status of the newly regulated activities. On the one hand, a dramatic shift in official labelling takes place, as exemplified by an article in a Soviet magazine, which praises the initiative of a newly formed co-operative whose

> six young members travel to the south, buy up vegetables, fruits and flowers grown by individuals and farms, and sell them at . . . open markets . . . Quite recently [they] would have been labeled speculators, possibly liable to prosecution, but under the new conditions of restructuring, their activity is now viewed as useful (Komrakov, 1987: 6).

On the other hand, the Soviet press expresses several concerns common among officials at various levels of the economic hierarchy: that co-operatives will 'entail an outflow of manpower from state enterprises', that they will pose 'undesirable competition' to the state economy, and that 'under cover of the new law, underground production activity and illicit operations will develop' (Feofanov, 1987: 8). But the media also refer to the fears of potential entrepreneurs who 'remember the fate of the "Nepmen". And they remember how afterwards – after the industrial cooperatives were done away with – some people found themselves a long way from home' (Dmitrenko, 1987: 4). The reformist camp seems haunted by the ghosts of earlier periods as evidenced in inevitable parallels with the NEP era made by various Soviet commentators. An historian from the USSR Academy of Sciences sums up the lessons of that experiment:

> the NEP . . . laid bare the state's economic weakness . . . And the faster we moved into the NEP, the sooner it laid bare the contradictions between the state's capabilities, on the one hand, and the potential of capitalist and small-scale production, on the other (Dmitrenko, 1987: 1).

Perhaps to offset these perils, the CPSU Central Committee passed a special resolution in November 1987 to ensure that the ostensibly promoted private activities are not left to develop spontaneously:

> The USSR Ministry of Finance, the USSR State Planning Committee, the USSR State Price Committee, the USSR Ministry of Justice, the USSR Ministry of Internal Affairs and the USSR Prosecutor's Office have been instructed to step up supervision over the cooperatives' economic activity. They are to put a stop to instances of deception of the state, speculation and the improper distribution of income ('The Cooperative . . .', 1987: 10).

Both the reforms within the state economy and those promoting some measure of privatisation and legalisation of the second economy are likely to lead to selective and arbitrary price increases. Yet prices cannot be moulded by market forces because of the fluidity of non-convertible domestic currencies, whose value is determined by administrative decisions. The whole system of calculation of prices is therefore distorted by selective state subsidies for some producer- and consumer-goods and by the Marxist tradition of operating on the basis of the volume of goods, and not their exchange value. Price increases, instead of reducing market imbalances, tend thus to exacerbate them, and further to weaken the local currency. This leads, in turn, to a broader expansion of the barter economy that at this stage, involves even whole units of the state economy.[8] Furthermore, the role of 'hard' (convertible) currencies expands rapidly, and increasing areas of black-market operations are conducted exclusively in foreign currency. If the state experiences difficulties in meeting its foreign debt obligations or import requirements, it too is likely to turn to the black market to tap its resources. Additionally, the government may lengthen the list of goods which are available solely or primarily through the state-run hard-currency stores.[9] Such policies both stimulate black markets in foreign currency and channel this currency into the state coffers.

The above-mentioned market-oriented reforms repudiate the ideology of equality and, in reality, trigger growing economic disparities. This is, however, due not so much to the greater differentiation of official wage scales but, above all, to greater – both legal and illegal – private opportunities for profits and the growing role of hard currencies. By the same token, inflation – both official and within the second economy – has an uneven impact on different groups and strata, aggravating existing divisions.

While the market-oriented reforms aim both at the first and the second economy, each of these economies reacts to them differently. The second economy – being already market-based – responds quickly by both branching out into newly legalised areas and by exploiting illegal opportunities created by contradictory and difficult transformations within the first economy. The first economy, on the other hand, resists reforms at all levels of its bureaucratic and political organisation. According to the estimate by Gorbachev's top economic advisor, Professor Aganbegyan, it will take 20 to 30 years to implement the current reforms in the Soviet Union ('The Soviet Economy', 1988: 4). Rural reforms may be easier, however, and due to the relative isolation of the village economy, local officials may be able to redefine their roles from the enforcers of the plan to gatekeepers and mediators between the privatised economy and the state. This, indeed, is the case in rural China, where in the early 1980s state quotas were replaced by contractual arrangements between peasants and the state. According to the research conducted by Oi:

> once it became clear that the reforms were here to stay, the cadres quickly and easily moved into positions as the new middlemen in the system, ready and able to broker available opportunities and gain control over as many resources as possible ... They have securely entrenched themselves as the middlemen in this transitional system that is somewhere between plan and market (Oi, 1986: 15).

Yet, probably the most important implication of economic reforms for the second economy is the fact that the distinction between legal and illegal markets becomes blurred. This is especially true when reforms are vaguely formulated and communicated differently to different economic actors, as has been the case with most reforms within Marxist states. Finally, while some parts of the illegal second economy may be targeted for successful prosecution, its shifting definitions create confusion and its growth appears by and large uncontrollable. Therefore, in place of an image of a powerful control apparatus, there emerges a perception of a system of control which is erratic, corruptible, torn by contradictions and saturated by a feudal-style bureaucracy.

The Post-reformist Decadence

This stage is reached by those countries where – as in Yugoslavia, Hungary, and Poland – a whole range of economic reforms have been tried and failed. Far from being uniform, this stage has assumed a very different form in each of the three countries mentioned.

Yugoslavia, with its uncontrollable inflation, considerable unemployment problem, the underdeveloped state economy, the hard-currency-based second economy and the decentralised state, is verging on total chaos.

Hungary has become increasingly economically polarised, with its large entrepreneurial élite being gradually alienated from the impoverished society, and the state economy petrified and exhausted after a succession of promising but in the long run unsuccessful reforms.

Poland has become a *de facto* dual power society where the state's futile attempts at reforming from above are countered by a massive resistance of a semi-organised unofficial society with its unique forms of labour solidarity, Church-protected grass-roots organising, a well-developed second culture, and the vast second economy.

The protracted political stalemate and deepening economic crisis in all three of these countries can be linked to the weakening of the authoritarian state by the countless, yet barren, reforms which have contributed to the severe aggravation of the long-present contradictions of the 'market state socialism' model.

Typical for this stage, a forced marriage of the state- and market-economies not only heightens their respective intrinsic contradictions, but it also triggers attempts on the part of each economy to exploit the other in a largely parasitic, politicised and economically non-competitive manner. The controllers of the first economy want to have its problems solved through the second economy, but to protect the state economy's long-term hegemony. The market-oriented second economy operators – forced into a short-term perspective – fight for a greater share of the scarce producer goods, but their contribution to the supply and quality of the consumer goods is out of proportion to the increased money circulation achieved through the underground employment and speculative business profits. As well, the private market production is increasingly oriented towards luxury goods to satisfy demand of relatively enriched groups, leaving the general population unable to use the market economy to their own ends. The pressure of the unsatisfied demand is thus increased rather than decreased, and the society at large is torn between the state and the market, both of which lack effective restraints on labour exploitation and manipulation.

In fact, by permitting informal market employment opportunities for state employees, the state is able to maximise exploitation not only of the workers themselves, but also their families. The extra employment often involves efforts of other family members and the extensive use of informal networks and resources simply to achieve a minimal standard of living which should be provided by labour wages alone. In this sense, the informal economy appears to subsidise wages in the official economy.[10] This strategy allows the state to maintain a suppressed wage structure, even in the face of inflationary tendencies released by the reforms. On the other hand, the universal problems of the market economy – and especially the contradiction between private capital and labour – are aggravated in the situation where privately employed workers are unlikely to be protected by labour legislations and social security provisions. This forces many of them to handle two jobs in order to secure social insurance benefits offered by state employment. The first and second economy pressures on the worker are thus mutually reinforcing.

Additional problems and contradictions stem from the fact that the authorised limited privatisation assumes the existence of only one model of a supplementary quasi-market economy. Yet, within the social consciousness the unofficial economic activities belong to several quite separate spheres: the capitalist-style market economy, petty commodity economy, and self-help economy. Each of them is ruled by its own customary laws and economic logic. The partial legitimisation and uniform regulation of these spheres by the state prevent them from developing along their distinct lines, and may obstruct rather than facilitate the pursuit of legitimate goals of the population.

With regard to the external economic pressures, the state economy's subordination to the supreme policy of integration within the

Council of Mutual Economic Assistance (CMEA or Comecon) hampers the market-oriented reforms in member countries, as well as their search for independent solutions. So far, the reforms of the internal CMEA rules, initiated by the Soviet leadership in 1986, have not significantly alleviated the situation. And their attempts to accommodate Soviet economic reforms imply in part a greater direct integration between Soviet enterprises and those in other bloc countries (Åslund, 1988; also van Brabant, 1987). The non-member Marxist states, on the other hand, must face the incompatible demands and pressures of their integration into the world economy of both capitalist and Marxist types.

CONCLUSIONS AND FINAL COMPARISONS

The most general view confirmed in many studies, both in the East and the West, maintains that the second economy grows with greater regulation and increased size of the public sector, which automatically suggests a prominent role of the second economy in Marxist states (Choksi, 1979; Gulhati and Sekhar, 1981; Grossman, 1982; Gutmann, 1977: 26; Pendse, 1984: 5; Ray, 1981: 6; Singh, 1984: 25–36; Tanzi, 1983).

More specific causes of the second economy within the Western world have been identified as high taxation, the increased role of trade unions and labour legislations, recession and unemployment, the existence of marginalised – often immigrant – populations; and pressures of competition (including foreign competition). The latter pushes underground the more labour-intensive branches of legitimate firms to avoid taxes and other costs.

In East European countries, on the other hand, the system-specific causes of the second economy include the general ineffectiveness and bureaucratisation of the first economy, inherent problems of the central planning, underemployment and hidden labour reserves, state control of industrial input, central regulation of prices and related market imbalances, mechanical policies of equalisation (including rationing of basic goods), overregulation of the private sector and coercive policies towards the essentially family-oriented agriculture. These factors are present also in developing Marxist states, where – however – they operate jointly with other structural factors responsible for stimulating the second economy in Third World countries. They include rapid growth of the impoverished urban population, the clash between traditional and modern modes of production, colonial strategies of dual economy and other aspects of colonial heritage, patterns of dependence, external trade and foreign aid.

As demonstrated in this chapter, different stages of the Marxist development stimulate – or even necessitate – certain informal economic practices. A complex, cumulative process seems to be taking place whereby the patterns of the second economy formed at earlier stages become entrenched with time and are further developed, revised, and supplemented by new practices, at later stages. The process of the growth of the second economy cannot, however, be separated from the process of development of the official economy, as they both constitute the necessary mutually dependent aspects of the 'ideal–typical' sequence of the Marxist development.

Likewise, the capitalist second economy is not a fixed, stable and ahistorical feature, but is highly dependent on the cyclical nature of capitalist development. In those countries, too, different formations are likely to co-exist, and their relationships are sensitive to economic changes at both national and world levels. Economic crises and recession are likely to cause a movement from the formal to the informal economy (Grancelli, 1987; Cassel and Cichy, 1987). As established by Portes and Sassen-Koob, during the recession of the mid-1970s large industries 'with a vertically organized and tightly controlled waged labour force, proved ill-adapted to the new economic circumstances' whereby demand was rapidly contracting and production costs were rising due to the oil-related price increases (1987: 53). They also found:

> informalisation [to be] most likely when a profit squeeze, brought about by increasing labor costs or competition from cheaper foreign goods [usually manufactured in the Third World countries], combines with the possibility of decentralizing work arrangements and the availability of a labor force to do so ... [T]he very circumstances of the economic crisis and efforts to cope with it create an abundant labor supply that further encourages and facilitates informalisation (Portes and Sassen-Koob, 1987: 54, 55).

Based on his observations of the Italian economy, Grancelli also argues that the 1970s' recession and related fiscal problems caused a sharp increase in the second economy, decentralisation of entrepreneurial functions, re-emergence of the local community, and the diminished role of the state and trade unions. Moonlighting opportunities helped contain the industrial conflict and maintain social integration. It thus appears that when the dominant forms of the economy experience an acute crisis, pre-existing patterns of economic and social organisation re-emerge and bring about a measure of de-regulation and de-formalisation (Grancelli, 1987: 260–6). In addition to having a politically mollifying effect, the informalisation reaction in the West is likely to stimulate the official economy, as it increases demand due to unofficial incomes which are used in part to buy products from the official sector. Moreover, 'most activities in the second economy require certain crude products from the official economy', thus causing positive spillover effects into the first economy (Cassel and Cichy, 1987: 140). As was shown earlier, the increased demand in Marxist countries exacerbates the crisis by aggravating market imbalances.

In contrast to Marxist states, the informal economy in industrial capitalist societies does not represent a viable competition, and does not pose a long-term threat to the dominant economic relations. It acts as a built-in stabiliser without undermining the core socio–economic structure. The second economy in Marxist states, on the other hand, presents a serious economic and ideological competition, and a long-term threat to the party-state economy. When attempts to counter-balance it by solidifying the first economy's structure along the orthodox ideological lines provoke instead more developed forms of the second economy, quasi-market reforms are undertaken to neutralise and co-opt them. Tensions and contradictory pressures – both economic and political – resulting from the attempts to accommodate two radically different ideologies in a mechanically constructed model are not likely, however, to enhance the performance of the Marxist economy in a lasting manner. The stage of post-reformist decadence, which follows the reformist phase, reveals several significant facts and possibilities:

- The process of Marxist development leads eventually to the weakening of the monopolistic state, and may therefore force it to seek legitimacy in totally new ways – based, for example, on far-reaching privatisation and marketisation of the economy and, thus, inevitable convergence with the capitalist system.
- The weakening of the state may also provoke an introduction of a military rule in lesser Marxist states, or engagement in new military ventures by the Soviet Union; but these developments, instead of ameliorating economic problems, could only compound them.

- The gradual withdrawal from the ideological dogmas of the earlier era signals a pivotal shift from the ideological–totalitarian to the pragmatic–authoritarian mode of thinking. And since narrow pragmatists both in the East and the West see the mixed market-state economy option as a viable and workable long-term goal for Soviet-style economies, a broad co-operation between the East and the West – mediated by international economic organisations – is likely to develop, whereby the ideological differences will ostensibly lose significance. The Marxist states will not overcome their under-development, but they will break their isolation. Eventually, however, the pragmatic model's potential for maintaining order will be exhausted and the chaotic phase of decadence may spread throughout the Marxist world, leaving individual nations free to decide independently on their path to recovery.

NOTES

1. On this point, the authors of Chapter 7, Michalowski and Zatz, differ somewhat from such authors as Eckstein, 1985; Mesa-Lago, 1981; Packenham, 1986; Pérez-Lopez, 1986.
2. It has been argued that Cuba has benefitted economically from its foreign trade concentration within the CMEA community (for example, Carciofi, 1983: 216–20), and indeed the Soviet Union has been subsidising Cuba heavily for geopolitical reasons. Yet this policy has also had clearly negative consequences for Cuba's development. Since the CMEA countries are interested in Cuban sugar and minerals but not in its industrial products, its manufacturing sector remains backward. Moreover, due to conditions imposed by the CMEA, Cuba cannot use the export revenues earned from the Soviet bloc to purchase technologically more advanced Western goods (Eckstein, 1985: 228–9, 242; see also Pérez-Lopez, 1986: 21).
3. For an interesting, essentially socialist, discussion of the evolution and conflict within the Chinese model of the revolutionary development, see White (1983b).
4. Gordon White, in his overview of socialist development in the Third World, has distinguished three key phases: (i) revolutionary voluntarism; (ii) bureaucratic voluntarism (or the institutionalised revolution); (iii) reformism and market socialism (White, 1983a: 31–3). While my four stage model bears some similarity to White's portrayal of the socialist transition, it is more complex and broader in scope as it attempts to accommodate both the Third World states and the European Soviet bloc countries.
5. Several good examples of such legislations are provided in the preced-

ing chapters, among them the extremely harsh Law on Discipline at the Workplace in Angola and the similarly repressive Angolan Labour Code (both enacted in the late 1970s – see Chapter 10), as well as the Human Resources Deployment Act and the Economic Sabotage Act in Tanzania (passed in 1983 – see Chapter 11). Moreover, in the post-Stalinist consolidation period the Soviet bloc countries in Europe replaced the earlier *ad hoc* legislations and decrees, that criminalised labour indiscipline, with expanded penal code sections on economic crimes, which included the death penalty for exceptionally serious categories (see, for example, Łoś, 1988: 209; van den Berg, 1983: 154–74). As well, during the 1960s all East European countries, with the exception of Poland, emulated the 1961 Soviet anti-parasite legislation which formalised the duty to work and backed it with criminal sanctions (see Łoś, 1988: 78–104). Finally, Cuba – which in the second part of the 1980s has experienced a vigorous return of the monopolisation policies – has expanded its list of economic crimes, increased penalties for the existing ones, and revised its law on social parasitism despite a general tendency to reduce the number of offences in its new Penal Code passed in 1988 (Planas, 1988).

6.   Within Marxist theory, 'use value' relates to a product's ability to satisfy a human need, and 'exchange value' concerns 'the product's relation to other goods on the market, and is established . . . by the amount of labor time socially necessary to produce it' (Solinger, 1984: 14).

7.   See chapters on Poland, Hungary, Romania, China, Angola and Tanzania in this volume. See also Selden, 1985: 276–85 on the 1940s land reform and 1953–6 process of collectivisation in China; Eckstein, 1985, on two stage (1959 and 1963) land reform in Cuba; Wädekin (1973) on post-Stalinist measures against private plots in the USSR (1958–60) and the extensive literature on the Stalinist methods of collectivisation.

8.   Tarkowski, for example, talks about a 'parallel barter economy' organised by the state institutions in Poland of the 1980s (1983: 502), and dos Santos, in Chapter 10, maintains that Angolan official enterprises increasingly revert to barter as currency continues to lose its value.

9.   For example, in Poland during the early 1970s, the period of modernisation of industry which relied heavily on Western imports, alcohol sales in hard-currency stores increased by more than 24 times between 1970 and 76 (Wald *et al.*, 1981).

10.   A similar phenomenon has been noted by Portes (1978) in Latin America.

REFERENCES

Adler Lomnitz, L., 'Informal Exchange Networks in Formal Systems: A Theoretical Model', *American Anthropologist*, 901 (1) (1988) pp. 42–55.

Alavi, H., 'The State in Post-Colonial Societies – Pakistan and Bangladesh', *New Left Review*, 74 (July–August, 1972) pp. 59–81.

Åslund, A., *Private Enterprise in Eastern Europe* (London: Macmillan, 1985).

Åslund, A., 'The New Soviet Policy Towards International Economic Organisations', *The World Today* (February 1988) pp. 27–30.

Bednarski, M., 'Gospodarka drugiego obiegu a kryzys lat 80-tych' (The Second Economy and the 1980s' crisis), in M. Marody and A. Sułek (eds), *Rzeczywistość Polska i Sposoby Radzenia Sobie z Nią* (Warsaw: UW, 1987).

Carciofi, R., 'Cuba in the Seventies', in G. White, R. Murray and Ch. White (eds), *Revolutionary Socialist Development in the Third World* (Lexington, Mass.: The University Press of Kentucky, 1983) pp. 193–233.

Cassel, D. and U. Cichy, 'The Shadow Economy and Economic Policy in East and West', in S. Alessandrini in B. Dallago (eds), *The Unofficial Economy* (Aldershot: Gower, 1987).

Choksi, A. M., *State Intervention in the Industrialization of Developing Countries: Selected Issues* (Washington, D.C.: The World Bank, July 1979).

'Cuba's New Image', *The Economist* (7 May 1988) pp. 36–7.

CUSO Journal, issue on *The Informal Economy* (Ottawa: CUSO, December 1987).

Dallago, B., 'The Underground Economy in the West and the East: A Comparative Approach', in S. Alessandrini and B. Dallago (eds), *The Unofficial Economy* (Aldershot: Gower, 1987) pp. 147–64.

Davis, P., *Where is Nicaragua?* (New York: Simon & Schuster, 1987).

Dmitrenko, V. P., 'Are "Real" Cooperatives a Lost Art?', *Izvestia* (3 October) in *The Current Digest of the Soviet Press* (11 November 1987) pp. 1–5.

Dyker, D. A., *The Future of the Soviet Economic Planning System* (London: Croom Helm, 1985).

Eckstein, S., 'State and Market Dynamic in Castro's Cuba', in P. Evans, D. Rueschemeyer and E. Huber Stephens (eds), *States Versus Markets in the World System* (Beverly Hills: Sage, 1985) pp. 217–45.

Eisenstadt, S. N. and L. Roninger, 'Clientelism in Communist Systems: A Comparative Perspective', *Studies in Comparative Communism*, XIV (2, 3) (1981) pp. 233–45.

Feofanov, Yu, 'Legal Dialogues', *Izvestia* (24 April) in *The Current Digest of the Soviet Press* (3 June 1987) pp. 8–9.

Fitzgerald, V., 'Some Aspects of Economic Management in the Nicaraguan Revolution', in G. White and K. Young (eds), *Nicaragua After the Revolution: Problems and Prospects* (Sussex: Institute of Development Studies, 1985) pp. 9–13.

Frolic, M. B., *Mao's People* (Cambridge, Mass.: Harvard University Press, 1980).

Gabor, I. R., 'The Second (Secondary) Economy', *Acta Oeconomica*, XXII (3–4) (1979) pp. 291–311.

Gershuny, J. I., 'The Informal Economy – its Role in Post-Industrial Society', *Futures* (April 1979) pp. 3–15.

Gorostiaga, X., 'The Dilemmas Confronting the Nicaraguan Economy', in G. White and K. Young (eds), *Nicaragua after the Revolution: Problems and Prospects* (Sussex: Institute of Development Studies, 1985) pp. 14–18.

Grancelli, B., 'Political Trade-offs, Collective Bargaining, Individual Tradings: Some Remarks on Industrial Relations in Italy', in S. Alessandrini and B. Dallago (eds), *The Unofficial Economy* (Aldershot: Gower, 1987) pp. 257–70.

Grossman, G., 'The "Second Economy" of the USSR', *Problems of Communism*, 26 (5) (1977) pp. 25–40.

Grossman, G., 'The Second Economy of the USSR', in V. Tanzi (ed.), *The Underground Economy in the United States and Abroad* (Lexington, Mass.: Lexington Books, 1982) pp. 245–69.

Gulhati, R. and U. Sekhar, *Industrial Strategy for Late Starters: The Experience of Kenya, Tanzania and Zambia* (Washington D.C.: The World Bank, May 1981).

Gutmann, P. M., 'The Subterranean Economy', *Financial Analysts Journal* (November–December 1977) pp. 26–7, 34.

Henry, S., *The Hidden Economy: The Context and Control of Boarderline Crime* (Oxford: Martin Robertson, 1978).

Izvestia (30 April, 9 September 1987).

Jowitt, K., 'Soviet Neotraditionalism: the Political Corruption of Leninist Regime', *Soviet Studies*, 35 (3) (1983) pp. 275–97.

Katsenelinboigen, A., 'Corruption in the USSR: Some Methodological Notes', in M. Clarke (ed.), *Corruption: Causes, Consequences and Control* (New York: Frances Pinter, 1983) pp. 220–38.

Kemeny, I., 'The Unregistered Economy in Hungary', *Soviet Studies*, 34 (3) (1982) pp. 349–66.

Kenedi, J., *Do It Yourself. Hungary's Hidden Economy* (London: Pluto Press, 1982).

Knight, P. T., *Economic Reform in Socialist Countries, The Experience of China, Hungary, Romania, and Yugoslavia* (Washington, D.C.: The World Bank, 1983).

Komrakov, G., 'Dealers? No, Intermediaries', *Moskovskiye Novosti* (27 September) in *The Current Digest of the Soviet Press* (11 November 1987) pp. 5–6.

Laky, T., 'The Hidden Mechanism of Recentralization in Hungary', *Acta Oeconomica*, 24 (1–2) (1980) pp. 95–106.

Landau, Z., 'Selected Problems of Unofficial Economy in Poland', in S. Alessandrini and B. Dallago (eds), *The Unofficial Economy* (Aldershot: Gower, 1987) pp. 175–90.

LeoGrande, W. M., 'Cuban Dependency: A Comparison of Pre-Revolutionary and Post-Revolutionary International Economic Relations', *Cuban Studies*, 9 (2) (1979) pp. 1–28.

Łoś, M., *Red-Collar Crime: Elite Crime in the USSR and Poland* (Washington, D.C.: Kennan Institute for Advanced Russian Studies, Occasional Paper, 216, 1987a).

Łoś, M., 'The Double Economic Structure of Communist Societies', *Contemporary Crises*, 11 (1987b) pp. 25–58.

Łoś, M., *Communist Ideology, Law and Crime* (London: Macmillan; New York: St Martin's Press, 1988).

Majchrzak, I., *Pracownicze Przestępstwo i Jego Sprawca* (White Collar Crime and Its Perpetrator) (Warsaw: KiW, 1965).

Marchetti, P., 'Agrarian Transformation and Popular Participation in Nicaragua', in G. White and K. Young (eds), *Nicaragua after the Revolution* (Sussex: Institute of Development Studies, 1985) pp. 19–27.

Mars, G. and Y. Altman, 'The Cultural Bases of Soviet Georgia's Second Economy', *Soviet Studies*, 35 (4) (1983) pp. 546–60.

Mars, G. and Y. Altman, 'Case Studies in Second Economy Production and Transportation in Soviet Georgia', and 'Case Studies in Second Economy Distribution in Soviet Georgia', in S. Alessandrini and B. Dallago (eds), *The Unofficial Economy* (Aldershot: Gower, 1987) pp. 197–245.

Marx, K., *Capital*, vol. 3 (Moscow: Foreign Language Publishing House, 1962).

Mesa-Lago, C., *The Economy of Socialist Cuba: A Two Decade Appraisal* (Albuquerque: University of Mexico Press, 1981).

Nicholls, W. M. and Dyson, W. A., *The Informal Economy. Where People Are the Bottom Line* (Ottawa: VIF Publications, 1983).

Oi, J. C., 'Communism and Clientelism: Rural Politics in China', *World Politics* (January 1985) pp. 238–66.

Oi, J. C., 'Commercializing China's Rural Cadres', *Problems of Communism*, 35 (5) (1986) pp. 1–15.

Packenham, A. R., 'Capitalist Dependency and Socialist Dependency: The Case of Cuba', in J. F. Triska (ed.), *Dominant Powers and Subordinate States* (Durham: Duke University Press, 1986) pp. 310–41.

Pawlik, W., 'Ekonomia życia codziennego społeczności lokalnej' (Daily Life Economy of a Local Community), in J. Kurczewski (ed.), *Umowa o Kartki* (Warsaw: U.W., 1985) pp. 152–97.

Pendse, D. R., 'Black Money: Determining Situation', in G. S. Monga and V. J. Sanctis (eds), *The Unsanctioned Economy in India* (Bombay: Himalaya Publishing House, 1984) pp. 5–19.

Pérez-Lopez, J., 'Cuban Economy in the 1980s', *Problems of Communism*, 35 (5) (1986) pp. 16–34.

Planas, J. R., 'Cuba Enacts a New Penal Code' (unpublished manuscript, Washington, D.C., 1988).

Portes, A., 'The Informal Sector and the World Economy: Notes on the Structure of Subsidised Labour' (Sussex: Institute of Development Studies, Bulletin, 9 (4) (June 1978).

Portes, A. and Sassen-Koob, S., 'Making It Underground: Comparative Material on the Informal Sector in Western Market Economies', *American Journal of Sociology*, 93 (1) (1987) pp. 30–61.

Pravda (8 June 1987).

Prybyla, J. S., 'China's Economic Experiment: From Mao to Market', *Problems of Communism*, 35 (1) (1986) pp. 21–38.

Prybyla, J. S., *Market and Plan under Socialism* (Stanford: Hoover Institution Press, 1987).

Ragin, Ch. and D. Zaret, 'Theory and Method in Comparative Research: Two Strategies', *Social Forces* 61 (1983) pp. 731–54.

Ray, S. K., *Economics of the Black Market* (Boulder, Col.: Westview Press, 1981).

Rumer, B., 'The "Second" Agriculture in the USSR', *Soviet Studies*, 5 (1981) pp. 560–72.

Sampson, S. L., 'Rich Families and Poor Collectives: An Anthropological Approach to Romania's "Second Economy"', *Bidrag til Öststatsforskning*, 11 (Uppsala 1983) pp. 44–77.

Sampson, S. L., 'The Informal Sector in Eastern Europe', *Telos*, 66 (1986) pp. 44–66.

Sampson, S. L., 'The Second Economy of the Soviet Union and Eastern Europe', *The Annals of the American Academy of Political and Social Science*, 493 (September 1987) pp. 120–36.

Saul, J. S., 'The State in Post-Colonial Societies: Tanzania', in D. Held *et al.* (eds) *States and Societies* (New York and London: New York University Press, 1983) pp. 457–74.

Sawer, M., *Marxism and the Question of the Asian Mode of Production* (The Hague: Martinus Nijhoff, 1977).

Selden, M., 'State, Market and Sectoral Inequality in Contemporary China', in P. Evans, D. Rueschemeyer, and E. Huber Stephens (eds), *States Versus Markets in the World System* (Beverly Hills: Sage, 1985) pp. 275–91.

Sethuraman, S. V. (ed.), *The Urban Informal Sector in Developing Countries* (Geneva: ILO, 1981).

Simis, K., *USSR: The Corrupt Society* (New York: Simon & Shuster, 1982).

Singh, S. K., 'Black Money: Some Vicious Circles', in G. S. Monga and V. J. Sanctis (eds), *The Unsanctioned Economy in India* (Bombay: Himalaya Publishing House, 1984) pp. 20–37.

Skocpol, T., 'States and Revolutions: France, Russia and China', in D. Held *et al.* (eds) *States and Societies* (New York and London: New York University Press, 1983) pp. 151–69.

Solinger, D., *Chinese Business under Socialism: The Politics of Domestic Commerce, 1949–80* (Berkeley: University of California Press, 1984).

Tanzi, V., 'The Underground Economy: the Causes and Consequences of this Worldwide Phenomenon', *Finance and Development, A Quarterly Publication of the International Monetary Fund and the World Bank*, 20 (4) (1983) pp. 10–13.

Tarkowski, J., 'Patronage in a Centralized Socialist System: The Case of Poland', *International Political Science Review*, 4 (4) (1983) pp. 495–518.

'The Cooperative System Develops Abuses', *Pravda* and *Izvestia* (25 November) *The Current Digest of the Soviet Press* (11 November 1987) pp. 9–10.

'The Soviet Economy', *The Economist* (9 April 1988) pp. 3–18.

Timofeev, L., 'Black Market Technology in the USSR: or the Peasants' Art of Starving', *Telos*, 51 (Spring 1982) pp. 5–21.

Van Brabant, J. M., 'Economic Adjustment and the Future of Socialist Economic Integration', *Eastern Economic Politics and Societies*, 1 (1) (1987) pp. 75–112.

Van den Berg, G. P., 'The Soviet Union and the Death Penalty', *Soviet Studies*, 35 (2) (1983) pp. 154–74.

Vilas, C. M., *The Sandinista Revolution* (New York: Monthly Review Press, 1986).

Vito, T. (ed.), *The Underground Economy in the United States and Abroad* (Lexington, Mass.: Lexington Books, 1982).

Wädekin, K. E., *The Private Sector in Soviet Agriculture* (Berkeley: University of California Press, 1973).

Wald, I. *et al.*, *Raport o Problemach Polityki w Zakresie Alkoholu* (A Report of Anti-Alcohol Policies) (Warsaw: Komisja Rady Ministrów do Spraw Walki z Alkoholizmem, 1981).

Wedel, J., *The Private Poland* (New York: Facts on File, 1986).

Westoby, A., 'Conceptions of Communist States', in D. Held, *et al.*, (eds), *States and Societies* (New York and London: New York University Press, 1983) pp. 219–40.

White, G., 'Revolutionary Socialist Development in the Third World: An Overview', in G. White, R. Murray and Ch. White (eds), *Revolutionary Socialist Development in the Third World* (Lexington, Mass.: The University Press of Kentucky, 1983a) pp. 1–33.

White, G., 'Chinese Development Strategy After Mao', in G. White *et al.* (eds), *Revolutionary Socialist Development in the Third World* (Lexington, Mass.: The University Press of Kentucky, 1983b) pp. 1–33.

Wittfogel, K., *Oriental Despotism*, revised edn (New Haven: Yale University Press, 1981). First published 1957.

Zieliński, J. G., *Polskie Reformy Gospodarcze* (Polish Economic Reforms) (London: Odnowa, 1974).

Index

Adams, President John Quincy, 104
Afghanistan, 18
Aganbegyan, Professor, 218
agrarian reform, 105–6, 125, 131,
    142, 208, 225 n 5
agriculture, 208–10
    Angola, 163–4, 168–9
    China, 143–4, 208
    Cuba, 105–6; export economy,
      106, 110, 197
    Hungary, 50, 51–5
    Nicaragua, 208; export economy,
      123, 125, 130–1, 133
    Poland, 34–6
    Romania, 70, 72–3, 74–5, 77–8, 82
      n 2
    Soviet Union, 15, 16
    Tanzania, 177, 183–4; export
      economy, 178
    theft of produce for sale, 12, 15,
      52–3, 74–5, 144
    Yugoslavia, 86–7
Agrokomerc, 95
aid
    Nicaragua, 134–5
    Tanzania, 179
alcohol, illegal production, Soviet
    Union, 18
Aliev, Party Secretary, 16
Alma-Ata, 13
Alves, Nito, 159
Angola, 198, 225 n 5, 225 n 8
    colonial rule, 157–9
    political structure, 159–61
    second economy, 161–72; role,
      166–71
Anti-Economic Saboteurs
    Operation, Tanzania, 188
anti-monopoly bill, Poland, 40
Arusha Declaration, 179, 180

Association of Private Trade and
    Services (Warsaw Branch), 32
autonomous groups, sub-
    contractors, Poland, 40
Azerbaidzhan, 16, 18

backdoor, 148, 210–11
balance of payments, Tanzania, 183
barter, 8–9, 128, 147, 164–5, 169–70,
    225 n 8
basic products distribution,
    Nicaragua, 131
Batista, Fulgencio, 105
Beijing, 145
black market, 8, 18–19, 206–7, 217–
    18
    Angola, 169
    China, 150, 152
    Cuba, 108, 112–18; controlling,
      114–15; understanding, 116–18
    Nicaragua, 127–8, 128–30
    Poland, 31, 37, 38, 42, 44
    Romania, 74–5, 79, 80
    Soviet Union, 18–19, 22, 23
    Tanzania, 189–90
    Yugoslavia, 87–9
Bosnia, 95, 96
bribery, 8, 59, 110, 215
    China, 148, 152
    Poland, 30, 31, 32, 37, 42–3
    Romania, 74, 75, 78
    Soviet Union, 15, 16, 19, 21, 23
    see also corruption
Britain, 3, 176, 179
bureaucracy, 44, 57, 195
    expansion of, 203
    Poland, 30–1
    Tanzania, 184; colonial, 177–8

campesinos, Nicaragua, 123, 125, 133
candongas, 1962, 167, 169–70, 171
capital, flight of, Nicaragua, 130
capital investment, Hungary, 65
capitalism, 61, 123, 176, 222
capitalist societies, second economy, 221, 222–3
cash crops, Cuba, 106
Castro, Fidel, 104, 108, 109, 116, 117
CCM, 182
Ceausescu, Nicolae, 81
central planning, 6–7, 14, 56–7, 195, 203, 205–6
    China, 141
    Cuba, 104–7, 116
    market-oriented revisions, 214–15
    Nicaragua, 135
    Poland, 28, 31, 45
    Romania, 71, 76
    Soviet Union, 14, 17, 21–2
China, 196, 198, 211, 213, 218
    economic reforms, 145–6, 154–5, 213, 215, 218
    second economy, 140–55, 201; historical background, 142–8; ideological status, 148–9; official control, 150–4
Chinese Communist Party, 140, 142, 149, 152, 153–5
Chipenda, Daniel, 159
client–patron relationships, 204
CMEA, 197, 221, 224 n 2
coffee, 128–9, 116, 177
collectivisation, 194, 200, 201
    agriculture, 34–5, 51–5, 194, 208–10, 225 n 7
    businesses, 147
Colonial Pact, 157, 158
colonial rule
    Angola, 157–9
    Tanzania, 176–8
Comites de Defensa Sandinista, 131–2
Commission on the Economic Reform, Poland, 33
Commission on the Struggle against Speculation, Poland, 38
Committees for the Defence of the

Revolution, Cuba, 115
communes, China, 143–4, 145
Communist Party, *see* Chinese Communist Party; Hungarian Communist Party
consensus, self-management and, 90
consumer goods
    Angola, 165, 172
    Cuba, 110, 113
    free-market allocation, 214
    Nicaragua, 131, 132
    Poland, 38–9, 42
    Romania, 71, 75, 76, 79
    Soviet Union, 13, 15–16, 18–19
    Tanzania, 184, 187
    Yugoslavia, 88
contrato system, 157
co-operatives, 64,216
    agricultural: Angola, 164; China, 143–4, 145; Hungary, 54–5, 59; Poland, 35, 36
    industrial, 56–7, 147
corruption, 128, 178, 195, 212
    Angola, 170
    China, 152
    Cuba, 110–11
    high-level, 204–5
    Nicaragua, 128, 129, 130
    party functionaries, 77
    Poland, 32, 42–3, 44, 45
    Romania, 77
    Soviet Union, 11, 15–16, 19, 24 n 2
    Tanzania, 186–7
cotton, Tanzania, 177
Council for Mutual Economic Assistance, *see* CMEA
crime, 95, 123–4, 126
    economic, *see* economic crimes
Croatia, 88, 89, 95, 97
Cuba, 101–2, 208, 209, 210, 213, 224 n 2, 225 n 5
    central planning, 104–7, 197
    economic dependency, 196–7
    second economy, 107–18, 201; controlling black markets, 114–18; inside first economy, 110–11; outside first economy, 111–14; today, 109; transition to socialism, 107–9

Cultural Revolution, 145

Dalmatia, 89
Dar es Salaam, 189
'dead souls', 17
debt
    Angola, 165
    Nicaragua, 124–5
    Yugoslavia, 91
    see also loans
decapitalisation, 130
decentralisation, economy, 214–15
decision-making, investment,
        Yugoslavia, 95–7
Deng Xiao-ping, 144
Department of Industry and
        Commerce, China, 152
dependency
    Cuba, 104, 197
    Tanzania, 179, 181, 190
de-state-ification, 63
developing countries, 195
    second economy, 211–12
development policy
    Angola, 160–1
    Tanzania, 179–81
diamonds, Angola, 166, 167
discrimination, China, 150–1
distribution, economic, 206
    Angola, 163
    Nicaragua, 131
    Poland, 37–9
dollars, 37, 113–14, 129–30, 169
drugs, illicit, Soviet Union, 18
durable goods, black and grey
        markets, Cuba, 113

economic activity, hidden, 58–9
economic agreement, Poland–Soviet
        Union, 29
economic crimes
    China, 142, 151–4
    Cuba, 115
    legislation, 224 n 5
    Nicaragua, 126
    Poland, 32, 38, 42
    Soviet Union, 19–21
    Yugoslavia, 95, 96–7, 98
economic crisis, 222–3

Poland, 35
Romania, 78–9
Tanzania, 183, 186–7
Yugoslavia, 91–3
economic measures, against black
        markets, Nicaragua, 130–1
economic policy
    Nicaragua, 130–1, 133
    Tanzania, 178, 181–4
    Yugoslavia, 92
economic reforms, 213–19
    China, 145–6, 154–5, 213, 215, 218
    Cuba, 106–9, 197
    failure of, 219–21
    Hungary, 50–1, 55–6, 63–6, 213,
        215
    Poland, 28, 29, 33, 40–1, 215
    Soviet Union, 213, 215, 216–17,
        218, 221
    Tanzania, 213
economic relations, 103, 118 n 2
Economic Sabotage (Special
        Provisions) Act, Tanzania, 188–
        9, 225 n 5
education, corruption in, Soviet
        Union, 16
élites, 6, 204–5
    Angola, 170–1
    China, 141, 153–4
    ideology, 3–4
    Nicaragua, 123
    Poland, 36, 44
    produced by second economy, 7–
        8, 23, 81, 186
    Tanzania, 186–7
embezzlement, 15, 21, 22, 32, 153
entrepreneurship, 8, 205–6, 215
    Angola, 169–70
    China, 141–2, 145, 146
    Hungary, 64–6
    Poland, 29–34, 36, 43, 201
    Soviet Union, 13
enterprise managers, election,
        Yugoslavia, 95
esquemas, 161–2, 164, 167, 169–70,
        171
Esso, 106
exchange economy, informal, *see*
        barter

exchange rates
  Angola, 170
  China, 152
  Nicaragua, 133
  Yugoslavia, 88
export earnings, repatriation,
  Yugoslavia, 94–5
exports, agricultural
  Cuba, 106, 110, 197
  Nicaragua, 123, 125, 130–1, 133
  Tanzania, 178

factories
  China, 147
  Hungary, 56–7, 60–1
  Nicaragua, 126
  underground, Soviet Union, 17
family plots, *see* household plots
farmers' market, Cuba, 115
favours, trading, 110–11
first economy, 5, 27–9, 45, 102
  entrepreneurship within, 205–6
  forced marriage with second, 219–
    20
  ideology and, 194–9
  Poland, 27–9, 45
First Law of Agrarian Reform,
  Cuba, 105–6
FNLA, 158, 166
food
  black and grey markets, Cuba, 112
  distribution, 108–9, 131
  shortages, 53, 79, 107
foreign credits, *see* loans
foreign currency, black markets,
  169, 190, 217–18
  China, 152
  Cuba, 113–14
  Poland, 37
  Romania, 75
  Tanzania, 190
  Yugoslavia, 87–9, 94, 98
foreign trade
  Cuba, 224 n 2
  unofficial activities, Yugoslavia,
    93–5
fraud, China, 153

Georgia, 16, 20, 212

German occupation, Poland, 43–4,
  46, 212
ghost workers, 17
Gierek, Edward, 34, 36
GMKs, 64–5
gold, 19, 190
Gorbachev, Mikhail, 11, 13, 22, 216,
  218
Government Control Task Force,
  Tanzania, 183
government intervention, economy,
  177, 178, 195
government officials, election,
  Yugoslavia, 95
Great Leap Forward, 143–4
grey markets, 112–13, 127–8, 210
grey money printing, 96–7
Guardia Nacional, Nicaragua, 124

hard currency, *see* foreign currency
Havana, 113, 114
heavy industry, Poland, 27, 28
hidden economy, *see* second
  economy
high structure, society, 57–8
hoarding, 200
home brewing, 18
Hong Kong, 152
household plots, 35, 53, 72–3, 145,
  209
households, mixed, 86–7
housing, 73, 89
Human Resources Deployment Act,
  Tanzania, 187–8, 225 n 5
Hungarian Communist Party, 62–3
Hungarian Revolution 1956, 50, 52,
  60, 63
Hungary, 40, 219, 225 n 7
  collectivisation of agriculture, 51–
    5
  economic reforms, 50–1, 55–6, 63–
    6, 213, 215
  second economy, 56–63, 212;
    social implications, 62–3

ideological status, second economy
  Angola, 172
  China, 145, 148–9, 155
  Poland, 32, 33

Tanzania, 191
ideology
first economy and, 194–9
second economy and, 2–4
illegal second economy, 103–4, 205–8, 215
Angola, 161–72
China, 141–55
Cuba, 110–18
Hungary, 56–63
Nicaragua, 127–30
Poland, 36–9, 41–3
Romania, 74–6
Soviet Union, 14–19
Tanzania, 185–90
Yugoslavia, 86–98
import licences, Yugoslavia, 93–4
imports
Angola, 164
Cuba, 110
income distribution, Cuba, 116, 117
incomes, *see* wages
India, 195
individuals, autonomous decisions, 56–7
industrial co-operatives, 56–7, 147
industrial sector, Soviet Union, 17
industrialisation, 201
Angola, 158
China, 142
Cuba, 110
Poland, 27–8
Romania, 70–1
Stalinist model, 197, 198
industry, small-scale, Poland, 29–30
inflation
Nicaragua, 127, 129
Yugoslavia, 91
informal economy, 8–9, 210–13, 222
household, 2–3, 200
see also second economy
innovative firms, 40
instrumental behaviour, workers, 61
intermediaries, 147–8
investment
central planning, 214–15
decision-making, Yugoslavia, 95–7
Poland, 27–8, 35

US, in Cuba, 105
Italy, 222–3

jewels, 19

Kazakhstan, 15
KGB, 21
Kiev, 13
King Ranch, Cuba, 105
Kishinev, 13
kisszövetkezets, 64
Kosygin, A. N., 213

labour activity, illegal, Soviet Union, 12–14, 16–17, 22
labour exchanges, 87
Labour Code, Angola, 167, 225 n 5
land
ownership, 34, 53, 72–3, 106, 146, 163–4
private sales, Yugoslavia, 89
redistribution, *see* agrarian reform
Lange, Oskar, 214
law enforcement,
Angola, 170–1, 172
China, 151–3, 155
Cuba, 114–15
Nicaragua, 132
Poland, 32, 38
Romania, 78, 80
Soviet Union, 16–17, 19–21
Tanzania, 188–9
Law of Discipline at the Work Place, Angola, 167, 225 n 5
Law on Combatting Speculation, Poland, 38
leadership code, Tanzania, 180
legal second economy, 5–6, 206–7
China, 141–2
Cuba, 109
Nicaragua, 126–7
Poland, 29–36
Romania, 72–4
Soviet Union, 12–14
Tanzania, 185
legislation, 203, 224–5
Nicaragua, 132
Poland, 29, 30, 38–9, 40
Soviet Union, 12–14, 22

Lenin, V. I., 149, 213
liberalisation, Tanzania, 189–90
liberation movements, Angola, 158–9
licences
  private entrepreneurs, Poland, 30–1
  second economy activities, 13
livestock, private production, Romania, 78, 79–80
living standards
  Cuba, 105
  Romania, 69, 71
loans, 215
  Angola, 165
  Nicaragua, 134
  Western, Poland, 28–9
  Yugoslavia, 91
low structure, society, 57–8
Luanda, 167, 168

Macedonia, 95
Machado, Gerardo, 105
malnutrition, Cuba, 105, 107, 116
managers, 14, 61, 76
  second economy; Poland, 38, 45; Romania, 76; Soviet Union, 17, 20–1, 22; Yugoslavia, 93
Managua, 126
Mao Ze-dong, 148, 149, 198, 213
marginal economy, Nicaragua, 126–7, 128, 135–6
market economy, attacks on, 200
market forces, 189, 191
market socialism, 60, 89–91, 214–19
Marxist economic development, 199–200, 222
  monopolisation, period, 203–13
  post-reformist decadence, 219–21
  radical transformation stage, 200–3
  reformist stage, 213–19
masses, mobilisation, 201–2
migration, 87, 212–13
milionarios da kwanza, 169, 171, 172
militarisation, society, 202
military build-up, US, Nicaragua, 134
military debt, Angola, 165

military production, Poland, 27–8
militsiia, 21
mining, Angola, 157
mixed economy, Nicaragua, 125, 133, 197–8
mixed households, Yugoslavia, 86–7
moonlighting, 8, 14, 23, 59, 87
Moscow, 13, 16
MPLA, 159–60, 169
mutual favour networks, 8, 110–11, 205

Nagy, Imre, 55, 60, 62
National Anti-Economic Sabotage Tribunal, Tanzania, 188–9
National Basic Food Corporation, Nicaragua, 131
National Board for the Distribution of Foodstuffs, Cuba, 108
National Crafts Council, Poland, 32
national output, contribution of hidden economy, 59
national planning, 195
  see also central planning
National Price Commission, Tanzania, 183
National Union of Farmers and Stockraisers, Nicaragua, 131
nationalisation, 194, 200
  Angola, 163
  Cuba, 106–7, 108, 196
  Hungary, 62–3
  Tanzania, 180, 185
Neto, Agostinho, 159
networks, informal second economy, 210–11
New Democratic Reform, China, 142, 143
New Economic and Financial Mechanism, Romania, 71
New Economic Policy
  Angola, 172
  Soviet Union, 11, 213, 216–17
New Socialist Person, 109
Nicaragua, 122–4, 208, 212
  mixed economy, 197–8
  Sandinism, 124–5
  second economy, 126–36, 201–2; responses to, 130–2

Somozism, 123–4
US intervention, 134–5
nomenklatura, Romania, 81, 82 n 3
Nyerere, J. K., 182

OBKhSS, 21
officials, *see* élites; state employees
oil
  Angola, 163, 164, 167
  Cuba, 106–7
ownership
  industry, 13, 59–61, 141, 146, 163
  land, 34, 53, 72–3, 106, 146, 163–4

parallel markets, Cuba, 115
parametric state management, 28
parastatals, Tanzania, 178–9, 180–1,
  186
party élites, *see* élites
party members
  corruption, 11, 77
  economic crimes, Soviet Union,
    20
passive resistance, 52
peasants, 208–10, 212
  Angola, 168–9
  China, 218
  Hungary, 51, 52, 55
  Nicaragua, 123, 208
  Poland, 34
  Romania, 209
  Soviet Union, 209
  Tanzania, 183–4, 208–9
people's stores, Angola, 163, 164
personnel policy, unofficial
  activities, Yugoslavia, 95
Peter, György, 55
petty business classes, roles in
  socialist revolution, 202
Pingtree Ranch, Cuba, 105
PJTs, 64, 65
planning, 195
  see also central planning
Platt Amendment, 104–5
Poland, 69, 219, 225 n 8, 225 n 9
  economic reforms, 29, 33, 40–1,
    213, 215
  first economy, 27–9, 45
  German occupation, 43–4, 212
  illegal economy, 36–8, 41–3

second economy, 29–46, 200–1;
  illegal, 36–40, 41–3; legal rural,
  34–6; legal urban, 29–34, 40–1;
  past and present, 43–6
  Stalinist period, 27–8, 36, 44–5,
    200–1
police state, Poland, 36
political terror, 198
Polonian firms, Poland, 30, 40
Popular Supply Committees,
  Nicaragua, 132
Portugal, 157–9, 166
poverty, Cuba, 105, 107, 117
Preventive Detention Act,
  Tanzania, 188
Price Controls Act, Tanzania, 183
prices, 217–18
  Cuba, 108–9
  Poland, 41
  Romania, 77, 79
  Tanzania, 183, 189
private agriculture
  Angola, 164
  Cuba, 106
  Hungary, 53–5
  Poland, 34–6
  Romania, 72–3, 77–8, 79–80, 82
    n 2
  Yugoslavia, 86–7
private businesses, *see*
  entrepreneurship
private capital, attacks on, 200
private homes, 16, 73
private sector
  Angola, 163
  China, 143, 146, 150–1
  legal and black market, 206–7, 216
  Nicaragua, 126, 133
  Poland, 29–34
  Romania, 73–77
  State regulation, *see* state
    regulation
  Tanzania, 180, 184, 190
privatisation, Tanzania, 189
procuracy, 21
producer goods, 70, 214, 215
production
  campaigns to increase, Angola,
    167–8

production – *cont.*
  planning, Cuba, 106
  Poland, 39, 41–2
  unlicensed, Soviet Union, 18
production quotas, 60–1, 79–80
production supplies, role of second
    economy, 147–8
productivity, Yugoslavia, 91
professionals, Soviet Union, 23
profit ceilings, food, Cuba, 108–9
proletarianisation, 60, 157
promissory notes, 96
property rights, 103
prosecutions
  Angola, 167
  Cuba, 115
  Poland, 32
  Soviet Union, 16–17, 19–21
  Yugoslavia, 96–7, 98
  see also economic crimes; law
    enforcement
prostitution, Soviet Union, 18
public sector, 221
  Tanzania, 178, 180, 181, 182
purchasing power, 117–18

quasi-private sector, Hungary, 64–5
quotas
  production, 60–1, 79–80
  supply, 31

racketeering, Tanzania, 182
Rakosi, Matyas, 63
rationing, 203, 210
  Angola, 167
  Cuba, 108–9, 112, 114, 115
  Romania, 79
Reagan, President Ronald, 134
registration, second economy, Soviet
    Union, 13
relations of production, 148–9
remittances, Yugoslav workers', 87
repression, 150, 167
Rhodesia, 179
Romania, 69–70, 209, 211, 212, 225
    n 7
  post-war economy, 70–1
  second economy, 71–80; factors
    explaining rise, 76–8; illegal,

74–6; legal, 72–4; recent
    growth, 78–80
rural second economy, 208–9
  China, 144, 145, 147
  Poland, 34–6
  Romania, 74–5, 78, 79–80, 81
Rural Solidarity Union, 35
rural–urban migration, 212

salaries, *see* wages
samogon, 18
Sandinistas, 123, 124–5, 129, 130,
    133, 136, 198
Sanfan Movement, 153
Santiago de Cuba, 111
second economy, 5–10
  Angola, 161–72
  capitalist societies, 221, 222–3
  causes, 221–2
  China, 140–55, 201
  concept of, 102–4, 140–2
  Cuba, 107–18, 201
  cultural tradition of, 212–13
  definition, 2–4
  developing countries, 211–12,
    221–2
  dispersed activities, 4
  forced marriage with first, 219–20
  growth of, 75, 222–4
  Hungary, 56–63, 212
  Marxist states, 223–4
  Nicaragua, 126–36, 201–2
  partial legitimisation, 215–17; *see
    also* legislation
  Poland, 29–46, 200–1
  Romania, 71–80
  Soviet Union, 11–23, 201
  strategies against, 7
  stratification, 7–8, 23, 81, 186
  Tanzania, 181–91
  under economic reform, 213–19
  under monopolistic stage of
    development, 203–13
  under socialism, 199–200
  Yugoslavia, 86–98
secondary plants, Hungary, 56–7
self-help strategies, 210
self-management, Yugoslavia, 89–91
self-reliance, Tanzania, 179–81

Serbia, 95
service sector
  Angola, 165
  Poland, 33, 37, 42
  Romania, 73, 76
  Soviet Union, 13
shabashniki, 16–17
share-cropping, Hungary, 53, 54
share-holding, proposed, Poland, 40
Shell, 106
smuggling
  China, 152, 153–4
  Nicaragua, 127–8
  Tanzania, 190
  Yugoslavia, 94
Social Accounting Service,
  Yugoslavia, 93, 96–7
social ownership, Yugoslavia, 89–90
social services
  Cuba, 101, 117
  Tanzania, 181
social welfare programmes, China,
  151
socialised sector
  Poland, 35–6
  Yugoslavia, 93–8
socialism
  China, 142–3, 149
  Cuba, 107–9, 116–17
Socialism and Self-Reliance, 179–81
societies, high and low structure, 57–
  8
Solidarity Union, 29
Somoza dictators, 124, 125, 130
South Africa, 159, 163, 166, 171
Soviet Union, 1, 118 n 4, 196, 197,
  198, 212
  agreement with Poland, 29
  Angola's debt, 165
  collective farms, 209–10
  economic reforms, 213, 215, 216–
    17, 218, 221
  second economy, 11–23, 201;
    illegal, 14–19; law enforcement,
    19–21; legal, 12–14
speculation, 200
  Nicaragua, 131
  Poland, 33, 37–9, 41
  Soviet Union, 18–19

Spence, Silvia Marjorie, 111
Stalin, J. V., 27, 201
Stalinism, 70, 198–9, 200–1
Stalinist period, Poland, 27–8, 36,
  44–5, 200–1
State Administration for Industry
  and Commerce, China, 146
state employees, working in second
  economy, 8, 220
  China, 148
  Hungary, 64–5
  Poland, 37, 39, 40, 42–3
  Romania, 74, 75
  Yugoslavia, 93
state farms, 208–9
  Angola, 164
  Hungary, 51–3
  Poland, 36
state monopoly, stage of Marxist
  development, 203–13
state officials, *see* élites; state
  employees
state property, theft of, *see* theft
state regulation, private sector, 194,
  216
  China, 145, 146, 150–1
  Poland, 34
  Tanzania, 184
State Trade Inspection, Poland, 39
subcontracting teams, Poland, 40
subsistence cultivation, Cuba, 106
substandard goods, 38, 39
sub-institutional forces, 56–7
sugar, 106, 107
supplies, quotas, Poland, 31
SUTA, 163
szövetkezeti szakcsoports, 63

Tallinn, 13
Tanganyika, 176, 178
  see also Tanzania
TANU, 179–80, 183
Tanzania, 175, 198, 225 n 5
  economic reforms, 213
  history of the economy, 176–81;
    colonial phase 176–8;
    development policy 179–81;
    post-independence period 178–9
  second economy, 181–91;

Tanzania – *cont.*
    government response, 184–90
    villagisation, 183–4, 208–9
taxation, 13, 31–2, 177
Texaco, 106
theft, 52–3, 77, 90, 152
    for sale, 208–9; Cuba, 113;
        Nicaragua, 129; Poland, 38, 41,
        42; Soviet Union, 15
tobacco, 106
    Angola, 163, 167
tourism, Yugoslavia, 87–8
tourist shops, Cuba, 113–14
trading favours, 8, 110–11, 205
tutoring, private, 13, 24 n 4, 74

Ukraine, 15
underdevelopment
    Nicaragua, 124–5
    Tanzania, 184, 190
underground factories, Soviet
    Union, 17
unemployment, resettlement,
    Tanzania, 187–8
unemployment, Yugoslavia, 91
UNITA, 159, 166, 171
United Fruit, 105
United Kingdom, *see* Britain
United States, 3, 110–11, 159, 179
    Cuba and, 104–5, 106–7
    intervention in Nicaragua, 134–5,
        136
    second economy, 102
urban explosion, Angola, 168
urban second economy
    Poland, 29–34
    Romania, 75–6, 78, 81
urbanisation, Romania, 70
US dollars, 37, 113–14, 129–30, 169
USSR, *see* Soviet Union

Van Dunem, José, 159
Varadero, 114
VGMKs, 63–4
vigilantism, 201–2
villagisation 183–4, 208–9
Vilnius, 13
Vojvodina, 87

wages, 220
    Angola, 165
    Cuba, 117
    Hungary, 50, 62, 63, 66
    Nicaragua, 126, 127, 133
    for non-existent jobs, 17, 111
    Poland, 43
    Romania, 76, 77, 79
    Yugoslavia, 91
War against *Ulanguzi*, Tanzania,
    188
Warsaw, 42
Warsaw Pact, 28
West Germany, 179
wildcatters, 16–17
work environment, negative
    features, 92–3
working pools, state enterprises,
    Hungary, 63–4
World Bank, 107, 134–5, 195

Yugoslavia, 85, 198, 199, 214, 219
    economic crisis, 91–3
    economic growth, 86
    self-management paradigm, 89–91
    size and scope of second economy,
        86–9
    socialised sector, 93–8

Zagreb, 89
Zanzibar, 176, 178
    see also Tanzania